Argument Structure

phs

ditor

Argument Structure   Jane Grimshaw

The MIT Press
Cambridge, Massachusetts
London, England

This book was set in Times Roman by Asco Trade Typesetting Ltd., Hong Kong, and printed and bound in the United States of America.

Library of Congress Cataloging-in-Publication Data

Grimshaw, Jane B. (Jane Barbara), 1951–
  Argument structure/Jane Grimshaw.

    p. cm.—(Linguistic inquiry monographs; 18)
  Includes bibliographical references.
  ISBN 0-262-07125-8
  1. Grammar, Comparative and general—Syntax. 2. Semantics.
I. Title. II. Series.
P295.G68   1990
415—dc20
                                    89-13972
                                       CIP

Contents

Contents

Acknowledgments

The research discussed here was conducted with the support of grants IST-8420073 and IRI-8808286 to Brandeis University. For one year, when I was supposed to be finishing this book, I enjoyed the hospitality of the MIT Center for Cognitive Science.

Parts of this work have been in existence for a while under various guises, and many people have commented on these earlier versions, contributing important suggestions or clarifications. They include Mark Baker, Robert Beard, Adriana Belletti, Luigi Burzio, Noam Chomsky, Martin Everaert, Lyn Frazier, Isabelle Haïk, Lars Hellan, Ray Jackendoff, Alana Johns, Richard Kayne, Beth Levin, Joan Maling, Alec Marantz, Armin Mester, David Pesetsky, Steven Pinker, Alan Prince, James Pustejovsky, Malka Rappaport, Eduardo Raposo, Ian Roberts, Tom Roeper, Sara Rosen, Carol Tenny, Esther Torrego, Sten Vikner, Edwin Williams, Ellen Woolford, and Maria-Luisa Zubizarreta.

While working on this monograph, I have had many extensive discussions of the material with Steven Pinker, Edwin Williams, Beth Levin, Alan Prince, and Maria Luisa Zubizarreta. The final product reflects their benign influence in numerous respects.

Detailed comments on the manuscript or on various components thereof were kindly provided by Mark Baker, Piero Bottari, Martin Everaert, Guglielmo Cinque, Norbert Hornstein, and Beth Levin. Where I have not been able to act upon their suggestions the book is doubtless the worse for it.

Parts of this work were presented at various times at the University of Connecticut, Yale University, the West Coast Conference on Formal Linguistics at the University of Washington, the University of North Carolina, the Amsterdam Workshop on Syntactic and Lexical Structure, the NYU Conference on Alternative Conceptions of Phrase Structure, McGill University, the University of Quebec at Montreal, the

University of Maryland, Princeton University, MIT, and the University of Massachusetts at Amherst. Audiences at all of these places made valuable suggestions that have found their place, though perhaps not always their rightful place, in the final version.

Those attending the Topics in Syntax course at Brandeis last spring provided vigorous and spirited discussion of much of the material in this book. I thank in particular John Aberdeen, Claudia Borgonoro, Piroska Csuri, Sumana Dixit, Kevin Hegg, Arild Hestvik, Mark Hewitt, Soo Won Kim, Henrietta Hung, Gyanam Mahajan, Sara Rosen, Dan Silverman, and Saeko Urushibara. Finally, special thanks to Claudia Borgonoro for last minute assistance with the manuscript.

Argument Structure

Chapter 1
Principles of Argument-
Structure Representation

Only ten years ago argument structure was equated with the number of arguments related by predicate, a construct of some use but of limited interest. With the increasingly important role played by principles such as the Theta Criterion and the Projection Principle in Government-Binding Theory, beginning with Chomsky (1981), and with the development of lexicalist theories like Lexical Functional Grammar (Bresnan (1982c)), a new view has emerged in which argument structure represents a complex of information critical to the syntactic behavior of a lexical item. Recent work has used argument structure theory to explain properties of adjectival and verbal passives, middles, light verb constructions, verbal compounds, causatives, and nominals, among many other topics (Levin and Rappaport (1986, 1988), Zubizarreta (1985, 1987), Grimshaw (1986b), Hale and Keyser (1986a, 1986b, 1988), di Sciullo and Williams (1987), Grimshaw and Mester (1988), Li (1990)).

This monograph is a study of the representation of argument structure (a-structure). The term refers to the lexical representation of grammatical information about a predicate. The a-structure of a lexical item is thus part of its lexical entry. Argument structure interfaces with two other kinds of representation. One is lexical semantic structure, which represents lexical meaning. Hale and Keyser (1986a, 1986b, 1988), Jackendoff (1983, 1987, 1990), Rappaport and Levin (1986), and Zubizarreta (1985, 1987) posit lexical conceptual structure or lexical semantic representation. The second representation which a-structure interfaces with is deep structure (d-structure). Argument structure is projected from lexical semantic structure, and d-structure is projected from argument structure and principles of X-bar theory. In the strongest possible theory the a-structure of a lexical item is predictable from its meaning, and the d-structure the item appears in is predictable from its a-structure in interaction with independent parametric characteristics of the language. The theory of a-structure is the theory of how this is achieved, and a core component of this is the primary concern of the present study: the nature and internal organization of a-structure representation itself.

Out of the earlier work cited has emerged a more or less standard view of argument structure as consisting of a *set* of arguments represented either by theta role labels (Williams (1981a), Marantz (1984), di Sciullo and Williams (1987), Belletti and Rizzi (1988)) or by variables over arguments (Levin and Rappaport (1986), Rappaport and Levin (1986), Zubizarrreta (1987)). Further information about the status of these arguments is required for their correct deployment; it is necessary, for example, to represent the external/internal argument distinction, first introduced in Williams (1981a). To encode such additional properties of arguments, various word-processing resources are employed.

Williams (1981a) and much subsequent work uses underlining to pick out the "external" argument. Other notational systems use angled backets around the internal arguments to identify the external. These are equivalent means of expressing the distinction and are equivalent in turn to, say, capitalizing the external argument. Some systems also designate the "direct argument," an argument which receives its theta role directly from the verb (Marantz (1984), Levin and Rappaport (1986)).

Representative argument structures drawn from these works are given in (1) through (5):

(1) see($\underline{A}$, Th)   (di Sciullo and Williams (1987, 29))

(2) give(*theme*, goal)
    put(*theme*, location)
    steal(*theme*, source)   (Marantz (1984, 18))

(3) temere 'fear' [*Experiencer*, Theme]
    preoccupare 'worry' [Experiencer, Theme]
    piacere 'please' [Experiencer, Theme]
    (Belletti and Rizzi (1988, 344))

(4) put: x <y, P-loc z>   (Rappaport and Levin (1986, 9))

(5) work, x
    arrive^y
    hit^y,
    put^y, x; Loc P^z   (Zubizarreta (1987, 8–9))

In these analyses the argument structure of a predicate is a *set* of elements, with the external or internal status of an argument indicated by various notational devices. These make it possible to recognize the asymmetry between internal arguments, which are within the scope of the predicate in some sense (Zubizarreta 1987, to appear), and external arguments, which are not.

This monograph explores a view of a rather different kind: the hypothesis that argument structure is a structured representation over which relations of prominence are defined. An early version of this idea is presented in Grimshaw (1987) and Grimshaw and Mester (1988). It is really a development of the proposal for Warlpiri in Hale (1983), in which the external agrument is in effect higher in the argument structure than internal agruments and counts as asymmetrically c-commanding internal arguments for purposes of the Binding Theory.

The *prominence theory* of a-structure contrasts in a number of respects with the view that a-structures are sets. The fundamental assumption is that the a-structure of a predicate has its own internal structure, which affects the grammatical behavior of the predicate in many ways. The organization of the a-structure for a predicate is taken to be a reflection of its lexical semantics, so that the a-structure of a predicate should be derivable from key characteristics of its meaning. As a consequence of this, a-structure cannot be freely altered by rules, since an argument has whatever a-structure properties it has by virtue of its role in the lexical meaning of the predicate and not by stipulation. Finally, the prominence theory gives an organic characterization of some of the properties of arguments that are otherwise represented by unexplained diacritics. The prime example is the concept of an external argument, which has a natural definition in a theory of structured argument structure, as the most prominent argument.

The fundamental goal of this enterprise is to derive a-structure from semantics and then to derive the lexical behavior of a predicate and its d-structure from its argument structure representation. Current research on the acquisition of lexical items make it clear that the same issues of learnability arise with respect to the lexicon as elsewhere (Landau and Gleitman (1985), Pinker 1989)). The position taken in much earlier work, that the lexicon is idiosyncratic and is acquired piece by piece, simply cannot be maintained. It fails to explain the high degree of regularity of the lexical system as well as how children come to acquire lexical information.

Despite its commitment to deriving a syntactic representation (a-structure) from properties of a semantic representation, this is not a reductionist program. It is the syntactic representation of a predicate that determines its *syntactic* behavior; the syntactic properties of predicates are not reduced to their semantics. For example, I argue that the restrictions on passivization follow from the formal character of passivization interacting with the a-structure properties of particular lexical items; passivization affects an external argument. A verb with no external argument will not passivize. The fact that whether a verb has an external argument or not is predictable does not mean that we can or should dispense with a-structure representation altogether. It is only by positing a-structure that we can *explain* the limits on passivizability, for example. (See Pinker (1989) for a recent discussion of learning issues here.)

The basic assumptions of the theory are the following.

1   A-structure is a structured representation which represents prominence relations among arguments. The prominence relations are jointly determined by the thematic properties of the predicate (via the thematic hierarchy) and by the aspectual properties of the predicate. I will represent the structure using parentheses. For a verb like *announce*, with an external Agent and an internal Theme and Goal, the a-structure prominence relations are those indicated in (6). Here the Agent is more prominent than the other arguments, which are more deeply embedded in the representation. Other arguments also bear relations of relative prominence to each other; the Goal is more prominent than the Theme, for example.

(6) *announce*(Agent (Goal (Theme)))

Although this asymmetry has no official status in most earlier theories, it is implicit in the tradition of listing the Agent before the Theme in a-structure.

The general idea that a-structure is a structured representation has major ramifications extending throughout the material to be presented in this monograph. It figures centrally in the theory of external arguments and in the characterization of long-distance anaphora. The structure of a-structure also governs theta-marking in compounds and in the light verb construction analyzed in Grimshaw and Mester (1988).

2   As in earlier research, especially that of Rappaport and Levin (1986) and Zubizarreta (1987), theta-role labels are not present in a-structure, hence operations defined over a-structure must be blind to thematic roles and depend solely on the formal characteristics of a-structure itself. However, the prominence theory differs from earlier views in that the internal organization of the a-structure results (in part) from the thematic hierarchy, so the prominence relations reflect thematic information of a very limited kind, namely whether a given argument is higher or lower on the thematic hierarchy than another. Some apparently thematically governed restrictions, such as those affecting experiencer predicates, will be shown to follow from the principles of a-structure without explicit reference to the thematic roles involved.

3 The concept of an external argument can be explicated in terms of a-structure prominence. The external argument is the most prominent argument in the a-structure of a predicate. In fact, it must be the most prominent along two dimensions: thematic and aspectual. Thus an argument is external or internal by virtue of its intrinsic relations to other arguments. Its status cannot be changed except by the introduction of another argument. This gives an argument structure theoretic definition of external arguments, one that turns out not to be equivalent to the notion of a d-structure subject.

4 I distinguish between grammatical arguments and semantic participants. Not all semantically relational lexical items have a syntactic a-structure and take syntactic arguments. I will argue that only nouns that refer to what I call complex events—nouns that have an internal aspectual analysis—have a-structure. Hence, only they have obligatory grammatical arguments of the kind that verbs have. Each verb and noun has a lexico-semantic representation (a lexical conceptual structure or lcs) that includes, among other things, the participants in the activities or states described by the verb (see Jackendoff (1987, 1990), Levin and Rappaport (1986), Hale and Keyser (1986a, 1986b), Zubizarreta (1987)). Some of these participants are realized as grammatical arguments and projected into an a-structure representation. However, the ability to project arguments in this way is limited among nouns to a subclass that I will refer to as *process* or *event nominals*. Other nouns do not have a-structure as part of their lexical representation, even though they may very well have semantic arguments appearing in their lcs definitions. I will argue that gerunds always have a-structure and that derived nominals are typically ambiguous in this respect. The distinction between the two kinds of nominals can be shown to correlate with a large number of other grammatical differences, which can be unified by the hypothesis that the two kinds of nouns have different external arguments.

This veiw distinguishes sharply between nouns that are in a sense semantically relational and nouns that are syntactically relational in that they admit grammatical arguments, and equally sharply between the *semantic* representation of arguments in lcs and their *syntactic* representation in a-structure. An a-structure is a lexico-syntactic representation assembled from a set of elements identified by the lcs of the predicate.

5 The argument structure and theta-marking properties of lexical items vary across syntactic categories. I will first argue that nouns, even though they have argument structure if they are of the right semantic kind, never theta-mark directly but only via prepositions. The evidence for this is that nouns never take bare arguments, even when the arguments do not require case. Hence, nouns never have sentential arguments, for example. I will suggest that this is because nouns are not governors, and government is required for theta-marking. Second, I will show that the argument structure of nouns and passive verbs are different from that of active verbs. In nominalization and passivization the external argument of a predicate undergoes suppression, and suppressed positions cannot be satisfied by syntactic arguments, although they can license *argument adjuncts*. This explains many properties of passives and nominals: the distribution of *by* phrases and possessives, the absence of passivization and nominalization of certain verb classes, and the behavior of passives and nominals with respect to control, for example.

The data for this study comes primarily from compounds, verb classes (including the psychological predicates), verbal and adjectival passives, and nominals.

Chapter 2
The Structure of Argument Structure

A central claim of the theory under development here is that argument structure does *not* consist of just a set of arguments but is rather a structured representation over which relations of prominence are defined. The external argument is the most prominent, and the internal arguments also have prominence relative to each other. One kind of evidence comes from theta-marking in light verb and compound constructions, where the structure of the a-structure of the head is reflected in restrictions on theta-marking (see 2.2). The behavior of the psychological verbs provides another kind of evidence for positing a structured argument structure: their behavior can be understood as resulting from a mismatch between their thematic prominence relations and their other properties. In later sections I will explore the interaction of thematic prominence with aspectual prominence, developing a theory of one class of the psychological predicates which explains many of their properties. This leads to a theory of external arguments which predicts properties of externals and explains restrictions on nominalization and passivization, including the existence of the Thematic Hierarchy Condition on passives (see 2.5.1 and 4.3). All of these results depend crucially on a structured representation for argument structure.

2.1 Structured Argument Structure: The Thematic Dimension

Early work on thematic relations suggested the existence of a thematic hierarchy (Jackendoff (1972, 43)). My proposal is that the hierarchy is properly understood as the organizing principle of a-structures. Argument structures are constructed in accordance with the thematic hierarchy, so the structural organization of the argument array is determined by universal principles based on the semantic properties of the arguments. I will assume a version of the hierarchy in which the Agent is always the highest argument. Next ranked is Experiencer, then Goal/ Source/Location, and finally Theme, a scheme that gives the proto-argument-structure in (1).[1]

(1) (Agent (Experiencer (Goal/Source/Location (Theme)))))

For an agentive verb like *murder*, the a-structure prominence relations are those given in (2). For agentive verbs the Agent is always the most prominent argument.

(2) *murder* (x   (y))
       Agent Theme

This is not a surprising result, since the argument that is most prominent in the a-structure is also the most syntactically prominent argument, the subject. However, this is not always true. Suppose we apply these principles to experiencer or psychological verbs, which have an Experiencer argument and another argument that I will call a Theme, although its exact label is not important for the point at hand so long as it has a role that is lower in the hierarchy than that of Experiencer. The resulting argument-structure prominence relations are those of (3), with the Experiencer as the most prominent argument and Theme as the less prominent.

(3) (x   (y))
       Exp Theme

As is well known, there is more than one kind of pyschological predicate. In one set, the Experiencer is relaized as a subject, and the Theme as an object. This is what happens with verbs like *fear*, *hate*, and *admire* (the *temere* class of Belletti and Rizzi (1988)).[2]

(4) They fear/hate/admire thunder.

The other set does not pattern this way; it includes verbs like *frighten*, and *disturb* (the *preoccupare* class of Belletti and Rizzi).[3] Here the Experiencer appears as a postverbal object, and the Theme occupies the subject position, as in (5).

(5) Thunder frightens/disturbs them.

For the *fear* class, like agentive predicates, the prominence relations of the a-structure are maintained configurationally, with the most prominent element in the a-structure acting as the subject of the verb. For the *frighten* psych verbs, however, this is conspicuously not the case, since the Experiencer has maximal thematic prominence but is not realized as a subject.

Here, then, we have an interesting situation in which the thematic prominence relations of a-structure do not match expectations based on constituent structure. (The thematic prominence relations assigned by the thematic hierarchy are confirmed by the behavior of theta-marking, as we will see in the next section.) This is critical to the behavior of the psychological verbs, which have figured prominently in both earlier and recent research (Postal (1971), Ruwet (1972), Giorgi (1983–1984), Hermon (1985), Georgopoulos (1987), Belletti and Rizzi (1988), Pesetsky (1987), Hoekstra (1988), Baker (1988c), Zubizarreta (to appear)). I will argue that the prominence theory of argument structure supports an explanation for the properties of these verbs which exploits the prominence relations provided by the representation of argument structure. The central idea is that the two classes of verbs have the same thematic prominence relations, although they differ with respect to their aspectual properties (see 2.3) and hence with respect to the d-structure realization of their arguments.

The thematic hierarchy (in various versions) has been given several functions in the literature. It has been thought to govern control (see Nishigauchi (1984) for a recent example), passivization (Jackendoff (1972)), and linking or argument realization (as proposed in, e.g., Carrier-Duncan (1985), L. Levin (1985), Bresnan and Kanerva (1989)). It has even been suggested that it governs anaphoric relations (see, for example, Jackendoff (1972), Giorgi (1983–1984), Hellan (1988)). The hierarchy has had, however, no real status in the theory. The proposal that I will be developing has at its core the idea that the hierarchy has the effects it has because it is what governs the structure of argument structure. It follows that any syntactic effects of the thematic hierarchy must be attributable at least indirectly to argument structure, since organizing argument structures is the *only* syntactic role the hierarchy plays in the theory. Only processes sensitive to a-structure can be sensitive to the hierarchy.

One very general consequence of this position is that the hierarchy can determine relations only among arguments of a single predicate, since only co-arguments are listed together in an a-structure. In chapter 4 we will see that the effects of the hierarchy in constraining passivization can be rather precisely delineated under this view, which explains the otherwise odd restriction that the effect of the hierarchy on passivization is limited exactly to co-arguments. So the location of the thematic hierarchy as a matter of a-structure representation plays a substantial role in delineating the functions of the hierarchy and its interaction with grammar. The hierarchy itself plays only one role, and this is located strictly in the interface between lexical conceptual structure and argument structure.

As will become clear in 2.6, the hypothesis that a-structure is structured in the ways described makes it possible to maintain a highly principled characterization of the role of theta-role labels. The a-structure contains no information about particular theta roles but only information about the relative prominence of the arguments. Hence, two verbs with different theta roles but the same prominence relations will be indistinguishable as far as a-structure is concerned, a possible example being an agentive predicate and a *fear* class of psychological predicates under the analysis for the latter suggested in 2.3.4. I will argue that this provides precisely enough information to support theta-marking and lexical operations, which do not refer to specific theta-role labels.[4] Without structured a-structure, reference to thematic role labels seems to be indispensable.

A practical matter arises here, however: argument structures are incomprehensible if the thematic role labels are omitted, especially in the kinds of cases at issue here, where the argument structure and syntactic structure do not match. For purposes of maintaining comprehensibility, then, I will use thematic role labels to identify arguments. The reader should bear in mind though that the theory gives no status to this information, so that (6a) is just a convenient way of representing (6b).

(6) a. (x   (y   (z)))
       Agent Goal Theme

    b. (x   (y   (z)))

One final question arises in this connection. Is it necessary to stipulate the hierarchical organization of arguments in (1)? The thematic role labels used to construct a-structures are read off from the lexical semantic representation of a predicate. It seems rather reasonable to assume that in fact the prominence relations expressed there are simply a reflection of the nature of the lexical semantic representations from which a-structure is projected, which consist of the kind of semantico-conceptual structures explored recently in Hale and Laughren (1983), Hale and Keyser (1986a), Rappaport, Laughren, and Levin (1987), and Jackendoff (1983, 1990). In this case the hierarchy need not be stipulated, which is obviously the desired result.

2.2 Theta-Marking and the Structure of A-Structure

2.2.1 Theta-Marking with Light Verbs

Grimshaw and Mester (1988) analyze a Japanese construction involving the verb *suru*, a "light" verb with an empty argument structure (see also Miyagawa (1987, 1989) and Tsujimura (1988)). When *suru* occurs as the main verb of a clause, it is accompanied by a direct object NP, and it is the head Noun of this NP that supplies the a-structure which licenses arguments. The distribution of arguments in this construction is a matter of some complexity. What concerns us here is simply the fact that though in general any argument can occur outside the NP, when both a Theme and a Goal argument occur, either both must be outside the NP, or the Theme must be inside and the Goal outside. It is not possible for the Goal to be inside and the Theme to be outside. (Nor, in fact, can both be inside, but for reasons that are not relevant for the present argument.)

From examples with *shoomei* 'proof', we can see that the arguments of a Noun can be split between the inside and outside positions. This is shown in (9a) and (10a) below. However, switching the positions of the arguments makes these examples ungrammatical. The data is presented schematically in (7) and (8). The Goal can be outside the NP with the Theme inside, but the Theme cannot be outside with the Goal inside.

(7)

(8)

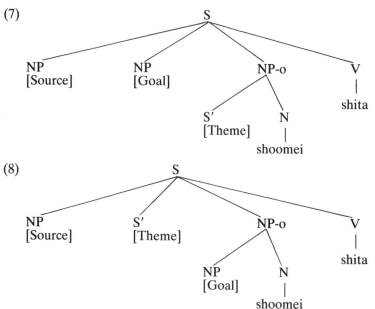

(9) a. Sono deeta-ga   wareware-ni [[kare-no   riron -ga
        that data -NOM   us   -to he -GEN   theory-NOM

        machigatteiru-to]-no   SHOOMEI]-o   shiteiru.
        mistaken be -C -GEN   prove   -ACC suru

        'That data proves to us that this his theory is mistaken.'

    b. *Sono deeta-ga   [kare-no   riron -ga   machigatte iru
         that data -NOM he -GEN theory-NOM mistaken   be

        -to] [wareware-e -no   SHOOMEI]-o   shiteiru.
        -C   us   -to-GEN   prove   -ACC suru

(10) a. Sono hookokusho-wa   Mary-ni   [[kaiketsu-no
        that report   -TOP   Mary-to   solution -GEN

        hookoo] -no   SHISA-o   shiteiru.
        direction -GEN suggest-ACC   suru

        'That report suggests to Mary the direction of the solution.'

    b. *[kaiketsu-no   hookoo -wa]   sono   hookokusho-ga
         solution -GEN   direction-TOP   that   report   -NOM

        Mary-e -no   SHISA-o   shiteiru.
        Mary-to-GEN   suggest-ACC   suru

Grimshaw and Mester argue that it is not the absolute positions of the
individual arguments that is responsible for the ungrammaticality of
(9b) and (10b). Instead, the *relative* position is the important matter: the
combination of an outside Theme and an inside Goal is ill-formed.

The generalization seems to be this: the Theme must not be further
from the theta marker than the Goal is. Yet if the Goal and Theme are
just items in a *set* of a-structure elements, we expect them to be inter-
changeable. This phenomenon thus indicates the existence of an asymmetry between the Theme and the Goal. Grimshaw and Mester propose
that the Goal-Theme asymmetry is a reflection of the organization of
argument structure, in which Theme is less prominent than Goal.
Shoomei 'proof' and *shisa* 'suggestion' then have the a-structure given in
(11):[5]

(11) (x   (y   (z)))
     Agent Goal   Theme

Two assumptions about theta-marking are needed to explain the
observed data. Suppose that theta-marking respects the organization of
the a-structure, the lowest element being theta-marked first and the

highest last. In addition, suppose that the NP constitutes one theta-marking domain and the clause constitutes another. All theta-marking within the NP precedes all theta-marking in the clause, according to a familiar cyclicity principle. Now the difference in grammaticality between (9a) and (9b) and between (10a) and (10b) is explained. The ungrammatical cases necessarily involve theta-marking the Goal, which is inside the NP, before theta-marking the Theme, which is outside. This is inconsistent with the a-structure representation of the theta-marker.

The light verb construction has one crucial property which makes it informative: it contains two theta-marking domains, the NP and the entire clause, even though it contains only one theta-marker. The theta-marking principle appealed to here is irrelevant for theta-marking *within* a domain, so it does not affect the positional realization of arguments within, say, a clause. As a result, nothing prevents the more prominent Experiencer of *frighten* from being realized as a complement while the less prominent Theme is realized as a subject.

Baker (1989, 545) suggests an alternative account for the light-verb data. He proposes that the ungrammaticality of examples like (9b) and (10b) should be explained by case theory as follows: since the Theme usually gets marked with *-o* and this case marker is already assigned to the NP containing the theta-marking Noun and the Goal, no case remains to be assigned to the Theme. However, this explanation cannot be right. As Grimshaw and Mester (1988) showed, it is fully grammatical to have both the Theme *and* the Goal arguments outside the NP. In this case the NP is still marked with *-o*, and the Theme is case-marked with *-wa* (see example (26a) in Grimshaw and Mester (1988)). Since there is case available for the Theme when both the Theme and the Goal are outside the NP, there must be case available for the Theme when it alone is outside the NP. A second consideration which shows that case cannot be what is at stake is that the same effect obtains even when the Theme is a clausal argument and hence is not case-marked, at least under the usual assumptions (Stowell (1981)). (The critical examples are (23) and (47) in Grimshaw and Mester (1988).) Furthermore, as we will see in 2.2.2, the same phenomenon occurs in compounds, and here again case-marking cannot be the explanation. For all of these reasons the asymmetry must be explained by theta theory and not by case theory, and thus it provides evidence about the nature of a-structure. Li (1990) shows that theta-marking in verbal compounds in Chinese also implicates hierarchical organization in a-structure.

2.2.2 English compounds

A similar case for structured a-structure can be made for English compounds of the kind usually called verbal or synthetic. I will argue in chapter 3 that these are distinguished from root compounds by having an argument-taking head.[6] The non-head of a synthetic compound satisfies an argument position in the a-structure of the head. As with light verbs, evidence for a structured a-structure representation can be drawn from constraints on the positions in which the non-head elements can occur.

The key assumptions are these: the non-head is theta-marked by the head, the a-structure of the head is structured in the now familiar way, and elements inside a compound are theta-marked prior to elements outside a compound. Like the NP object of *suru* in the light verb construction, the inside of a compound forms a domain for theta-marking.

Suppose, then, that we take a verb with two internal arguments, like *give*. It will be assigned the a-structure in (12), with the Agent as the most prominent argument, then the Goal, and finally the Theme.

(12) $(x \quad (y \quad (z)))$
       Agent Goal Theme

If theta-marking respects the organization of a-structure, the argument corresponding to the Theme must be theta-marked first, followed by the Goal. This predicts exactly the contrast in (13). The phrase in (13a), where the Theme is inside the compound and the Goal is outside, is grammatical. The phrase in (13b), with the Goal inside and the Theme outside, is impossible.[7]

(13) a.   Gift-giving to children
     b.   *Child-giving of gifts

The well-formedness of (14) suggests that there is nothing else wrong with (13b); *of gifts* in (14) apparently satisfies the a-structure of *giving* quite adequately.

(14) The giving of gifts to children

Thus English compounds exhibit the same Goal-Theme asymmetry as the Japanese light verb construction and similarly support the idea that argument structure represents the relative prominence of Theme and Goal in the way proposed.

The more general prediction for compounding is that when the head takes more than one internal argument, the least prominent must be inside the compound, and the more prominent outside. Examples like those in (15), which have this form, are consistently far better than examples like those in (16), which do not.

(15) a. Flower-arranging in vases
     b. Cookie-baking for children

(16) a. *Vase-arranging of flowers
     b. *Child-baking of cookies

N. Hornstein points out in a personal communication that (17) is comparatively well-formed, although it does not seem to fit the characterization given here:

(17) National Science Foundation submissions of psycholinguistic experiments went up last year.

However, it is very likely that *National Science Foundation submissions* is a root compound and not a synthetic compound, in which case theta-marking is irrelevant for its well-formedness. (We will see in chapter 3 that theta-marking Nouns do not pluralize, so that plural Nouns do not head synthetic compounds.)

In this way the prominence theory explains why all arguments are not equally available for compounding. Although the cases and explanations are both different, the essence of the First Sister Principle of Roeper and Siegel (1978) follows from the prominence theory.

The same reasoning explains a rather unexpected asymmetry between psychological verbs of the *fear* class and those of the *frighten* class:

(18) a. Man fears god.
     b. A god-fearing man

(19) a. Teenagers love fun.
     b. A fun-loving teenager

(20) a. God frightens man.
     b. *A man-frightening god

(21) a. This exploit appalls parents.
     b. *A parent-appalling exploit

While the object of *fear* can form a compound with *fearing*, this is not possible for the object of *frighten*. With the a-structure prominence relations already posited for these verbs and our assumptions about theta-marking in compounds, the explanation for (18) through (21) is already in place.

(22) a. *fear*(x   (y))
    Exp Theme

   b. *frighten*(x   (y))
      Exp Theme

As for *give*, the least prominent argument in the a-structure must be satisfied first, and the highest last. Thus the argument satisfied within the compound must be lower in the a-structure than the argument satisfied externally. For psychological verbs, the Theme is always lower in the a-structure than the Experiencer. Hence, if any argument position is satisfied within the compound, it must be this one. An example like *god-fearing* is consistent with this, since it is the Theme of *fearing* that is satisfied inside the compound and the Experiencer that is satisfied externally. In *man-frightening*, on the other hand, *man* inside the compound corresponds to the Experiencer, while the Theme is satisfied outside.[8] Hence the arrangement of arguments is inconsistent with the principle that theta-marking must respect the structure of argument structure.[9]

In sum, the properties of argument satisfaction in synthetic compounds give us a second piece of evidence for positing internal structure in a-structure. Both light verb constructions and synthetic compounds define two distinct theta-marking domains with a single predicate responsible for theta-marking within them. The properties of argument satisfaction in such cases reveal the internal structure of a-structure.[10]

Note again that left-to-right ordering inside the VP and theta-marking inside versus outside the VP are *not* restricted by the interaction of theta-marking and the structure of a-structure, which affects only theta-marking across domains. Otherwise, verbs in the *frighten* class would be unable to realize their arguments as they do, since their more prominent arguments are always theta-marked inside VPs and their less prominent outside. (We will see in 2.4 that the Theme of the *frighten* verbs *is* a d-structure subject in this theory, unlike in the Belletti and Rizzi account). Evidently, the VP does not define a domain for theta-marking, perhaps because all subjects are generated and theta-marked inside VPs, as has been suggested recently by Kuroda (1986), Koopman and Sportiche (1988), and Sportiche (1988).

An additional prediction of the structured a-structure hypothesis is that compounding of an external argument will be impossible when the predicate takes an internal argument in addition to the external.

(23) a.   Flower-arranging by novices
    b.   *Novice-arranging of flowers

(24) a. Book-reading by students
     b. *Student-reading of books

As we will see in 2.5, the external argument is always the most prominent argument in a-structure, hence by the reasoning followed here, it must always be the last to be satisfied. The ungrammatical examples (23b) and (24b) involve illegitimately theta-marking the less prominent argument outside the compound and the more prominent argument inside.

The only way for an external argument to occur inside a compound is for *all* of the arguments of the head to be inside the compound, so that the prominence relations can be respected by theta-marking. In such a situation, however, the a-structure of the head is saturated and has no open position. This, I assume, is ruled out by the general theory of predicates and arguments (see Grimshaw and Mester (1988) for a discussion of this point in connection with light verbs).

Selkirk (1982, 34) cites examples like (25) to illustrate the prohibition against compounding of externals:[11]

(25) a. *The hours for girl-swimming at this pool are quite restricted.
     b. *Kid-eating makes such a mess.

According to the reasoning followed here, there is really nothing special about an external argument beyond the fact that it is always the last to be theta-marked. If what prohibits theta-marking of an external inside a compound is the requirement that the head must be unsaturated, internal arguments should not compound either when they are the only argument. Thus to Selkirk's examples we can add those in (26) with unaccusative predicates:

(26) a. *Leaf-falling makes a big mess.
     b. *Glass-breaking can be caused by sound waves.

Why is it not possible for all the arguments of the head to be realized inside a compound? Let us examine the case where the compound has an adjectival head. (Note that compounds are headed either by adjectives or nouns in English, never verbs, since English allows no verb-headed compounds.) Adjectives are integrated into an NP when their external argument is identified with that of a noun (Higginbotham (1985)). Alternatively, their external argument is satisfied by a subject via predication.

Consider, for example, the adjective *fierce* in (27).

(27) a. The tiger is fierce.
     b. I saw a fierce tiger.

Fierce has an argument structure containing one open position, as does *tiger*. In (27b) the two positions are identified, or co-indexed, and hence satisfied together. In (27a) *the tiger* satisfies the open position in *fierce* by predication.

In examples like *a man-eating tiger* compounding does not affect the basic mode of argument satisfaction. *Eating* has two arguments, one of which (the "eaten"argument) is satisfied within the compound and the other of which is identified with the *R* argument of *tiger* (See 3.3 on *R*).

(28) a. *eating*(x (y))
      b. *man-eating*(x) & *tiger*(R)   x = R

Similarly, in *a god-fearing man*, *fearing* has two arguments, one satisfied inside the compound and the most prominent satisfied by identification with the *R* argument of *man*.

(29) a. *fearing*(x (y))
      b. *god-fearing*(x) & *man*(R)   x = R

What would happen if an adjective had all its arguments satisfied internally by compounding? Consider the form *shouting* in (30):

(30) a. *shouting*(x)
      b. *man-shouting*( )

After compounding has produced *man-shouting*, the adjective has no open position. Hence, there is no way for its external argument to be identified with the *R* external argument of a head noun. Thus there is no way for the adjective to modify a noun.[12] The same reasoning holds even if the compounded argument is internal. Hence, adjectives like *leaf-fallen* cannot exist, just as *man-shouting* cannot. Structures that resemble these but have very different interpretations are possible as root compounds precisely because root compounds to do not involve a-structure satisfaction (see 3.4).

Related reasoning explains the fact that external arguments do not incorporate, a point argued by Baker (1988) to follow from the Empty Category Principle (ECP). One type of incorporation seems to be just compounding (di Sciullo and Williams (1987), Rosen (1989a)).[13] As with compounding, then, if an external argument is satisfied inside a compound, all arguments of the head must be. Otherwise, theta-marking would not be respecting the prominence relations of the a-structure. In an incorporation structure like *meat-eat*, *meat* will satisfy the internal argument of *eat*, and the external argument remains open for syntactic satisfaction. In a case like *people-work*, however, the verb has no open arguments at all. Hence, it does not constitute a well-formed predicate, and there is no way for it to be integrated into the clause.

In sum, then, the hypothesis that argument structure is structured in accordance with the thematic hierarchy, together with the assumption that cross-domain theta-marking must respect the structure of the argument structure, allows us to explain a cluster of properties of light verbs and compounds. At least one argument must be satisfied outside the compound, and the prominence theory guarantees that this will always be the most prominent argument.

2.3 Structured Argument Structure: The Aspectual Dimension

The a-structure representation proposed in 2.1 always assigns the Experiencer more prominence than the Theme for both *fear* and *frighten*, which explains the compounding facts of 2.2.2. Why, then, is the Experiencer realized as the subject in one class and not in the other? The syntactic realization of arguments is obviously not a direct reflection of their thematic prominence. The answer lies, I argue, in the existence of a second kind of semantic analysis which assigns a different status to the Experiencer of *frighten* and the Experiencer of *fear* and leads to their realizations. The interaction of this second analysis, which is aspectual in character, with the thematic analysis, provides a general theory of external arguments.

2.3.1 The inadequacy of thematic reanalysis
One reason that the *fear* and *frighten* classes might differ is that the apparent identity of their thematic roles is misleading. Suppose that in reality what I have been calling the Experiencer is not really a unified category: perhaps the thematic role involved for *fear* is different from the one involved for *frighten*. Or perhaps the Theme is not really the same in the two cases (whatever else this argument may be, it certainly is not a Theme by the generally accepted definition used in Jackendoff (1972)).[14]

Within the present theory there are major limits on the usefulness of thematic reanalysis of the verb types. If an alternative analysis does not alter relative prominence of the arguments, the a-structure representation will be identical in all relevant respects. All that will be changed is the thematic role labels themselves, but they are not part of the argument structure. (Recall that the only role that thematic labels play in this account is to determine the relative prominence of an argument in a-structure.) If the prominence relations are left unchanged, nothing is gained in the present terms, since *frighten* and *fear* will have identical a-structure representations:

(31) a. x *frightens* y   *frighten*(y (x))
     b. y *fears* x   *fear*(y (x))

If, on the other hand, the prominence relations of *frighten* are reversed as a result of the thematic reanalysis, which would make the subject of *frighten* higher in the argument structure than the object, *frighten* will look just like, say, *arrest* or any other well-behaved verb.

(32) a. x *frightens* y   *frighten*(x (y))
     b. x *arrests* y   *arrest*(x (y))

Though this appears to make sense of the fact that the *x* argument is the subject, it makes sense of no other facts. The problem is precisely that the *frighten* class does not behave like other verb classes: its members exhibit a cluster of properties that appears to be systematic. Consider, for example, the explanation offered in 2.2.2 for the restrictions on compounding. This explanation relies crucially on the idea that the a-structure prominence relations for the *frighten* class are not the same as those for *fear*. If the *frighten* verbs are analyzed as in (32), they should behave just like any other dyadic predicates, but they don't. Similar points hold for the passivization and nominalization properties of the *frighten* class (see chapter 4) and their behavior with respect to anaphora (see chapter 5). An analysis like the one that gives (32) leaves no opening for explaining the cluster. In fact, the very claim that the psychological predicates exhibit a cluster of significantly related grammatical properties must inevitably be denied.

Pesetsky's (1987) proposal along these lines is that the subject of *frighten* has the role "cause of emotion," while the object of *fear* has the role "target of emotion." This proposal has exactly the property just discussed, that it assimilates the *frighten* class of psychological verbs to other classes and thus cannot provide a basis for explaining their properties. In Pesetsky's account, their interaction with anaphora, for example, is quite independent of their other properties.

In addition, there is one piece of evidence that the subject of *frighten* and the object of *fear* do indeed have the same theta role. If we assume some version of what is sometimes called thematic uniqueness, no verb can have multiple occurrences of a single thematic role.[15] If the subject of *frighten* and the object of *fear* have the same role, no verb could have both kinds of argument. As Pesetsky (in preparation a) points out, it does not seem possible for the two to co-occur.

(33) a.   Mary was frightened of the ghost.
     b.   *The movie frightened Mary of the ghost.

If the *of* phrase in examples like (33a) has the same theta role as the subject of *frighten*, (33b) will violate thematic uniqueness, and its ungrammaticality can be explained.[16] Of course, this explanation critically relies on the idea that the verbs are *thematically* related, either absolutely identical or identical at least up to whatever determines co-occurrence. Any account that denies thematic identity must offer a completely different explanation for the generalization.

In sum, thematic relabeling will not solve the problems to be addressed here. If it changes the prominence relations for *frighten*, it will overregularize the verb. If it does not change them, it will have no effects at all. The conclusion is, then, that there is a systematic relationship between the theta roles of the two classes, which can be captured by treating them as thematically identical.

2.3.2   The inadequacy of lexical case marking

If the theta roles of *fear* and *frighten* are identical, what distinguishes them? Belletti and Rizzi (1988) propose that the difference between *fear* and *frighten* is that the Experiencer argument of *frighten* is associated with a lexical accusative case-marker, which anchors it to a postverbal position. If we incorporate this analysis into the present account, we get an argument structure like (34).

(34) *frighten*(x-acc (y))
          Exp   Theme

The case feature specifies an association between the Experiencer and a particular syntactic realization, an accusative-case-marked position. The intention is that this pre-linking prevents the Experiencer argument from being realized as subject, since its [-acc] specification would be contradicted if nominative assignment is obligatory, a point due to N. Hornstein.

Pre-linking treats the difference between *fear* and *frighten* as the result of an arbitrary lexical stipulation. Yet in fact there are systematic differences between the two classes, which cannot be connected in any way to the case feature on *frighten*: the verbs in the *fear* class are Dowty-Vendler states, while those in the *frighten* class are not. Clearly, we must seek a solution that relates the realization of the arguments to

other properties of the Verbs. Moreover, the difference in argument
realization is cross-linguistically stable: for example, the psychological
verbs in Tagalog have the same realization properties (Carrier-Duncan
(1985, 8)). All of this suggests that it is not possible for a verb meaning
what *fear* means, to have its arguments realized like *frighten*, nor vice
versa. Hence, lexical stipulation cannot be the source of the differences
between them.

Nevertheless, there is some evidence, given in Grimshaw (1987), that
the behavior of the *frighten* class is connected to lexical case-marking in
some important respects. One serious puzzle for a lexical case solution
such as Belletti and Rizzi's is why an Agent argument can never be
associated with accusative case. If an Experiencer can be, why not an
Agent? This would yield an agentive verb with its Agent in object position, just as the representation in (34) yields an experiencer verb with its
Experiencer in object position. It turns out that this gap appears also in
the overt lexical case-marking system of Icelandic: lexical case-marking
of Agents is prohibited, so Agents are always nominative (Andrews
(1982), Yip, Maling, and Jackendoff (1987)). Moreover, we will see in
chapter 4 that the behavior of lexically case-marked subjects in Icelandic parallels that of the Experiencer argument of the *frighten* class
in one other major respect: neither one undergoes the suppression process crucially involved in passivization and nominalization. This suggests that realized lexical case in Icelandic, and whatever distinguishes
the *frighten* class, do share some crucial properties. The theory of external arguments given in 2.5 unifies these observations. It follows from
the interaction of their thematic and aspectual properties that Agents
are inevitably external arguments, while Experiencers are not, and
both the distribution of quirky case and the limits on passives and
nominals result from this difference.

2.3.3 Another dimension of semantic analysis
The critical difference between the two classes seems to be that the
frighten class and the *fear* class belong to different aspectual subclasses
according to the Vendler-Dowty classification. In particular, the *frighten*
verbs have a causative meaning not shared by the *fear* class (Chomsky
(1970), Ruwet (1972), Pesetsky (1987, in prep. a)), the subject causing a
change of psychological state in the object. Accordingly, (35b) is a
reasonable paraphrase of (35a).

(35) a. The storm frightened us.
    b. The storm caused us to experience fear.

Verbs in the *frighten* class are causative and not stative. Those in the *fear* class, on the other hand, are always stative and never have an event reading:

(36) a.   The storm was frightening us.
     b.   *We were fearing the storm.

There is a tendency for the morphology to reflect the causative character of these verbs also, as we can see from the *en* forms in (37). (M. Everaert points out that *enjoy*, a member of the *fear* class, shows that the morphology is not always helpful).

(37) a.   The movie *en*raged the audience.
     b.   The move fright*en*ed the audience.

In other languages, such as Japanese, the morphology is transparently that of a causative (Pesetsky (in prep. a)). Finally, the vast majority of verbs in the *frighten* class (for example, *frighten*, *annoy*, *bother*) have an agentive counterpart with an obviously causative meaning.

Yet the strongest reason for considering verbs of the *frighten* class to be causative is that, as we noted above in connection with Pesetsky's proposal concerning the thematic analysis of *frighten*, it provides immediate insight into their argument realization: the cause arguments of causative predicates are always subjects. The *frighten* class simply behaves in just the same way as any other causative in this respect. Hence, the fact that the argument corresponding to the cause is realized as the subject for the *frighten* class is no longer a mystery.

Zubizarreta (to appear) argues against a causative analysis for the *frighten* class. She suggests that the causative interpretation is due to the presence of an implied causal adjunct, metonymically related to the subject of the predicate, as in (38).

(38) The article angered Bill *by its content.*

This view seems to leave unexplained the argument realization of these predicates and the aspectual differences between the two psychological classes. Moreover, the adjunct analysis may itself presuppose the causative character of the *frighten* class, since causal adjuncts themselves seem to be limited to causative predicates:

(39) a.   John killed Bill by his foolish action.
     b.   *Bill died by his foolish action.
     c.   ?The storm frightened the children by its noise.
     d.   *The children feared the storm by its noise.

If this is true, the very possibility of having the causal adjunct in (38) argues in favor of the causative analysis for the *frighten* class.

The basic idea, then, is that the arguments of *fear* and *frighten* are thematically the same but they differ fundamentally in that for *frighten* the Theme is a cause, and in the *fear* class it is not. The causal status of this argument determines whether it is the grammatical subject of its clause; if it is a cause it must be realized as a subject. To express this generalization, the lexical representation must express the causal status of an argument. It could be treated as a kind of diacritic if we have recourse to some rule like "Assign subject realization to a cause argument." Or causal status could be treated as a property that contributes probabilistically to the likelihood of an argument being a subject, as Dowty (1989) proposes. We have alrealy seen that building it into the thematic role labels and subdividing these labels into smaller and smaller units does not result in an illuminating solution.

A more interesting interpretation is that the importance of the causal status of the argument is indicative of a dimension of prominence relations distinct and autonomous from the thematic dimension. This develops within the prominence theory a notion of multiple semantic analyses, tiers perhaps, like those proposed in Jackendoff (1987, 1990). The causal structure of a predicate also defines a hierarchy, just as the thematic structure does, a hierarchy in which the Cause argument is most prominent:

(40) a. (Agent (Experiencer (Goal/Source/Location (Theme))))
     b. (Cause (other (. . .)))

How do the two hierarchies combine in a lexical representation? The lexical semantic representation of a predicate projects the set of its grammatical arguments and a specification of their thematic and causal status. Each of the two hierarchies imposes its own set of prominence relations on this collection of arguments, as illustrated in (32) for *break*.

(41) a. The girl broke the window.
     b. *break*(x   (y))
             Agent Patient
             Cause . . .

The argument in the subject position of *break* is more prominent than the object along both dimensions, since it is a cause and a thematic Agent.

For the *frighten* verbs, however, the first position in the thematic organization does not correspond to the first position in the cause dimension, since they are not occupied by the same semantic argument. Instead, the second element in the thematic dimension is associated with the first element in the causal dimension, and the first element in the thematic dimension corresponds to the second position in the causal dimension.

(42) a. The building frightened the tourists.

    b. *frighten*(x   (y))

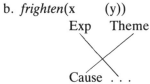

The special character of the non-agentive *frighten* class has its source, according to this proposal, in a conflict between two hierarchies, the subject being most prominent in the causal hierarchy but not in the thematic hierarchy.

This view about the *frighten* class allows us to complete the picture of compounding begun in 2.2.2. The ungrammaticality of examples like (43a) was explained there as a violation of the theta criterion. But why is (43b) not possible?

(43) a. *A child-frightening storm
    b. *A storm-frightening child

The answer is that (43a) is impossible because it requires the Theme to be theta-marked in a wider domain than the Experiencer, and (43b) is impossible because it requires the non-Cause to be theta-marked in a wider domain than the Cause. Since there is no way to theta mark without violating one or the other of the two sets of prominence relations, there is no well-formed compound corresponding to non-agentive *frighten*.

2.3.4 The aspectual dimension

A more general understanding of the special character of the subject of the *frighten* class can be achieved if the status of the cause argument is examined in terms of event structure or aspect. If the special characteristics associated with the *frighten* class follow from the misalignment of the two dimensions, verb classes which do not show these characteristics should resemble agentive predicates like the *break* causative in having perfect alignment of the two dimensions. None of the peculiarities associated with the *frighten* class with respect to anaphora, compounding, passive and nominalization, etc., are found with agentive verbs like *arrest* or unergative verbs like *work* (see 2.5.2 on unaccusatives). Moreover, the *fear* class, at least in English and Italian, seems to behave like the agentive predicates. For these verbs, therefore, the prominence relations in the two hierarchies must coincide.

As this shows, the notion of cause is too narrow, since verbs like *arrest*, *work*, and *fear* are not causatives. Despite this, the subject of *fear*, the subject of an agentive predicate, and a cause, must all have some property in common, which qualifies an argument for maximal prominence in the second dimension. This property is clearly not thematic, since it does not coincide with the theta roles of the arguments. In fact, the relevant property cross-classifies with theta roles, and that is why *frighten* and *fear* can come out different.

My proposal is that the dimension is aspectual in character, since it is a projection of the event structure of the predicates. I assume that each verb has associated with it an event structure, which when combined with elements in the clause, provides an event structure for an entire sentence. The event structure represents the aspectual analysis of the clause, and determines such things as which adjuncts are admissible, what the scope of elements like *almost* will be and so forth (Vendler (1967), Dowty (1979), Bach (1986), Pustejovsky (1988) Tenny (1988, 1989a, 1989c)).

The event structure breaks down events into aspectual subparts. For example, a Vendler-Dowty "accomplishment" denotes a complex event (which consists of an activity) and a resulting state (see in particular Pustejovsky (1988) for a discussion).

(44)   event

        activity   state

An accomplishment like *x constructs y* is analyzed as an activity in which *x* engages in construction plus a resulting state in which existence is predicated of *y* . For *x breaks y*, the activity is one which *x* engages in breaking, and the resulting state is one in which *y* is broken.

Now a cause argument has a standard representation in such an analysis: it will always be associated with the first sub-event, which is causally related to the second sub-event. Thus we have a clue as to how the aspectual dimension is derived. The generalization is that an argument which participates in the first sub-event in an event structure is more prominent than an argument which participates in the second sub-event. A cause is always part of the first sub-event. Hence, it is always more prominent than the argument corresponding to the element whose state is changed.

If the aspectual analysis for the first sub-event involves more than one argument, which counts as most prominent? Suppose, for example, that *x breaks y* should be analyzed as an activity involving both x and y and a resulting state involving y. The definition must still pick out x as the aspectually most prominent argument even though two arguments are involved in the first subevent. There are a number of ways to achieve this result. Here we will just assume that an argument associated only with the first event counts as more prominent than an argument associated with both sub-events. This result can be obtained by indexing each argument with the number of the sub-event it appears in (a 1 if it appears in the first sub-event and a 2 if it appears in the second) and then choosing the argument indexed with just 1 as most prominent.[17]

Using event structure in this way will give us the result we want for accomplishments. How does it extend to the other verb classes? Simplifying Pustejovsky (1988) somewhat, we can give this analysis for an unergative verb like *work*:

(45) event

activity

Note that this resembles the first sub-event of the representation in (44) and hence seems to follow the general pattern. Since the argument engaged in the activity is in the first sub-event of the event structure, it will count as maximally prominent, as desired.

Obviously, it is critical exactly how the event structure is set up. Pustejovsky (1988) presents evidence bearing on its organization which stems from aspectual considerations. We also have as evidence the realization of arguments: the aspectually most prominent argument is realized as the subject. The proposed aspectual analysis thus allows a very simple statement of the principle of subject selection.

The case of psychological state verbs like *fear* is considerably more delicate. The desired result will follow if their Experiencer qualifies as the aspectually most prominent argument, since the two semantic dimensions will then coincide. Hence, members of this verb class have external arguments. This result seems to be the right one for Italian (Belletti and Rizzi (1988)) and for English, as I will argue. However, it must be admitted that in this case there is no independent evidence that the aspectual analysis will give this result, so for present purposes we must simply stipulate it. It is clear, then, that while the proposed two-dimensional view strongly entails that a verb in the *frighten* class has no external argument, it does not strongly entail the a-structure analysis of the psychological state predicates.

Now we can examine the interaction between the aspectual analysis and the thematic analysis for the major verb classes at issue. For agentive predicates, the Agent will be the aspectually most prominent argument for all aspectual classes of verbs. Since it is also thematically most prominent, the subject of an agentive verb like *arrest* is most prominent according to both hierarchies.

(46) *Transitive agentive*
    (Agent (Theme))
      1   2

(Since I have no particular evidence on the aspectual status of the Goal and Theme, I will indicate their ranking with an x.)

(47) *Ditransitive*
    (Agent (Goal (Theme)))
      1   x   x

The same holds for the subject of an unergative verb:

(48) *Unergative*
    (Agent)
      1

By hypothesis, even for the *fear* class, the alignment of the two tiers is the same as for the agentive class. The Experiencer is maximally prominent both thematically and aspectually.

(49) *Psychological state*
    (Exp (Theme))
      1   2

For the *frighten* class, however, the Experiencer is not the aspectually most prominent argument; the Theme is. Hence, we have the desired mismatch between the results of the aspectual and thematic analyses:

(50) *Psychological causative*
    (Exp (Theme))
      2   1

Finally, the agentive counterparts to the members of the *frighten* class will have the representation in (51), in which the two dimensions are perfectly aligned, just as they are for the agentive verbs in (46).

(51) *Agentive psychological causative*
   (Agent (Exp))
     1   2

None of the characteristic effects found with the non-agentive experiencer verbs should be matched in the agentive cases.

The analysis that thus emerges for the psychological causatives is very clearcut. If all of this is correct, there is nothing particularly difficult about this class. From their semantics their a-structure inevitably, follows and hence also their grammatical behavior.

As we have seen, however, the issue of how the *fear* class should be analyzed is a much more delicate one. First, there is no well-established independent analysis of their aspectual structure that would guarantee that the Experiencer will be aspectually more prominent than the Theme. Second, while the psychological causatives seem to be extremely stable cross-linguistically, the same is not true of the psychological state predicates. While verbs in the *fear* class in English and Italian behave as if they have external arguments, undergoing passivization and so forth, in other grammatical systems (Old English and Icelandic, for example) verbs with the same *apparent* meaning can get quirky case-marked arguments (Allen (1986), Sigurðsson (1989)) and fail to undergo operations like passivization. In the prominence theory, this must be attributed to their lacking an external argument. Third, there is yet another sub-class of the psychological predicates which will not yield to the analysis proposed here. It includes verbs like *please* and *concern*, which share the realization of their arguments with *frighten* but are not accomplishments. They are, in fact, states (note that they do not occur in the progressive).

(52) a.   The weather pleased/pleases us.
     b.   *The weather was/is pleasing us.

(53) a.   The news concerned/concerns us.
     b.   *The news was/is concerning us.

To this extent, at least, these verbs share their basic semantics with the *fear* class, despite the difference in argument realization. In Dutch and Italian this class is easy to detect because it consists of verbs that are self-evidently unaccusative; they select the perfect auxiliary of the unaccusatives, for example. These true unaccusatives are the *piacere* 'please' class of Belletti and Rizzi (1988), the *ontvallen* 'escape' and *bevallen* 'please' class that Everaert (1986, 112–115) discusses and con-

trasts with verbs like *ergeren* 'annoy', and perhaps also the dative experiencer cases of Legendre (1989).

What should be said of such cases? It is quite conceivable that the event structure or thematic analysis of these verbs is subtly different from those of the English/Italian *fear* class and leads to their displaying a thematic/aspectual mismatch and hence to their having no external argument. How the realization of their arguments can be predicted under such an analysis or whether such an analysis is even tenable remains to be seen. It is always possible, though unlikely, that there is nothing interesting to be said about the psychological state verbs and that learners must decide on the correct analysis for each instance (see Pinker (1989) for a detailed discussion of the learning of lexical verb classes).

One question raised here as well as by Belletti and Rizzi's (1988) analysis of psychological predicates is why the *frighten* class does not behave as unaccusatives do with respect to auxiliary selection and *ne* cliticization in Italian if they lack an external argument, like the true unaccusatives. In the analysis given here, *frighten* verbs and the unaccusatives differ in that only unaccusatives involve NP movement. Since the subject of a *frighten* verb is never in object position, *ne* cliticization is correctly ruled out. As for auxiliary selection, the difference in transitivity between the *frighten* class and the unaccusatives could be involved in the auxiliary selection. Or if we follow Burzio (1986), the choice of *essere* may be based on the presence or absence of an underlying subject and not on whether a predicate has an external argument. This would distinguish the unaccusatives from the psychological predicates in the appropriate way.

2.4 Consequences of Thematic and Aspectual Prominence for Linking

The two-dimensional proposal has a number of consequences for a general theory of argument realization, or linking as it is sometimes called (Fillmore (1968), Carrier-Duncan (1985), Ostler (1979), L. Levin (1985), Carter (1988), Tenny (1989a), Bresnan and Kanerva (1989), Jackendoff (1990)).

First, the existence of verbs like the *frighten* class with Experiencer objects and Theme subjects is expected. The proposal locates the special property of the *frighten* class of verbs in the relation between its thematic and aspectual analyses. This is not a matter of lexical idiosyncracy; it is a principled consequence of the dimensions of meaning in

natural languages, and their interactions. Since there are two dimensions of prominence, there is no particular reason why they should always coincide. It is no mystery, then, that languages have verbs for which the two dimensions do not match. Far from being exceptional, their existence is inevitable once the dimensions of prominence have been set up.

Second, the aspectual hierarchy determines which argument gets realized as the subject.[18] (It seems possible, then, that in general this dimension determines the configurational realization of arguments, with the thematic analysis governing such matters as Preposition choice. Tenny (1989a) discusses the effects of aspect on argument realization.) If the aspectually most prominent argument is always the grammatical subject, the realization of the arguments of both the *frighten* class and the *fear* class of psychological predicates is fully predictable.[19]

This contrasts with most recent proposals, which treat the realization of the arguments either as essentially unpredictable (for example, Belleti and Rizzi (1988)) or as determined probabilistically (Dowty (1987)). In the Belletti and Rizzi account nothing makes it possible to predict whether or not a given occurrence of an argument with the Experiencer role will be associated with [acc], so there is no way to predict that the subject of *frighten*, but not of *fear*, is generated in the postverbal position. Dowty (1987) suggests a probabilistic account of "subject selection," defining an "Agent Proto-Role" with the following properties: it has volition or sentience/perception, it causes the event, it moves, its referent exists independently of the action of the verb. The basic idea is that the more of these properties an argument has, the more likely it is to be a subject. Dowty's proposal is a response to the failure of purely thematic theory to provide illuminating accounts of argument realization. It is certainly clear that thematic roles alone do not determine linking (consider, for example, the alternation in realization of Goals and Themes in the dative construction or the realization of Experiencers in subject and object position). Nevertheless, it is undesirable to retreat to a probabilistic theory such as Dowty's because some of the restrictions are absolute and can *never* be overridden. Agents and causes are always subjects, for instance, no matter what their other properties may be. Descriptively, the cluster of properties that Dowty isolates seems quite accurate. This is precisely because the proposal essentially lists properties of thematically most prominent arguments and aspectually most prominent arguments. Positing an aspectual dimension of prominence interacting with the thematic dimension provides another kind of solution to the linking problem.

The third consequence for linking is that if the d-structure realization of arguments is determined by the aspectual dimension, the subject of the *frighten* verbs must be a d-structure subject. Causes are always associated with subject position, and it would presumably complicate rather than simplify the linking if we generated the cause/Theme argument anywhere other than in subject position.[20] Moreover, Zubizarreta (to appear) presents evidence that the subject of a psychological predicate is indeed in a Theta position. Zubizarreta observes that in French the pronoun *ça* appears as an argument, while *il* appears as an expletive:

(54) a. C'est possible (que Marie ait peur des mouches).
    'It is possible (that Marie fears flies).'
   b. Il semble que Marie a peur des mouches
    'It seems that Marie fears flies.'

If the subject position of the *frighten* class is a non-theta position, it should be occupied by *il* when the Verb has a sentential complement. As (55) shows, the prediction is false. The verb *amuser* acts like a transitive verb in this respect.

(55) a. Ça m'amuse (que Marie ait peur des mouches).
    'It amuses me (that Marie fears flies).'
   b. *Il m'amuse que Marie ait peur des mouches.

This argument of Zubizarreta's supports the conclusion that the *frighten* psychological verbs have an underlying subject. It follows that the kind of analysis given in Hermon (1985) and Belletti and Rizzi (1988), which relies on the idea that the subjects of psychological predicates are derived subjects, is not available in this theory for causative psychological predicates. The properties of the *frighten* class must follow, then, from a-structure representation and not from a subjectless d-structure status. Of course, this theory does not rule out NP movement in principle, and NP movement in the derivation of passives and unaccusatives remains available (see 2.5.3).

Belletti and Rizzi (1988) present evidence from extraction that the superficial object of the Italian counterpart to the *frighten* class is not really an object but a sister of V'. This conclusion suggests an instantiation of the linking principles which places the Experiencer outside V' even though there is no direct object present. In the other direction, Levin (1987) points out several respects in which the Experiencer acts like other direct objects, for example, middle formation (*She frightens easily*). The two sets of observations about the Experiencer—that is does not extract like an object and that it does seem to act like other objects with respect to lexical operations—can be reconciled if the Experiencer is an internal argument generated outside V'. As with external arguments, this requires a clear separation of the a-structure notion *internal* from the configuration notion *NP of V'*.

Finally, this proposal for linking predicts that Agents will always be subjects (see chapter 4 on the status of *by* phrases in passives). Why are Agents so well behaved? Under the two-dimension proposal we have an answer to this question: the behaviour of Agents is just a special case of the more general behavior of causes; they are always subjects. Since Agents are always maximally prominent on the aspectual dimension, the two dimensions always coincide for Agents, and their subject status is assured. This has given the impression, I believe, that the thematic properties of Agents *alone* determine their realization, which leads to a general commitment to the idea that thematic roles should always suffice to predict realization. However, the case of Agents is now seen to be misleading, for it is really the combination of the aspectual and thematic analyses that determine the subject status of Agents. In all likelihood the very notion *Agent* encodes both aspectual status and thematic status, hence its success as a predictor of realization (see Jackendoff (1987, 1990)).

Thus the general idea that a-structure representation is derived from a combination of thematic analysis and aspectual analysis allows us to explain a number of properties of the argument realization system. The existence of verbs like the *frighten* class which exhibit mismatches between the two dimensions is predicted, the realization of Experiencers in the two classes of psychological predicates follows, and we can explain the reliable subject status of Agents.

2.5 External Arguments and A-Structure Prominence

2.5.1 A theory of external arguments

The notion of *maximal prominence*, together with the two dimensions along which prominence is determined, makes possible a new characterization of the concept of an *external argument*. If we define an external argument as an argument that is maximally prominent in both dimensions, a number of important properties of external arguments immediately follow.

The notion of an external argument was first introduced in Williams (1981a) and has been shown to figure extensively in morpho-syntactic theory (e.g., Marantz (1984), Zubizarreta (1985, 1987), Levin and Rappaport (1886), di Sciullo and Williams (1987)). In Williams's theory of a-structure and in much subsequent work, the external argument of a predicate is indicated by underlining. Thus the a-structure of *arrest* is that given in (56).

(56) *arrest*($\underline{x}$, y)   or   (Agent, Theme)

Williams defines the external argument of a predicate as the argument that is realized outside the maximal projection of the predicate, the d-structure subject for a Verb.

While it is clear that the concept is essential to understanding lexical representation, the external argument has a somewhat mysterious status. Why should there be such a thing as an argument distinguished in this way? Why can there be only one such distinguished argument? What principles determine which argument, if any, should count as external? Why is an Agent always external if there is one?

The same questions arise in other theories of a-structure representation, like that of Rappaport and Levin (1986). They use angle brackets as diacritics to distinguish internal from external arguments—the single argument outside the brackets is external, and the others are internal.

(57) put: x < *y* P-loc z>

In (57), (7) of Rappaport and Levin (1986), italicization distinguishes the direct argument of the head. Like Williams's (1981a) representation, this representation is based on diacritics. While it may very well encode the right information, it offers no basis for a principled theory of externality. Note that these representations do not actually *structure* the argument structure in any important sense, as in Grimshaw and Mester (1988) and here. The angle brackets are used simply as diacritics, equivalent to writing internal arguments in upper case, and play no other role in the theory.

The structured a-structure account offers solutions to the problems concerning external arguments, by grounding the concept of an external argument in a more articulated theory of a-structure representation. The theory relates the notion of an external argument to relationships among other arguments. Every argument in an a-structure has a certain prominence in each dimension relative to every other argument. An external argument is just the limiting case, an argument that is most prominent in both respects. Let us investigate how this view of externality answers some of the issues concerning external arguments.

First, this definition of an external argument allows us to derive the behavior of external arguments under theta-marking, as described in 2.2. It follows from the proposal that the external argument must always be the last one to be theta-marked, since theta-marking always proceeds from the least to the most prominent. It thus follows that if there are two theta-marking domains with a single theta marker, as with compounds and light verbs, the external will always be realized in the higher domain. This captures, I believe, the essential insight of Marantz's (1984) proposal. Marantz suggests that the external argument is not included in the a-structure at all and that this is why externals fail to interact with lexical processes of various types.[21] In the present theory the prominence relations allow us to derive this key effect while representing external arguments in the a-structure of predicates just like any other argument.[22] In any theta-marking calculation, the external argument is the last one to enter in. Thus, in effect, calculations performed over the internal arguments are done without reference to the external arguments, but any a-structure calculation involving the external arguments will of necessity involve the internal ones. The special properties of externals follow from their occupying the position of maximal prominence.

Second, there is no particular mystery to the idea of an external argument if it is defined as I am suggesting. It is a kind of argument that inevitably results when both dimensions of analysis pick out the same argument as most prominent.

Third, it is immediately obvious why no predicate has more than one such argument, since only one argument can meet the criterion of maximal prominence.

Fourth, from the two-dimensional account we can predict whether a predicate has an external argument, and if so, which of its arguments qualifies. An Agent must always be external if it is present. We have already seen that an Agent always qualifies for maximal thematic and causal prominence. Hence, it will always count as external, and an agentive verb will always have an external argument. The *fear* class of psychological predicates also has an external argument in the analysis in 2.3.4.

On the other hand, the *frighten* class of psychological verbs has no external argument. The Experiencer is the thematically most prominent argument of a *frighten* verb, but it is not the aspectually most prominent argument.[23] The cause argument is aspectually, but not thematically, the most prominent. Since no argument holds maximal prominence in both dimensions, the *frighten* class has no external argument.

As preliminary evidence for the claim that the members of the *frighten* class have no external arguments, consider the observation made by Zubizarreta (to appear) that these verbs do not participate in the causative/anticausative alternation, while causatives in general do:

(58) a. Someone broke the glass.   The glass broke.
      b. Someone frightened John.   *John frightened.

Zubizarreta's observation is straightforwardly explained in the prominence account if the alternation (like passivization and nominalization) affects only external arguments.[24] Zubizarreta points out that this data is problematic for Pesetsky's account of the *frighten* class, in which they are regular causatives with no distinguishing properties (see the discussion in 2.3.1). In the prominence account these psychological predicates differ from the other causatives precisely in that while agentive causatives have an external argument, the *frighten* verbs do not. As we will see in chapter 4, the fact that the *frighten* verbs lack external arguments also explains their failure to undergo certain operations. Since both nominalization and passivization involve suppression of an external argument, verbs of the *frighten* class cannot undergo either process. More generally, the prominence definition of external argument explains the existence of a Thematic Hierarchy Condition on passivization and an unexpected limitation on its effects (see 4.3.1). The fact that the *frighten* verbs have no external arguments is also the key to their behavior with respect to reflexive cliticization, as argued in chapter 5.

Fifth, the theory developed here distinguishes the notion of an external argument from that of a d-structure subject. The *frighten* verbs *do* have a d-structure subject (the cause), even though they have no external argument. Hence, this analysis agrees with Belletti and Rizzi's account in claiming that they have no external arguments but not in claiming that they have derived subjects. The most important difference is that in the prominence theory we can explain why they lack external arguments, something which had to be stipulated under Belletti and Rizzi's account. This notion of an external argument is conceptually quite different from the one proposed by Williams, who equates an external argument with a d-structure subject. In the prominence theory, *external argument* is an a-structure-theoretic concept. The two theories diverge for the *frighten* psychological predicates, which have no external arguments despite having underlying subjects.

Separating the a-structure notion *external* from the d-structure notion of *subject* makes it possible to accommodate new ideas about the configurational representation of subjects. Kuroda (1986), Sportiche (1988), Koopman and Sportiche (1988), and Rosen (1989b, 1989c) all argue that subjects are generated under the VP node and move to Specifier of IP for reasons of case rather than being generated under IP, as previously assumed. This view is actually inconsistent with a definition of an external argument that requires that an external argument be generated outside the maximal projection of the head. It might be possible to redefine the external argument as the argument generated outside the X-bar level, but it is quite unclear how this revision would include external arguments for other categories, NP in particular (see 3.3, 4.5.2). A definition of *external* based on a-structure representation and not on configurational representation unifies the various cases as a matter of principle.

A similar issue arises in Marantz's (1989) analysis of agreement in Georgian. Marantz argues that "dative subjects" (Experiencers and subjects of perfect predicates) are generated in Specifier of VP position, as are indirect objects. However, dative subjects "bear a projected government relation with respect to V'," which makes them subjects, while indirect objects do not count as subjects. The two behave differently in a number of respects. The distinction can be rephrased in terms of the theory proposed here: the dative subjects are actually external arguments, while the indirect objects are not.[25] Hence their different behavior.

2.5.2 External arguments and quirky case

The association of the thematic and aspectual dimensions suggests a hypothesis about "lexical" or "quirky" case assignment (Zaenen, Maling, and Thrainsson (1985), Van Valin (1989a), Maling and Kim (to appear)). As I mentioned in 2.3.2, there are some striking similarities between the behavior of verbs with lexically case marked arguments and the behavior of the *frighten* verbs. This similarity has a natural explanation in the present terms. Suppose that quirky argument realization can occur only when the thematically most prominent argument is not also the most prominent in the other dimension. We can view this as a situation in which the thematically most prominent argument is skipped in the aspectual analysis, as in (59). Hence, the realization of the argument will not be specified by the aspectual analysis; rather, it can be lexically specified, or *quirky*.

(59) Thematic dimension: (1 (2 (3)))
     Aspectual dimension: (1 . . .)

This immediately explains why Agents never get lexical case: they are always most prominent in both dimensions and so are never skipped in this way. More generally, the proposal predicts that external arguments are never quirkily case-marked, since all external arguments are maximally prominent in both analyses. Hence, only internal arguments can in principle get quirky case. This conclusion is essentially that reached also in Van Valin (1989a) and Sigurðsson (1989). (Note that once again we obtain the result that external arguments are exempt from a lexical process, quirky case marking this time, without appealing to Marantz's (1984) proposal that the external argument is not part of a lexical entry.) Quirky-case-marked subjects, then, are not external arguments, although they may well be d-structure subjects.

Most striking, this proposal concerning quirky case explains the fact, mentioned in 2.3.2, that verbs with quirky-case-marked subjects can never be passive (Zaenen, Maling, and Thrainsson (1985)). For an argument to get quirky case, it must not have maximal prominence in both dimensions, since quirky case arises only when there is imperfect alignment. But passivization involves suppression of an external argument (see 4.3.1), an external argument must be maximally prominent in both dimensions, and such an argument can never receive quirky case. Hence, passivization and a quirky-case-marked subject are incompatible.

2.5.3 Unaccusatives

In the two-dimensional system a verb lacks an external argument if no single argument is most prominent in both dimensions. We have seen that the *frighten* verbs lack such an argument. The other major class of verbs with no external argument is the *unaccusatives*. The conclusion that unaccusatives have no external argument is based on their behavior with respect to a large number of phenomena (see, e.g., Perlmutter (1978), Perlmutter and Postal (1984), Hoekstra (1984), Burzio (1986), Grimshaw (1987), Zaenen (1987a, 1987b), Van Valin (1989b), and Levin and Rappaport (1989)). This research has provided a fair understanding of the grammatical consequences of unaccusativity and also some initial insight into *why* unaccusativity exists and what determines the unaccusativity of certain semantic verb classes.

The two-dimensional theory tells us where to look for an explanation for the existence of unaccusativity. An argument will not count as external if it is not maximally prominent in both dimensions. Unaccusative predicates, then, must have arguments that fail to reach maximal prominence either in the aspectual dimension or in the thematic dimension (or both). However, many unaccusatives are monadic. If a Verb has only one argument, what would prevent that argument from being the most prominent in both dimensions?

One kind of answer could be adapted from Hale and Keyser (1988). The basic idea is that (at least for verbs which alternate between a causative and an inchoative use), the unaccusative version has a hidden lcs argument, something like a cause in the present system. This argument takes up the external slot, forcing all other arguments to be internal. In the present terms, the cause argument would count as most prominent on the aspectual analysis, so none of the overt arguments of the verb could qualify as external. The advantage of such an account is its ability to predict that the argument is internal. The disadvantage lies in the claim that the lexical semantic representation of the predicate really does contain a cause argument. In view of the large number of aspectual and other semantic differences between causatives and unaccusatives (not to mention middles, which they treat in the same way), the semantic analysis is hard to defend. Yet if only relative prominence is involved in calculating externality, it is hard to see any alternative to importing Hale and Keyser's extra argument, even for unaccusatives with no transitive variant. Apparently, more than *relative* prominence is involved; some measure of *absolute* prominence must contribute too.

Suppose that there are some absolute requirements on maximal prominence in either of the two dimensions. We might define a maximally prominent argument as one surrounded by a single set of parentheses and propose that the Theme is always surrounded by two sets. An unaccusative verb would have no external argument because the Theme would not count as maximally prominent even when there is no more prominent argument to compete for this assignment:

(60) ((x))
     Theme

Why should the Theme never count as external? The theory should give this argument a special status because of its role in the semantics of a predicate; I suggest that this status arises from the organization of the aspectual dimension. As has been pointed out by Zaenen (1987a, 1987b), Van Valin (1989a), and Tenny (1989c), the unaccusative predicates belong to particular aspectual classes; they express certain states or changes of state. The event structure of an unaccusative, then, corresponds to the *second* subpart of an accomplishment (as illustrated in (61) and (62)), whereas the event structure of an unergative corresponds to the first subpart.[26]

(61) accomplishment
      [[activity][state/change of state]]

(62) unergative   unaccusative
      [[activity]]   [state/change of state]

Presumably, it is not accidental that the argument involved in part 1 of (61) and the argument involved in the activity of (62) both count as external, while the argument involved in the second part of (61) and the argument involved in a simple existential state or inchoative do not. Recall that the aspectually most prominent argument is an argument associated with the *first* subevent.

All of this suggests, then, that the argument of an unaccusative can never meet the aspectual requirement for externality, because it intrinsically has the wrong status with respect to the event structure—it always has the aspectual prominence of the internal argument of an accomplishment rather than that of the external argument. This result will follow if what determines the aspectual hierarchy is an event-structure template which is fixed for all predicates rather than being projected from the lexical semantic representation of the individual predicate. The aspectual dimension, then, is a projection of an abstract event structure (e), which always includes two subparts, an activity (act) and a state or change of state (s/cos):[27]

(63)   e

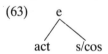

      act   s/cos

The event template determines prominence, assigning the maximally prominent position in the aspectual dimension only to an argument participating in the first subevent, regardless of the actual lexical semantic representation of the predicate. If all events are constrained by this template, activities will always fit the first slot in the template, and an existential state or a change of state will always fit the second slot. Thus the single argument of an unaccusative will never count as maximally prominent and will never qualify as external.

This proposal does not change anything in the analysis of the verb classes discussed in 2.3.4. The agentive predicates (both transitive and unergative) and presumably the *fear* class will have an aspectually and thematically most prominent argument. The *frighten* psychological verbs will have an argument that has maximal aspectual prominence but does not have maximal thematic prominence and does not qualify as external. The unaccusatives will lack a first sub-event and hence will lack an external argument.

For purposes of the present investigation, the important distinctions are between external and internal arguments and between thematically more and less prominent arguments. I posit the representations in (64), using the convention that an external argument is one surrounded by only one set of parentheses. Because of their aspectual/thematic properties, neither unaccusatives nor the *frighten* class have such an argument. Otherwise, prominence is represented as before.

(64) a. *Transitive agentive*
     (x   (y))
     Agent Theme

   b. *Ditransitive*
     (x   (y   (z)))
     Agent Goal   Theme

   c. *Unergative*
     (x)
     Agent

   d. *Psychological state*
     (x   (y))
     Exp Theme

   e. *Psychological causative*
     ((x   (y)))
      Exp Theme

   f. *Psychological agentive*
     (x   (y))
     Agent   Exp

   g. *Unaccusative*
     ((x))
      Theme

What are the implications of this proposal for the syntactic analysis of unaccusatives? Is the single NP argument of an unaccusative generated as a d-structure subject or as a d-structure object? Most versions of the unaccusative hypothesis assume that the surface subject of an unaccusative is a d-structure object and not *just* an internal argument. There are two reasons for this. The first is conceptual and has no force within the current framework of assumptions. If the internal/external distinction is equated with the VP-internal/VP-external distinction, as in Williams's original proposal, an internal argument must by definition occur within the VP at d-structure. Hence, it would be incoherent to have an unaccusative predicate with a d-structure subject but no external argument. However, the prominence theory has already separated the notion of an external argument, an a-structure notion, from the notion of a subject, a configurational notion.

The second reason for analyzing the internal argument of an unaccusative as a d-structure object is that some of the phenomena associated with unaccusativity are not likely to reduce to the a-structure status of this argument. Consider, for example, *ne* cliticization in Italian (See Burzio (1986) and references there). We can *stipulate* that only certain arguments allow *ne* cliticization (Van Valin (1989a), for example, proposes that only predicates with a State predicate in their semantic analyses allow *ne* cliticization), but it seems unlikely that an explanation for the behavior of *ne* cliticization can be couched in terms of a purely semantic analysis, like Van Valin's, or a purely a-structure theoretic analysis. It seems considerably more likely that the system of government or related syntactic notions lie behind the phenomenon, as is usually assumed. Such an explanation implies that the argument of an unaccusative must be governed and hence must be an object, not a subject.

I conclude that the aspectual status of the unaccusative argument makes it internal and places it in d-structure object position, not subject position. The aspectual status of the Theme argument of a *frighten* psychological predicate guarantees that it is realized as a d-structure subject. Thus although both are internal arguments, their d-structure positions are different because their aspectual status is different. All external arguments are d-structure subjects, but not all d-structure subjects are external arguments. To be a d-structure subject is necessary but not sufficient for external argument status.

With a definition of external arguments that requires an external to be maximally prominent along both dimensions of semantic analysis, and with the event structure analyses proposed in 2.3.4, we arrive at an analysis in which all agentive verbs and psychological state verbs of the *fear* class have external arguments. Verbs of the (non-agentive) *frighten* class and the unaccusatives have no external arguments. In this way a-structure representations which support explanations for the properties of the various verb classes can be derived from the prominence theory.

2.6 Theta Role Labels

An important property of the prominence theory of argument structure is that it makes no use of theta role labels in the a-structure representation. Argument structure represents the argument-licensing capacity of a predicate without specifying any semantic information about its arguments, except for their relative prominence.

Consider, for example, the explanation for argument distribution in light verb and compound constructions given in 2.1. The actual theta role labels play no role in the solution. Instead, there is a general characterization of the constraint obeyed by theta-marking in these constructions from which the specific facts for individual verb classes follow. A similar point holds for the definition of external arguments and for the principles of argument realization involved in selecting subjects. Defining relations of prominence along the thematic and aspectual dimensions makes it possible to define *external argument*, and to determine which verbs have one and which do not, all without referring to labels like Agent, Experiencer, and so forth. Moreover, I have been able to explain the three special characteristics of Agents: that they are always subjects, that they always count as external arguments, and that they are never quirky case-marked. Again, once the prominence relations are in place, no further reference to the thematic or aspectual status of the argument is required.

In a similar vein I will argue that the existence of apparently thematic constraints on passivization and nominalization in fact follows from the grammatical representations of the predicates interacting with general principles of a-structure and not from stipulations about theta roles. Even the fact that the psychological predicates behave oddly in a number of respects does not require reference to theta role labels. Statements like "Do such and such to the Theme" or "Do such and such to a verb with an Experiencer argument" play no role in explaining the grammatical properties of these verbs.

Thus, the introduction of prominence relations into the a-structure makes it possible to eliminate reference to the theta role labels themselves. In this way a-structure prominence makes it possible to maintain the view of Rappaport and Levin (1986) and Zubizarreta (1987) that thematic role labels should be eliminated from argument structure.

Thematic roles, in this view, are purely lexical conceptual labels and do not project into the grammatical representation. Thematic role labels provide convenient terminology for *describing* many lexico-syntactic problems, but they do not figure in *solving* them. The solutions depend only on relative prominence among arguments and on the general principles which refer to the structure of a-structure.

2.7 Summary

The general thesis of this chapter is that argument structure has internal organization and that this internal organization is not stipulated for each predicate but is projected from lexical semantic representation. In particular, I have proposed that the theory of external arguments depends on the results of two separate semantic analyses: one in terms of aspectual properties and one in terms of thematic properties. This makes it possible to explicate some of the core properties of external arguments, to understand how theta-marking works in cases of multiple theta-marking domains, and ultimately to explain the grammatical behavior of various verb classes.

This theory differs from other theories of a-structure in one further respect: there is no sense in which the external or internal status of an argument can be changed by a lexical operation. An argument is external or internal by virtue of its intrinsic semantic properties. Thus the core operations defined in Williams (1981a), externalization and internalization, must be reinterpreted in the prominence theory. Later sections will present analyses of verbal passives, nominals, adjectival passives, and causatives which do not stipulate alterations in the internal/external status of arguments.

Chapter 3
Nominalization

The general question of the relationship between nouns and verbs has occupied a central place in theoretical investigation since Chomsky (1970). Although it is now generally agreed that nouns differ from verbs in not being able to assign case, the extent and character of similarities and differences with respect to argument structure and theta theory is still an open issue. It is often asserted, for example, that nouns take arguments only optionally (for various versions of this idea, see Anderson (1983–1984), Higginbotham (1983), Dowty (1989)).

One of the primary goals of this chapter is to show that this not correct. Nouns can and do take obligatory arguments. This property of nouns has been obscured by the fact that many nouns are ambiguous between an interpretation in which they do take arguments obligatorily and other interpretations in which they do not. My claim will be that nouns denoting *complex* events, which have an associated event structure of the kind discussed in chapter 2, also have an argument structure. The argument structure of such a noun must be satisfied, hence the obligatoriness of its arguments. Other nouns—those that denote what I call *simple* events, and the *result* nominals—have no argument structure. A similar argument is made for Italian by Bottari (1989). These nouns do, of course, have a meaning, sometimes even a relational meaning, expressed by their lcs representation. I will document a large set of differences between nouns in the argument-taking class and other nouns, all of which can be connected up under the hypothesis that the two types of nouns have different kinds of external arguments.

The view that lexical heads can be either theta-marking or not makes it possible to characterize the difference between synthetic compounds like those discussed in chapter 2, and root compounds. The hypothesis is that synthetic compounds have heads with argument structure, which take the non-heads as arguments, while root compounds have heads that don't theta mark.

With the basic differences established between nouns that theta-mark and nouns that do not, we can investigate the behavior of what are often called passive nominals. Suprisingly, they turn out to behave exactly like result nominals and simple event nominals. Perhaps even more surprising, the same is true of nouns with sentential complements. Neither of these two types of nominals behaves in any way like the complex event nominals that have a-structure. I will argue that this follows from the hypothesis that even nouns with a-structure are defective and require the aid of Prepositions to act as theta-markers.

Finally, those satellite phrases which are not arguments themselves break down into types. What I call *complements* are found with simple event nominals. They correspond to lcs arguments and hence obey selectional requirements of these arguments. *Modifiers*, on the other hand, do not correspond to lcs arguments, except indirectly, when the external arguments of the nouns they are modifying are bound to lcs positions. The modifier-modifiee relation, but not the complement-head relation, can be established by predication across a copula as well as by modification. The principles governing complements and modifiers explain many characteristics of passive nominals and nominals with clauses as modifiers and complements. We can explain why nouns like *decision* and *belief* behave differently from nouns like *attempt* and *knowledge*. Moreover, the long-standing puzzle of why sentential complements are impossible with -*er* nominals is solved within this system.

3.1 Ambiguity in the Nominal System

In some fundamental respects verbs and nouns seem to share complement-taking properties. This was established in Chomsky (1970) and is illustrated by the famous pair in (1).

(1) a. The enemy destroyed the city.
    b. The enemy's destruction of the city.

The range of elements that can occur after nouns is closely related to the range that can occur after verbs, apart from the failure of nouns to take bare NPs.

(2) a. *CP complement*
       The physicists claimed that the earth is round.
       The physicists' claim that the earth is round.

b. *Infinitival complement*
   They attempted to leave.
   Their attempt to leave.

c. *Locative PP complement*
   The train arrived at the station.
   The train's arrival at the station.

Examples like these might suggest that nouns and verbs have the same a-structure representation, are governed by the same principles of argument realization, and differ only in their case-assigning properties. There are two primary stumbling blocks to this view. One is the fact that subjects of clauses, at least tensed clauses, are strictly obligatory, while what look like the subjects of noun phrases are equally strictly optional. This is explained in the terms of the theory under development here as a function of an a-structure difference between nouns and verbs. This analysis, sketched in chapter 1, will be developed further in chapter 4.

The other important difference concerns non-subject arguments. Here too it appears that nouns optionally take arguments, while verbs take them obligatorily. So we find sets of data like (3):

(3) a. *The doctor examined.
    b. The doctor's examination (of the patient) was successful.
    c. *They attempted.
    d. Their attempt (to reach the top) was successful.

The data in (3) might be construed as showing that the nouns *examination and attempt* are simply indifferent to the presence or absence of their complements while the verbs absolutely require their presence. By such reasoning we would reach the conclusion that nouns take arguments only optionally and so differ quite fundamentally in their theta-marking properties from verbs.

However, appearances are misleading here. The flexibility exhibited by the nouns in (3) is due to a fundamental and persistent ambiguity within the nominal system: nouns do not behave uniformly. Some are systematically like verbs in their argument-taking capacities. Other classes of nouns are quite different and in fact take no arguments at all. This situation is obscured by the fact that many nouns are like *examination* in being ambiguous between the two classes. Once the ambiguity is factored out, the apparent complexity of the behavior of nouns reduces to a basic division between nouns that take arguments and nouns that do not.

The existence of highly significant ambiguities within the system of nominalization has long been recognized, of course. Most work on nominals acknowledges a distinction between concrete and abstract nouns or between result and process nouns. This research incorporates various views about the grammatical effects of the ambiguity (Anderson (1983–1984), Randall (1984), Grimshaw (1986b), Lebeaux (1986), Roeper (1987), Zubizarreta (1987), Bottari (1989), and following some of this work, Levin and Rappaport (1988) and Rappaport and Levin (1989)).

The fundamental ambiguity in nominalization correlates with ambiguity in the interpretation of phrases in construction with the noun. When a noun is ambiguous between the two readings, as *examination* is, an associated possessive is also ambiguous between the modifier reading found with concrete nouns and the a-structure-related reading in which the possessive provides information about a position in the argument structure of the noun (see chapter 4 for more information on how this is accomplished). So a possessive modifying *examination* can be the possessor, author, or taker of the exam, as in (4a). Alternatively, it can have an a-structure-related interpretation as in (4b), where *John* is interpreted as the agent of an action.

(4) a. John's examination was long.
    b. John's examination of the patients took a long time.

This is essentially the conclusion of the study of possessive NPs in Anderson (1983–1984). Anderson concluded that prenominal genitives are of two different types, depending on the kind of noun they are modifying. When possessives are associated with concrete nouns, they can be modifiers, which are uniformly non-theta-assigning. With abstract nouns, possessives can either be modifiers or have a subject-like role. Anderson suggests that abstract nouns can in principle be either theta-assigning or not. When they are not theta-assigning, they behave like concrete nouns in taking possessive modifiers. When they are theta-assigning, they take a subject-like argument. Anderson based her distinction on the specifier system, but we can show that the very same distinction pervades the complement system for nouns and lies behind the apparent optionality of the arguments of nouns seen in (3).

3.2 Nominals and Event Structure

3.2.1 Event structure and argument structure in nominals

The division among nouns corresponds roughly to the well-known result versus process distinction. Result nominals name the output of a process or an element associated with the process; process nominals name a process or an event. The noun *examination*, for example, has two interpretations. In (5a) it can refer to a concrete entity; in (5b) it refers to an event. While *examination* is ambiguous, the abbreviated form *exam* is unambiguously a result nominal and does not occur in all the same contexts as the process nominal.

(5) a. The examination/exam was long/ on the table.

     b. The examination/*exam of the patients took a long time/*was on the table.

The *result* and *process* labels, however, do not provide an illuminating way of characterizing the entire range of relevant cases. I will argue that the real distinction is between nouns that have an associated event structure of the kind discussed in chapter 2, which I will call *complex event nominals*, and nouns that do not. (Even nouns that denote events behave like result nominals unless they have an event structure which provides them with an internal event analysis.) Since argument structure is composed from the aspectual and thematic analyses of a predicate, we can now hypothesize that any predicate lacking an aspectual analysis will also lack an argument structure and will never take any grammatical arguments at all.

3.2.2 The presence or absence of argument structure

Since complex event nominals have an event structure analysis, they have a-structure and take arguments. If the a-structure of a nominal has exactly the same status as that of a verb, it must be satisfied. The prediction is, then, that complements to complex event nominals will be obligatory. Of course, *obligatory* must mean the same for nouns as for verbs: capable in principle of being obligatory but perhaps subject to lexical variation. After all, even direct objects of verbs are sometimes optional.

The widespread ambiguity between the two types of nominals will complicate the process of testing the hypothesis, and various techniques of disambiguation must be invoked. In the simplest case we can just pick unambiguous nouns and see how they behave. Lebeaux (1986) cites *felling* and *destroying,* points out that they have only a process reading, and shows that they are identical to the corresponding verbs with respect to their objects, which are obligatory.

(6) a. The felling *(of the trees)
    b. They felled *(trees).
    c. The destroying *(of the city)
    d. They destroyed *(the city).

Gerundive nominals behave exactly as predicted if they are argument-taking: they take obligatory arguments. We will see later that they share the determiner system, and event properties of the other complex event nominals.

The disambiguation of other derived nominals supports the conclusion that complex event nominals take grammatical arguments. It is often possible to disambiguate nouns with both readings: certain modifiers occur only with the event interpretation of particular nouns. For instance, the modifier *frequent* forces the event reading of *expression* in (7). Once we disambiguate, we can see that the object of the event nominal is obligatory.

(7) a. The expression is desirable.
    b. *The frequent expression is desirable.
    c. The frequent expression of one's feelings is desirable.
    d. We express *(our feelings).

A similar explanation can be given for (8). In (8a) there is a result nominal, which of course does not require (or indeed allow) an argument. The addition of *constant* as in (8b) rules out the result reading, since *constant* cannot be construed as a modifier of *assignment* on its result reading, and forces the complex event reading of the noun. Hence, its a-structure must be satisfied, as in (8c), just as the a-structure of *assign* must be satisfied in (8d).

(8) a. The assignment is to be avoided.
    b. *The constant assignment is to be avoided.
    c. The constant assignment of unsolvable problems is to be avoided.
    d. We constantly assign *(unsolvable problems).

Why should *constant* and *frequent* have this effect? My suggestion is that when they modify singular count nouns, they must be licensed by event structure, like other aspectual modifiers. Thus they can occur with nouns like *assignment* and *expression* only when the nouns have an event structure, whence their disambiguating function. Of course, both *constant* and *frequent* have other uses, found with plural result nominals (and certain non-count nouns), which are not associated with an event.[1] Note the change in meaning from (8b) to (9), for example:

(9) The constant assignments were avoided by students.

A further kind of evidence for the obligatoriness of arguments with complex event nominals comes from the behavior of possessives. Recall that subject-like possessives are licensed by a-structure (see chapter 4 for evidence and more details). Thus when a possessive subject occurs, the noun must have an argument structure. So the presence of an possessive interpreted as a subject will force the complex event reading of the noun, where the noun has an argument structure to be satisfied. This in turn should lead to the appearance of obligatory objects.

This reasoning explains an observation made by Lebeaux (1986) that if a "subject" is present, the object of an action nominal is obligatory. Of course, this not strictly correct as stated: action or event nominals *always* take obligatory arguments. In reality, the presence of the subject serves to disambiguate the nominal in the direction of the event reading.

(10) a.   The examination took a long time.
      b.   (*)The instructor's examination took a long time.
      c.   The instructor's examination of the papers took a long time.
      d.   The instructor examined *(the papers).

The result nominal *examination* in (10a) is perfectly well-formed with no *of* phrase. When a possessive NP is added, as in (10b), there are two possible interpretations. If the possessive is construed as a possessive modifier, as just somehow associated with the noun, (10b) is grammatical. But if it is construed like a subject, (10b) is ungrammatical. So the instructor in (10b) cannot be the agent of *examination*. This point is hard to establish because clearly in the interpretation of the possessive modifier *does not exclude* a reading in which the "possessor" was the instigator. My claim is that this is different from a true subject reading, however, and that the "possessor" cannot be construed strictly as the agent. As evidence that this position is correct, note that if an agent-oriented adjective is included in the nominal in (10b), it becomes clearly ungrammatical, as in (11a), unless the argument structure of *examination* is satisfied, as in (11b):

(11) a.   *The instructor's intentional/deliberate examination took a long time.

b. The instructor's intentional/deliberate examination of the
papers took a long time.

So *deliberate* in (11a) has only a manner reading, and *intentional* has no
sensible interpretation.

As expected, the inclusion of an a-structure-related element requires
the argument-taking version of the noun, which takes obligatory arguments. The agent-oriented adjectives in (11) contribute by making the
possessive necessarily agentive and thus ruling out the modifier reading.
The addition of an *of* phrase as in (10c) satisfies the a-structure of the
head, just as addition of a direct object satisfies the a-structure of *examine* in (10d).

This pattern is entirely systematic. It is replicated for *development* and
destruction in (12) and (13); (12b) and (13b) are ungrammatical with the
possessive construed as Agent.

(12) a. The development was applauded.
b. * The city's development was applauded.
c. The city's development of inexpensive housing was
applauded.
d. The city developed *(inexpensive housing).

(13) a. The destruction was awful to see.
b. * The enemy's destruction was awful to watch.
c. The enemy's destruction of the city was awful to watch.
d. The enemy destroyed * (the city).

One other kind of subject-like element occurs in nominals, the *by*
phrase. Just like a possessive, the *by* phrase is licensed by a-structure
(see chapter 4). Hence, the prediction is that inclusion of a *by* phrase
will have the same effect as the addition of a possessive subject: disambiguating the nominal into an argument-taking reading and making
objects obligatory. Hornstein (1977, 148, n. 12) pointed out that a *by*
phrase renders the object obligatory, as is illustrated in (14).

(14) a. The expression * (of aggressive feelings) by patients
b. The assignment * (of unsolvable problems) by the instructor
c. The examination * (of the papers) by the instructor
d. The development * (of inexpensive housing) by the city
e. The destruction * (of the city) by the enemy

Like possessives, *by* phrases can occur as simple modifiers not related to
an argument structure at all. Only the subject-like *by* phrase will disambiguate the nominal in the direction of its argument-taking reading.

The modifier *by* phrase will not. Hence, examples like those in (15) are possible even without a complement because the nouns have no a-structure to be satisfied.

(15) a. An examination by a competent instructor will reveal. . .
    b. The assignment by Fred was no good.
    c. Pine Tree Hollow—a development by Homes Associates.

By manipulating the context to disambiguate nominals, it is possible to see that nominals do take obligatory objects, just as verbs do. But the existance of the ambiguity explains why objects might *seem* to be optional for nouns. If a noun is ambiguous in the relevant way, it will take an object in its theta-marking use and not take one otherwise. Using *expression* as an example, we find pairs like (16a, b): (16a) contains a non-theta-marker, and (16b) the theta-marker.

(16) a. The expression (on her face)
    b. The expression of her feelings

Initial inspection of such data may well give the appearance of optionality for the object, but it is only an appearance, since what is really involved is an alternation between two cases of the noun. When it has no a-structure, it behaves like a concrete noun in taking only modifiers, but when it has an a-structure, it behaves like a verb in taking, and indeed requiring, arguments. In this view, the kind of reasoning usually employed to show that arguments are optional for nouns is simply based on the wrong nouns, those that are not argument-takers at all. Dowty (1989), for example, shows that the noun *gift* is not obligatorily associated with any complements and concludes that event nouns do not take arguments, as verbs do. In fact, however, *gift* is simply not a complex event nominal in the first place. In fact, it is questionable whether it is even a simple-event nominal in view of the oddness of ??*The gift occured at six*. In any event, the failure of *gift* to take arguments certainly does not indicate that nouns in general fail to do so.

Dowty (1989) proposes that the way in which nouns compose with their arguments is fundamentally different from the way in which verbs do so. In view of the differences among nominals discussed here, this is too simple. Result nominals and simple event nominals are indeed not verb-like in the way they combine with their satellites. Complex event nominals are verb-like in having a-structure, although not in the way they theta-mark (see below).

My conclusion, then, is that nouns with a complex event interpretation have an argument structure, which must be satisfied, and other nouns do not. But, of course, even result nominals imply the existence of certain participants in the situations they are used in. For an exam to exist, someone must have made it up, for example. The proposal here crucially distinguishes between syntactic *arguments*, which stand in a grammatically significant relationship to predicates, and what we might call *participants*.

Nonetheless, even participants have a status in the theory. Verbs and nouns have meaning and are associated with a lexical semantic representation, a lexical conceptual structure (lcs), of the kind presupposed in chapters 1 and 2. Among other information, the lcs defines a set of participants involved in the meaning of a lexical item. Verbs project (at least some) participants into their a-structure and thus make their participants grammatical arguments. Complex event nominals do the same. Other nominals have participants even though they do not have grammatical arguments. We will see in 3.6 that the lcs status of a participant crucially affects its form through the effects of selection.

3.2.3 Properties of the determiner system

The distinction between argument-taking complex event nominals and other nominals correlates with a set of differences in the determiner system. The indefinite determiner and the numeral *one* occur only with result nominals; the same holds for demonstratives like *that*, which are compatible only with result nominals. Only the definite determiner *the* occurs with both kinds of Noun. These points can be seen clearly with the Noun *assignment*, which is ambiguous in much the same way as *examination*:

(17) a. They studied the/an/one/that assignment.
      b. They observed the/* an/* one/* that assignment of the problem.
      c. The assignment of that problem too early in the course always causes problems.

When *assignment* is associated with a grammatical argument structure, as it is in (17b, c), it admits only the definite determiner.

In addition, complex event nominals do not pluralize, while result nominals do. Moreover, with complex event nominals it is possible to have no determiner at all, as in (18c), although this is not generally possible with singular count nouns.

(18) a.   The assignments were long
      b. * The assignments of the problems took a long time.
      c.   Assignment of difficult problems always causes problems.

In these respects the head noun of a complex event nominal behaves like a non-count noun, allowing no determiner, but differs in allowing the plural form. The heads of other nominals can be either count or non-count, depending on their intrinsic properties.

Emmon Bach has pointed out to me that there is a further restriction on complex event nominals: they resist indefinite subjects:

(19) a. ??A teacher's assignment of the problem
     b. The assignment of the problem by a teacher

This is explained by the observation of Jackendoff (1969) and Fassi Fehri (1987) that the definiteness of a phrase is determined by that of its possessive. Consider the behavior of possessives in existential contexts:

(20) a. There's a man's shirt on the chair.
     b. * There's the man's shirt on the chair.

The examples in (20) show that the entire NP has the definiteness of the possessive even though the determiner is clearly associated with the possessor and not with the head. (Note that *man's shirt* in (20) is not a compound, as the phrasal stress on *shirt* shows.) This observation makes it possible to reduce Bach's generalization to the previous point, namely that event NPs cannot be indefinite. The presence of the indefinite possessive would make the entire NP indefinite, which is not permitted.[2] Note that this proposal also explains why the restriction does not hold of the *by* phrase in (19b), which is apparently in the same semantic relationship to the head as the possessive in (19a). The *by* phrase is not in a position from which definiteness is projected.

An important difference of another kind is that process nominals do not occur predicatively or even with equational *be*, while result nominals do:

(21) a. That was the/an assignment.
     b. * That was the/an assignment of the problem.

Since predicative NPs require an indefinite determiner and complex event nominals are never indefinite, this alone may explain the failure of predication.

In all of these cases there is a kind of secondary construal in which the complex event nominal behaves like the result nominal. I believe that this is due to a process of type shifting by which the event nominal can be treated as though it referred to an individual rather than an event. So an expression like *that assignment of the problem* might be well-formed with a meaning like *that instance/case of assignment of the problem*.

Under such a shifted interpretation a complex event nominal will systematically violate the criteria discussed here. It will take the determiner system of other nominals, and it will occur predicatively.

The cluster of properties that typifies the complex event nominals can be directly observed with -*ing* nominals. As we saw in 3.2.2, the nominal -*ing* affix is unambiguous. Apart from a few lexicalized cases (*handwriting*, for example), gerundive nominals pattern perfectly as complex event nominals. They allow only the definite determiner, never pluralize, and never occur predicatively:

(22) a. The shooting of rabbits is illegal.
     b. *A/one/that shooting of rabbits is illegal.
     c. *The shootings of rabbits are illegal.
     d. *That was the shooting of rabbits.

Work by Torrego (1988) on extraction from NPs in Spanish and French shows an important interaction between the determiner system and the extractability of modifiers and complements. This interaction partially implicates the very ambiguities in nominalization that are connected with argument-taking properties.

3.2.4 Unambiguous modifiers

It is already apparent that many phrases that appear in construction with nouns are ambiguous between argument-structure-related meanings and more modifier-like interpretations. Prenominal possessive, *by* phrases, and PPs introduced by *of* all have both uses. The possessive in a phrase like *John's book* is not related to an argument structure, while the possessive subjects in (10c), (12c), and (13c) are. The *by* phrases in (14) are related to a-structure, while those in examples like *a book by Chomsky* and *a picture by Picasso* are not. Other languages distinguish the two cases overtly; Esther Torrego has pointed out to me that Spanish *by* phrases can act in nominals and passives as a-structure-related expressions (as a-adjuncts in fact, see chapter 4) but not as modifiers (examples (23) and (24) are due to Claudia Borgonovo).

(23) a. El libro fue escrito por Chomsky.
         'The book was written by Chomsky'.
     b. La destruccion de la ciudad por el ejercito
         'The destruction of the city by the army'

(24) a. *Un libro por Chomsky
     b. Un libro de Chomsky
         'A book by Chomsky', 'Chomsky's book'

In contrast to the behavior of *by* phrases and possessives, some phrases occur only as modifiers and never have an a-structure-related interpretation. Postnominal genitives are unambiguously modifiers, co-occuring only with non-argument-taking nouns, so examples like *an examination of Bill's* are unambiguous. Certain possessives can never be interpreted as related to a-structure, since their meaning is such that they cannot contribute information about an argument position, at least information of the relevant kind. One example is temporal possessives like *yesterday's*, *last year's*, *this semester's*, which are disallowed, as expected, in complex event nominals.

(25) a.   This semester's assignment led to disaster.
     b.   *This semester's constant assignment of unsolvable problems led to disaster.
     c.   The constant assignment of unsolvable problems this semester led to disaster.

The nominal in (25a) is fine because *assignment* here is a result nominal. Sentence (25c) is also fully grammatical because *this semester* is an adverbial, the kind of phrase that can be associated with a complex event nominal. The ungrammaticality of (25b) shows that complex event nominals can take adjuncts but not modifiers. I conclude that these modifiers are associated only with nouns with no argument structure. This is obviously another reflection of the fact that non-argument-taking nouns refer to individuals and simple events and argument-taking nouns refer to complex events.

3.2.5 Aspectual differences

The third class of differences concerns the aspectual behavior of the two kinds of nominals.

First, there is a telling difference concerning the possibility of "event control." Nominals, like passives, allow control into an infinitival purpose clause. Lasnik (1988) and Williams (1985) argue that the controller in such cases is the "event" denoted by the clause or the nominal, rather than an implicit argument of the Noun, as proposed in Roeper (1987). This point will be taken up in detail in 4.4. As (26) shows, "event" control is possible with a passive, as in (26a), and with the complex event nominals in (26b, c).

(26) a.   The book was translated (in order) to make it available to a wider readership.

b. The translation of the book (in order) to make it available to a wider readership

c. (The) examination of the patient in order to determine whether . . .

Unambiguous result nominals never allow control:[3]

(27) a. *The translations of the book (in order) to make it available to a wide readership

b. *The exam in order to determine whether . . .

c. *The murder in order to preserve peace

d. *The solution (to the problem) in order to simplify the assigment

The difference is explicable if the control here is by an event and if only complex event nominals denote events in the relevant sense.

The two classes of nominals differ critically in their ability to license aspectual modifiers like *in an hour*, *for six weeks*, and as Lebeaux (1986) points out, *while* clauses. Complex event nominals admit the same aspectual modifiers as their verbal counterparts, a point discussed in Vendler (1967) and Dowty (1979).

(28) a. The total destruction of the city in only two days appalled everyone.

b. *The total destruction of the city for two days appalled everyone.

c. The bombing destroyed the city in only two days/*for two days.

(29) a. Only observation of the patient for several weeks can determine the most likely . . .

b. *Only observation of the patient in several weeks can determine the most likely . . .

c. They observed the patient for several weeks/*in several weeks.

It is important to see that this characterization of the critical class of nominals is not equivalent to labeling them event nominals. There are many nominals that seem to denote events but do not behave like the complex event nominals (see Zucchi 1988). Consider, for example, the nouns *race*, *trip*, *exam*, and even *event*. They do denote events in some sense at least. They certainly occur or take place, and they occur over time, for example. Hence, expressions like *took a long time* or *took place* can be sensibly predicated of them.

(30) The event/race/trip/exam took a long time/took place at 6:00 P.M.

This may be the right notion of an event for some purposes, but it is clearly not the right notion for distinguishing those nouns that take syntactic arguments from the others. Nouns of the type in (30), which I call *simple event nominals*, act just like result nominals in most respects (see 3.6 for differences). They share the determiner system of result nominals, occur only with optional modifiers and not with arguments, disallow *frequent* and *constant* unless they are in the plural, and disallow event control:

(31) a. That trip/event took three weeks.
      b. That trip/those trips took three weeks.
      c. *The frequent trip/event was a nuisance.
      d. The frequent trips/events were a nuisance.

(32) *That trip/event in order to . . .

Moreover, if we try to combine these nominals with the aspectual modifiers, following a suggestion made by Fred Landman personal communication, we find that while argument-taking nominals behave like their base verbs, the other nominals disallow aspectual modifiers of any kind (see Tenny (1989b)):

(33) a. *Jack's trip in five hours/for five hours was interesting.
      b. *The process in five hours/for five hours.

The distinction between complex event nominals and the others, then, is a matter not of having temporal extent but of the existence of an internal semantic analysis of the event provided by the event structures, as in chapter 2. Nouns in the result class and the simple event class (*event*, *trip*, etc.) lack this internal analysis. Hence, they all behave in the same way with respect to the issues at hand. Only the complex event nominals have the internal aspectual structure needed for event control and needed to license aspectual modifiers.

The proposal so far can be summarized as follows: Complex event nominals and corresponding simple event and result nominals have related lexical conceptual structures, or lexical meanings, but only complex event nominals have an event structure and a syntactic argument structure like verbs. The argument structure of complex event nominals licenses (and indeed requires) arguments. Complex event nominals are distinguished from the others in the range of determiners and adjuncts they occur with as well as in event control and predication.

3.2.6 Some alternatives

The recent literature contains a couple of alternative accounts for some of the data that motivates the ambiguity of nominals. Two of these have in common that they deny any fundamental ambiguity between argument-taking and non-argument-taking Nouns. Williams (1987b) reanalyzes some of the data in Grimshaw (1986b) and proposes that *by* be analyzed as an ergative marker, which can occur only if a theme (acting like an absolutive) is expressed. Hence the ungrammaticality of examples like (34):

(34) *The assignment by the teacher

Safir (1987) proposes that the realization of the external argument depends on the realization of the internal argument, and (on the assumption that the *by* phrase is an external argument) accounts for the ungrammaticality of such examples in this way.

   Both of these proposals are intended to make the ambiguity hypothesis redundant. In fact, however, each subsumes only a subset of the facts explained by the a-structure/no a-structure ambiguity hypothesis, which embodies an extremely simple prediction: if any of the characteristics of the complex event nominal are present, then all must be present, and the a-structure of the nominal must be satisfied. The dependency between the *by* phrase and the *of* phrase characterized by Williams's ergative-marker hypothesis is simply a special case of this. The presence of an a-structure related *by* phrase in (34) requires the head to be a complex event nominal with argument structure (otherwise the a-adjunct would be unlicensed). The noun, therefore, has an argument structure that must be satisfied. The presence of a possessive construed as an a-adjunct forces the argument-taking reading of the noun for the same reason, and similarly makes the arguments of the noun obligatory (note that Williams's hypothesis does not extend to this case). While *destruction* can occur at least marginally with no complement, *the enemy's destruction* cannot, as pointed out in 3.2.2, Lebeaux (1986), and Grimshaw (1986b).

   Safir's proposal is a degree more general in that it extends to the possessive case also, the principle being that the external argument can be realized only if the internal argument is realized. (Note that Safir's principle assumes that the external argument of the verb is also the external argument of the noun. See 3.3. on external arguments of nominals.) Since both the possessive NP and the *by* phrase are taken by Safir to be external arguments, Safir's proposal also predicts that the presence of one of these will make an object obligatory. This is still not general enough, however. For example, we saw in 3.2.2 that even the presence of certain modifiers like *constant* can have the effect of making the object obligatory. The explanation is simply that the modifier happens to be incompatible with the result reading of the noun, so it forces the argument-taking reading, which takes an obligatory object. Obviously this case has nothing to do with the realization of the external argument or with the presentce of a *by* phrase, so neither Safir's nor Williams's account can explain the phenomenon.

Moreover, the evidence adduced by Williams for the ergative-marker hypothesis is directly explained within the ambiguity hyothesis. Williams advances the argument that while *of* is possible in (35), *by* is not:

(35) John was the selection of/* by the committee.

He argues that the theme of *selection* is bound by R here (R being the external argument of *selection*; see 3.3) and since it is bound and not satisfied directly, a *by* phrase is not legitimate. However, the ungrammaticality of *by* here has a very simple explanation in terms of the ambiguity hypothesis, namely that event/process nominals cannot be used predicatively (except perhaps in highly marked quotation-like circumstances). Thus *selection* in (35) must be a result nominal and must not take arguments. The *by* phrase is not legitimate as an a-adjunct, since there is no argument structure to license it. It has to be a modifier. However, it cannot be a modfier, because, as Williams himself notes, the uses of the modifier *by* are limited to something like authorship, and this case is not within the range of possibilities. Hence, the *by* phrase in (35) is ruled out. The *of* phrase is legitimate, on the other hand, because it is an acceptable modifier for the result nominal. Note that *selection* in (35) shows the characteristics typical of result nominals: for example, it pluralizes, (*These are the selections of the committee, The selections of the committee will be announced shortly*), and it clearly refers to the individual selected, not to the event of selection. Williams argues that nominals like *selection* in (35) could not be result nominals, since they allow modification by *constant*, which (as we saw above) disambiguates certain nominals (like *assignment*) in the ambiguity hypothesis.

(36) The constant/frequent choice of the committee is Chablis.

But we saw in 3.2.2 that *constant* itself has several uses and meanings, and some of them are entirely compatible with *some* result nominals. Hence the well-formedness of nominals like *constant fears*. (Note that in

(36) *constant* has the meaning *fixed* or *unchanging*, not the meaning it has in (8c), where it implies a series of assignment events.)

Finally, Williams points to the contrast in (37):

(37) a. The promise to Bill was to leave.
    b. *The promise by Bill was to leave.

He claims that the ungrammaticality of (37b) is due to the omission of the theme argument required by the presence of *by*. However, (37b) remains equally ill-formed if the theme is expressed:

(38) a. *The promise to leave by Bill
    b. *The promise by Bill to leave

Evidently, the contrast in (37) has nothing to do with the absence of the theme. It probably lies in the semantic limitations on *by* phrases in nominals, an issue further discussed in chapter 4.

More generally, it is hard to see how particular hypotheses about *by* phrases or external arguments can accommodate the numerous differences between the two types of nominals, all of which have clear correlations with meaning. Williams cites the data in (39), based on Grimshaw (1986b), to illustrate his hypothesis:

(39) a. The expression of bad sentiments
    b. The expression of the patients
    c. *The expression of bad sentiments of the patients

The general idea is that *of* marks the theme in (39a) and the agent in (39b) but cannot be used to mark both, as in (39c). What this ignores, though, is the very obvious difference of meaning in (39a) and (39b). The first pertains to facial expression, and the second to the process of expressing something. For the sentence to be grammatical, *expression* in (39c) would have to simultaneously have both readings: the argument-taking reading to accommodate *of bad sentiments* and the non-argument-taking reading to accommodate *of the patients*. It is precisely the correlation between such meaning differences and a whole set of grammatical properties that the ambiguity hypothesis captures.

Lebeaux (1986) offers a different account of the distribution of arguments in nominals in which in different varieties of nominals represent nominalization at different levels of logical form (LF). Process nominals involve affix raising of the kind suggested in Pesetsky (1985), with the nominal affix adjoining to N' or N'' at LF. When the affix adjoins to N' it leaves a verbal configuration within N', and in this configuration theta-marking proceeds as usual for internal arguments. As a result, an object will appear, but no subject. When adjunction is to N″, the entire NP is verbal in character at LF, and theta-marking proceeds as usual for both internal and external arguments. Both subject and object must be present. When a subject is present, there must be N″ adjunction, and all arguments of the noun must be satisfied. When no subject occurs, there is N′ adjunction, and only the object will occur. Result nominals involve no affix raising at all. This account is similar to the one given here in that it recognizes ambiguity in the nominal system, ambiguity that leads to the conclusion that some nouns have arguments and others do not. It is an open question whether an affix-raising solution can be extended to the full range of cases considered here, including the determiner system, the interaction with event structure, and the failure of nominals to act as full theta markers (see 3.5).

3.3 The Lexical Representation of Nominals

How do all the differences between the two kinds of nouns discussed above connect up with each other? One way to view the cluster of properties exploits the idea that argument structure contains more than just the list of elements set into relationship by a predicate (the arguments a predicate is usually said to theta-mark). Following work by Williams (1981a), di Sciullo and Williams (1987), and Higginbotham (1985), let us suppose that lexical items also specify another kind of position involved in the syntactic and semantic integration of the lexical item into its containing units. These proposals posit a non-thematic argument R which serves as the external argument of nouns. R is distinguished from the more familar kind of argument by the fact that it does not appear as a complement to the head, nor is it the realization of a participant in the lcs of the word —there is no sense in which R is a Theme, a Goal, or an Agent of a predicate.

A second non-thematic argument has been proposed to play a role in a-structure. Following work of Davidson's Higginbotham (1985) introduces an event position designated by E into the argument structure of verbs. The literature contains various proposals for the role of E. For example, Kratzer (1989) argues that E is present only in the argument structure of "stage-level" predicates, and not "individual-level" predicates, while Higginbotham assumes that all verbs have this additional argument.

In fact, R and E turn out to be quite different from one another. First, Williams (1981a) and di Sciullo and Williams (1987) argue that R counts as the *external* argument of nouns (we will see additional evidence for this claim in chapter 4). But E, if present in the a-structure at all, certainly does not count as the external argument of verbs. The second major difference between R and E is that R can be identified with an lcs argument of the head (see in particular the analysis of sentential complements in 3.6). This is never possible for E. Since E does not interact with the syntactic a-structure representation of predicates in these ways, whereas R does, I will limit further discussion to properties of nonthematic arguments of nouns: R and what I call *Ev*.

The reason for positing R concerns the integration of heads into larger expressions (see di Sciullo and Williams (1987), chapter 4, and 3.6 below). Consider predication, for instance. In examples like those in (40a), *found* and *mad* are two place relations, and the external argument of the adjective is satisfied by predication. What, then, should be said about examples like (40b)?

(40) a. John is fond of Bill; John is mad at Bill.

  b. John is a man; he is a friend of mine.

If the two sets of cases are to be unified, the NPs *a man* and *a friend of mine* must have an external argument to be satisfied by predication, just as the adjective phrases in (40a) do.

How is this argument satisfied when the NP is not used predicatively? Here there seem to be two possibilities. According to Williams (1981a) and di Sciullo and Williams (1987), all NPs have an open position, which is satisfied by predication or reference. R is satisfied by reference in sentences like (41), where the NPs are not predicative:

(41) a. A man walked into the room.

  b. A friend of mine walked into the room.

Alternatively we could take the view that only predicative NPs have an unsatisfied external argument and that referential NPs have their R argument satisfied by a determiner. Higginbotham (1985) suggests that the determiner *a* does not satisfy R, or at least does not always satisfy R. Hence, an indefinite NP can have an open position which will be satisfied by predication. A definite NP, on the other hand, has no open position and cannot be used predicatively. In this analysis, nouns always have an open R position, but NPs have an open R position only when they are predicative.

No matter which of these alternatives we pursue, nouns always have an open argument. By this reasoning, then, all nouns have an external argument, even result nominals and simple event nominals:

(42) a. *dog*(R)
   b. *dissertation*(R)
   c. *observation/expression/exam*(R)

This non-thematic a-structure is involved in modification as well as predication. Modification is accomplished by "identification" of the external argument of the modifier with the external argument of the noun (Higginbotham (1985)). Hence, the expression *long dissertation* satisfies the theta criterion because *long* has an external argument, as does *dissertation*, and the two arguments are identified and then jointly satisfied.

In this sense, then, all nouns have an a-structure. Even if they have no other arguments, they have R as their external.[4] Nominals like those in (42), however, lack a *thematic* a-structure, an a-structure projection of their lcs participants, and this is what distinguishes them from complex event nominals.

The question that arises is how argument-taking complex event nominals fit into this picture. They always refer to events, and their modifiers modify the events they refer to. This follows if they have an external argument which does not correspond to one of their thematic arguments and which can be identified with the external argument of a modifier. On this analysis, they work just like result nominals with respect to modification. (Recall that they do not in general occur predicatively.) In a NP like *the unexpected observation of a black hole*, the external argument of *unexpected* will be identified with the external argument of *observation*, and both will be assigned together. Hence, the modifier modifies the event. Note that it would be completely incorrect to view the observer (or any other thematic argument of the noun) as the external argument of the noun, although it is the external argument of the verb *observe*. If the observer were the external argument, the modifier would be construed relative to this argument instead of relative to the event. Event nominals must have an external argument distinct from their thematic arguments.

Is this argument, which acts as the external argument for a complex event nominal, the same as the one that acts as the external argument for result and simple event nominals? The evidence points to the conclusion that they are different. First, note that the external argument of a complex event nominal never binds an lcs participant. These nominals always denote events. This could be because the projection of lcs arguments into an argument structure is inconsistent with lcs binding for some reason or because the external argument itself has a different character. The possibility that the external argument of a complex event nominal is not *R* but something else offers potential insight into the differences between complex event nominals and the others. Since the determiner and modifier systems are different for the two kinds of nouns, this can be attributed to their different external arguments. If the character of the external argument of the noun is to explain these differences, the external argument of a complex event nominal must not be *R*. I will designate it as *Ev*.

Ev, then, is the external argument of a complex event nominal. In the prominence theory of a-structure, it must be the most prominent argument, since it is external. All other arguments of a noun must be internal. Additional evidence for *Ev* being the *external* argument will be given in 5.2, where I will argue that the distribution of *by* phrases in nominals follows from the hypothesis that their external arguments are *Ev* rather than the external arguments of the corresponding verbs.

The nominalization of *observe* is given in (43): the verb is associated with an a-structure in which *x* is external. The nominal affix *-ing* is associated with an a-structure in which *Ev* is external, and *-ation* has this entry as one of its possibilities. When the verb combines with the affix, the result is a complex argument structure formed by combining the a-structure of the two. Since the affix is the head (see Williams (1981b), di Sciullo and Williams (1987), Grimshaw (1986a)), the derived form is a noun, and its external argument is the external argument of the whole.[5]

(43) a. *observe* V, (x (y))
     b. *-ing* N, (*Ev*)   *-ation* N, (Ev)
     c. *observing* N, (Ev (x (y)))
     d. *observation* N, (Ev (x (y)))

All result nominals have the same a-structure, which contains only an *R* position (see (42)). *R*, unlike *Ev*, can be bound to an lcs argument of the base. As pointed out in Sproat (1985), one of the arguments of the base verb acts as the external argument of the derived noun. We can construct a system with these properties in which *R* is identified with an argument of the base. Which argument it is identified with is a function of the affix that is added, so the affix must specify which kind of argument it binds. Roughly, the affix *-ee* binds a patient argument, *-er* binds an external argument (see Levin and Rappaport (1989)), and *-ion* binds something like a theme in cases like *observation*. The affix *-ness* presum-

ably binds a degree argument in the lcs of the head (the same argument
that licenses adverbials like *completely* with a degree interpretation).
This is the analysis of examples like *completeness* (see di Sciullo and
Williams (1987)).

(44) a. *detain*(x (y))   detainee(R = x) such that y detains x
     b. *teach*(x (y))   teacher(R = x) such that x teaches y
     c. *observe*(x (y))   observation(R = x) such that y observes x
     d. *fond*(x (y))   fondness(R = x) such that y is fond to degree x

Let us now examine how we can exploit the proposed *Ev/R* distinction
in characterizing the cluster of properties we have uncovered.

First, the basic distinction between nominals with event structure and
argument structure and those with neither is represented as an a-structure difference between them. A noun gets *Ev* as its external argument
if it has an event structure. Hence, no noun with *R* as its external can
ever have an event structure associated with it. Both result nominals
and simple event nominals have *R* as their external. It is the event structure that licenses modifiers like *frequent* and *constant* in their critical
disambiguating function, and it is the event structure that licenses
aspectual adjuncts like *for a day* and *in a day*. It follows that only
complex event nominals will occur with these expressions.[6]

Second, the morphological correlates of the ambiguities in the system
can be characterized by ambiguously specifying some affixes and unambiguously specifying others. Affixes like *-ation*, *-ment*, etc., are
ambiguously specified as introducing either *Ev* or *R*. Since they are
heads, their external argument will count as the external argument of
the entire expression. Zero derivation introduces *R*, and *-ing* is typically
specified for *Ev*. The result will be that zero-derived forms are not complex event nominals, *-ing* nominals characteristically are, and others are
characteristically ambiguous.

Third, the interaction between the determiner system and nominalizations can be characterized by means of the *R/Ev* distinction. One
way is to consider the determiners themselves to have a non-thematic
argument structure. For most determiners and the plural morpheme,
the argument structure contains *R*. Only *the* introduces *Ev* or *R*. The
argument of the determiner can now be identified with the external
argument of the noun, and the two can be satisfied together. If identification requires that the two arguments to be identified be of the same
type, it follows that only *the* can occur with complex event nominals,

while other possibilities exist for the other cases. The well-formed NPs are those of the forms given in (45).

(45) a. NP [Det(R) N(R)]

   b. NP [Det(Ev) N(Ev (x (y)))]

Alternatively, we could view the determiners as satisfying the external argument position of the noun (with the possible exception of the indefinite determiner, which might only optionally satisfy the position, and so leave it potentially open for predication.) In this case the determiners would have to be divided into those that satisfy R and those that satisfy Ev, the former being able to satisfy the external argument of a result nominal or a simple event nominal, and the latter to satisfy the external argument of a complex event nominal.

Finally, it is tempting to thinking that event control is a control relationship between Ev and PRO, and hence only complex event nominals participate in event control. A problem with this view, however, arises from the fact that verbs also allow event control, and we do not want to say that Ev is the external argument of verbs. Thus it is more likely that the event structure itself provides the controller for PRO, so that event control is limited to complex event nominals because only they have event structure rather than because only they have Ev as their external argument.

According to this analysis the various kinds of nominals are similar in that they have a non-thematic external argument, either R or Ev. They are dissimilar in that they have Ev if they are complex event nominals and R otherwise. In matters sensitive to which kind of external argument a noun has, the two types behave differently.

3.4 Componds and Argument Structure

The literature on compounds establishes that there are two kinds. One has been called "root" in the literature; the other has been called "verbal" or "synthetic" (Roeper (1987) provides a list of differences between the two types). Drawing on the results of our investigation of nouns, we can treat the differences between them as resulting from one fundamental difference: root compounds have heads with no a-structure, while the head of a synthetic compound is an argument-taking element (a noun or an adjective, since English does not allow compounds headed by verbs.) Since the head has an a-structure which must be satisfied, the non-head is theta-marked by the head.

There are two consequences of this proposal. First, the properties of the head of a nominal root compound should be those of a result nominal or a simple event nominal. Second, principles of a-structure representation are expected to affect the well-formedness of synthetic compounds but not that of root compounds, since root compounds do not involve a-structure satisfaction. Since the head of a root compound has no a-structure, principles of a-structure will not govern the formation of the compound. Instead, the compound represents a lexicalized modification structure expressing relations similar to those found in result and simple event nominals. The relationship of the non-head to the head is not one of a-structure satisfaction or theta-marking. The properties of synthetic compounds discussed in 2.2.2 should therefore not be replicated in root compounds.

Consider for example the observation, discussed in 2.2.2, that subjects (or perhaps external arguments) cannot appear in compounds. This restriction holds only for synthetic compounds. In root compounds, *apparent* subjects or external arguments can occur, as illustrated in (46), examples due to Jane Simpson and David Nash.

(46) a. a bee sting, bee stings
     b. a dog bite, dog bites

However, they are indeed impossible in synthetic compounds, where the non-head represents an argument of the head and not just a modifier.

(47) a. *bee-stinging
     b. *dog-biting

Similarly, it is possible to form a root compound with the apparent subject of an unaccusative predicate, which gives examples like those in (48), taken from Roeper (1987):

(48) rainfall, heartache, bus stop

As we in 2.2.2, this is never possible for synthetic compounds:

(49) *rain-falling, *heart-aching, *bus-stopping

The hypothesis that the head of a synthetic compound must have a-structure predicts that when the head of a compound is a plural noun, the compound must be a root compound, not a synthetic one, because argument-taking nominals do not occur in the plural. This lies behind an observation, due to Roeper (1987), that the compounds in (50) differ in interpretation, with (50a) involving a control relationship, where John is the one doing the baking, and (50b) involving no control.

(50) a. John enjoys clam baking.
      b. John enjoys clam bakings.

The reasoning is as follows: *Baking* can take arguments. Hence, John can be construed as controlling one of its arguments. *Bakings*, on the other hand, has no arguments, so control is impossible.

Finally, note that the characteristic morphology of the two types of nouns is replicated within the compound system in exactly the expected way. Compounds headed by *-ing* nominals (like the ones discussed in 2.2.2) are typically synthetic. Those headed by zero-derived forms, like those in (46) and (48), are typically root compounds. We expect to find, of course, ambiguity in the heads formed with affixes like *-ion*, *-ment*, since they can be either argument-taking or not.

The essential difference between root and synthetic compounds, then, is in the argument-taking properties of their heads. The characteristic differences between the two kinds of compounds follow from this difference.

3.5 Theta-Marking Properties of Argument-Taking Nominals

The conclusion so far is that nouns divide into two types. Complex event nominals have both an event structure and an argument structure, and other nominals have neither. Those nouns that have an argument structure show the same argument-taking properties as verbs in that their argument are fundamentally obligatory. Nonetheless, we will see that nouns do not behave as full argument-takers. Although they do take prepositional arguments, like the ones discussed in 3.2, they never take sentential arguments, nor do they take arguments in so-called *passive* nominals. The generalization is that nouns take arguments only when they combine with prepositions. The solution I will develop here builds on the proposal of Emonds (1985) that nouns have no direct theta-marking capacity. If we incorporate this idea about nouns into the proposal so far, argument-taking nouns have the same kind of a-structure representation as verbs, but nevertheless they cannot directly accept arguments because they are defective theta-markers.[7]

In the usual relationship of argument-taking, or theta-marking, two relationships hold. The predicate licenses a syntactic expression, and the syntactic expression satisfies a slot in the a-structure of a predicate. Although linguists usually group these two together under one label, the two relationships are logically distinct. (Indeed, the a-adjuncts to be discussed in chapter 4 show that they are empirically distinct, since a-adjuncts are licensed by a-structure but do not satisfy it.) If nouns do not take direct arguments, their participation in at least one of these relationships must be defective. Either an argument cannot satisfy the a-structure of a noun without help, or the a-structure of a noun cannot license an argument without help. The consequence of this is that nouns can take arguments only through the mediation of a preposition. Hence, the theta-marking configuration in (51a) is the only possible one, although all would be possible for verbs.

(51) a. N PP   b. N CP   c. N NP

Theta-marking requires two things: an argument structure and a theta marker. Verbs have argument structure and are theta markers. Complex event nouns have a-structure but are not theta markers.

Suppose that the prepositions that combine with nouns for theta-marking purposes also have a-structure, as in the entries for *to* and *of* in (52), but have no independent semantic roles to assign.

(52) *to*(y)   *of*(z)

Their argument structure can be satisfied by "identification" along the lines in Higginbotham (1985) and Li (1990). By identification, a position in one argument structure is linked to a position in a second argument structure in such a way that both are satisfied by a single syntactic expression. In the case at hand, the argument of the preposition will be identified with an argument of the noun. (If we take the further position that these prepositions have no independent lcs and that an lcs is required for theta-marking as opposed to identification, we can derive the conclusion that there is only one way their argument structures can be satisfied—by identification.) If nouns are defective theta markers, their a-structure can be satisfied only if each position is identified with a position in the a-structure of another (non-defective) theta marker. In (53) the *y* argument of *donation* (its Goal) has ben identified with the argument of *to*, and the *z* argument with the argument of *of*.

(53)

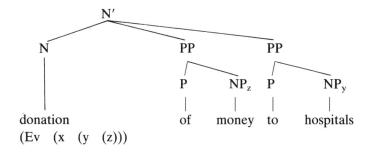

Similar suggestions have been raised in the domain of verbs, where semantically transparent prepositions can be viewed as participating in theta assignment. Marantz (1984) and Baker (1988b) propose that an instrumental receives its theta role from the verb directly, while a (prepositional) benefactive or Goal receives it through a preposition. Thus in an example like (54), *hospitals* can be said to get its role from the verb in concert with the preposition.

(54) They donated money to hospitals.

The verb makes the role available, and the preposition transfers it to the NP, the preposition acting to transmit a theta role from the verb to the NP. The present theory uses the same basic idea. Verbs can either directly theta-mark an argument, or they can do it indirectly via a preposition. The defective character of nouns lies in their failure to participate in one of these modes of theta-marking.

It might seem that case theory could be held responsible for these differences between nouns and verbs. To take direct NP arguments, the head must be able to assign case to the argument. So the fact that verbs do, and nouns do not, take direct arguments could be a function of their case-theoretic status, with verbs having, and nouns lacking, the capacity to assign case. The standard position at present is exactly that the intransitivity of nouns is a matter of case theory. However, the cases to be analyzed here do not follow from the case-theoretic properties of nouns. Case theory will not explain the absence of sentential (CP) arguments to nouns or the non-existence of passive nominals. CP arguments do not need case, according to the standard assumptions, and the hypothetically preposed NP in a passive nominal would be case-marked by the possessive, just as the preposed NP is case-marked in the subject position of a passive verb. So the noun-argument relations in (55) would be incorrectly allowed if only case assignment distinguishes nouns from verbs:

(55) a. N   CP
     b. NP's   N   [e]
        ↑_____|

If nouns are defective theta markers and not just defective case markers, nouns are intransitive in a more fundamental sense. They are intransitive with respect to theta-marking, not just with respect to case theory.

The structure of theta-marking with nouns requires that only prepositions that are theta transmitters will combine with nouns to take arguments. Other prepositions will not be qualified for the job, even though they are all case assigners. Critical in this solution is that the preposition *of* acts like the other prepositions with respect to theta-marking. It must transmit theta-marking. Otherwise, process nominals with *of* NP complements would violate the theta criterion, just as argument-taking nominals with CP complements do. Thus there is no reason to view *of* as inserted or as in any way special, at least vis-à-vis argument-taking nominals. This accords with Rappaport's (1983) argument to the effect that *of* is thematically restricted in nominals, just as other prepositions are. More generally, since the prepositions which occur with theta-marking nouns are always theta transmitters, it is no surprise that the prepositions that appear in these NPs are always semantically based. Thus we can explain Rappaport's (1983) observation that arguments are realized in a semantically transparent fashion inside NPs (compare (56a) and (56b), based on her examples).

(56) a. They ordered the troops to fire.
     b. Their orders to/* of the troops to fire.

Rappaport's proposal is that this is due to the absence of grammatical functions within the NP. However, the difference actually reduces to the difference between a true theta-marking head, the V, and a head which does not directly theta-mark, the N.

The general consequence of the idea that nouns are defective theta markers is that nominals can license only PPs and not bare maximal projections of any other kind. Thus when a noun occurs with a complement that is not introduced by a preposition, the complement cannot be a syntactic argument. As a result, the NP cannot be a complex event nominal. If it is construed as a complex event nominal, it will have an argument structure to be satisfied, but the maximal projection will not be able to satisfy it, because the proper predicate-argument relationship cannot be established without a preposition. Thus an NP whose head is a noun with a non-prepositional complement should not show any of the properties of complex event nominals. I will show that this is exactly the situation that obtains when nouns take preposition-less complements. There are two cases: sentential complements to nouns and passive nominals. In each case the behavior of the NP is that of a result nominal, or a simple event nominal.

3.5.1 Sentential complements to nouns
As expected, when we investigate nouns which appear with sentential complements, it emerges that these complements never behave like

arguments. Both nouns and verbs can take arguments in general, but only verbs can take sentential argumetns. The evidence is simply that nouns with sentential complements consistently and systematically act as result nominals or simple event nominals and not as complex event nominals.

The first point to note is that sentential complements to nouns are *always optional*, even when the corresponding verb takes an obligatory complement. In 3.2.2 I established that with nonsentential complements to nouns it is perfectly possible to manipulate the grammatical context so as to make the complement obligatory. This can *never* be done with sentential complements.

(57) a. The announcement/conclusion (that an investigation has been initiated) was inaccurate.
     b. * They announced./* They concluded.
     c. John's attempt (to convince people that he has initiated an investigation) was unsuccessful.
     d. * John attempted.

Thus the evidence from optionality suggests that sentential complements have a status quite different from that of other complements to nouns: they behave as though they are not regulated by a-structure at all.

The second point, made in Stowell (1981), is that nouns with sentential complements do not have the meaning of process nouns. Thus *the announcement that* seems to refer not to an event of announcing but to an announcement of which the complement specifies the content. Similarly, the noun *observation* in (57b) refers not to the fact, event, or process of observing but to the content of the observation.

(58) a. The/Their announcement that the position had been filled was a surprise.
     b. The/Their observation that the position had been filled surprised everyone.

There does seem to be an event reading for nouns like *attempt* in (59):

(59) Their attempt to climb the mountain.

The existence of this reading led Stowell to the hypothesis that infinitival sentential complements to nouns are true complements while apparent finite complements are really just modifiers. However, there is overwhelming evidence that the reading of *attempt* here is that of a simple event and not that of a complex event. *Attempt* clearly behaves like the result nominals, or simple event nominals, and not like those that denote complex events. We already saw that the complement to the noun *attempt* is optional, which is characteristic of a non-argument-taking noun. As (60) shows, the determiners for *attempt* are those of the result nominals, and pluralization is perfectly well-formed:

(60) a. This particular attempt to convince people that the procedure was fair was doomed to failure.

b. Their attempts to convince people that the procedure was fair were doomed to failure.

An NP headed by *attempt* can be used predicatively:

(61) a. This was their first attempt to climb Mt. Everest.

The modifiers *frequent* and *constant* are impossible unless the head noun is pluralized:

(62) a. *Their constant/frequent attempt to climb Mt. Everest

b. Their constant/frequent attempts to climb Mt. Everest

All in all, the behavior of the *attempt* class shows exactly the pattern of result nominals referring to simple events.

Note that this conclusion about nouns like *attempt* has important consequences for our understanding of control. The head has unambiguously non-argument-taking properties, so the controller in a case like (63) cannot possibly be a syntactic argument of *attempt*, since *attempt* has no syntactic arguments. Yet its control properties seem to be identical to those of the corresponding verb.

(63) a. The/His attempt to leave on time

b. All of his attempts to leave on time

c. These attempts of yours to leave on time

The control relation must be based on the lcs representation of *attempt*. Since the properties of the control relation seem to be identical in the case of nominals and that of complements to verbs, we must conclude that the principles governing the choice of controller access lcs rather than syntactic argument structure. This accords with a general line of research that holds that controller choice is a function of semantic properties of the predicate (see, e.g., Farkas (1987) and Jackendoff (1985)).

With some complications, the behavior of nouns with finite complements is also that of result nominals, or simple event nominals. As expected, if nouns with finite sentential complements are result nominals, they do not allow the adjuncts associated with complex event nominals.

(64) a. *Their frequent/constant announcement that they were the greatest eventually became tiresome.

b. * His frequent/constant statement that he was about to resign was intended to mislead.

The examples of (64) improve greatly when they are given plural heads, even though the plurals themselves are not perfect:

(65) a. ?Their frequent/constant announcements that they were the greatest eventually became tiresome.

b. ?His frequent/constant statements that he was about to resign were intended to mislead.

A plural head should be possible in principle if these are result nouns. Cases like (66) seem to be more or less impossible without the parenthesized material, as do the plural forms of nouns like *fact* and *idea* with no verbal source. The reason seems to be that the the clause specifies content, and it is not possible to give just one content for a plural head. Note the improvement in (66a, b) if the material in parentheses is included.

(66) a. ??The announcements that the problem was solved (and that no issues remained) were greeted with scepticism.

b. ??Their observations that the problem was solved (and that no issues remained) were greeted with scepticism.

Modifiers uniquely associated with result nominals (see 3.2.4) are certainly allowed by these nouns:

(67) a. *Yesterday's* statement that the president intends to retire in December was greeted with scepticism.

b. This announcement *of yours* that the president intends to retire in December will not pass muster.

c. That attempt *of his* to mislead everyone was extremely successful.

Also, as expected, no event control is possible with these nominals, so the purpose clauses in (68a) and (69a) are unambiguously associated with the lower clause, while the purpose clauses in (68b) and (69b) can be construed with either.

(68) a. Their statement that the president intends to retire in order to mislead the public was absurd.

b. They stated that the president intends to retire in order to mislead the public.

(69) a. Their attempt to mislead everyone in order to preserve their jobs was unsuccessful.

b. They attempted to mislead everyone in order to preserve their jobs.

If the verb in the lower clause is one, like an inchoative, that cannot participate in event control, examples like (68b) and (69b) become simply ungrammatical.

(70) a. *Their statement that the gun misfired in order to mislead the public was absurd.
 b. They stated that the gun misfired in order to mislead the public.

In all of these respects nouns with sentential complements contrast with nouns with nominal/prepositional complements. To take two examples, the noun in (71) admits an event modifier and a purpose clause. The very same noun in (72) admits neither.

(71) a. The constant announcement of inacurrate results should not be condoned.
 b. The announcement of inaccurate results in order to impress the public is not condoned.

(72) a. *The constant announcement that results have been achieved should not be condoned.
 b. *The announcement that results have been achieved in order to impress the public is not condoned.

Finally, if CPs never occur with theta-marking nouns, and if gerundive nominals are theta-marking, as we concluded in 3.2, they should be impossible with CP complements. The noun-verb ambiguity of -ing forms makes this prediction a little more difficult to test; examples like (73) are certainly grammatical, but then they are expected to be grammatical when the head is a verb.

(73) a. Their announcing that . . .
 b. Their deciding to . . .

However, (74) shows that the addition of an adjective makes these examples ungrammatical, while the addition of an adverb leaves their grammaticality unchanged, at least if (73) is unambiguously a verbal gerund, since verbal gerunds do not allow AP modifiers (see (74c)).

(74) a. Their *unexpected/unexpectedly announcing that . . .
 b. Their *unexpected/unexpectedly deciding to . . .
 c. Their *unexpected/unexpectedly announcing the solution

By the same token, substituting *the* for *their* in (73) results in ungrammaticality. This is because only nominal gerunds, and not verbal gerunds, occur with a determiner.

So the situation is exactly as predicted. Sentential complements are ungrammatical with the *-ing* nominal because it is unambiguously a complex event nominal with an argument structure. Examples like (73) and (74) are theta-criterion violations when the head is a noun but are grammatical when the head is a verb. The ungrammaticality follows from the hypothesis that nouns cannot theta-mark.

To sum up, then, sentential complements to nouns are never arguments. The evidence is that they are never obligatory, which suggests that they are not related to a-structure positions, and that the nouns they are associated with never behave in any respect like complex event nominals.

I conclude that nouns differ from verbs in that nouns never take sentential arguments. Since nouns do take prepositional arguments and verbs take both sentential and nominal/prepositional arguments, there must be critical differences between nouns and verbs and between prepositional and sentential complements. What I proposed above is that nouns are defective argument-takers, which require a preposition to transmit theta-marking from them to their complements. Hence, the combination of a noun plus a preposition accomplishes what a verb can do by itself. Unlike NPs, CPs cannot occur with prepositions, so this means of transmitting a theta role is not available. Hence, there is no way for a noun to theta-mark a sentential argument, and a CP argument with an argument-taking noun will always violate the theta criterion. Consider a case like that in (75), where the noun *announcement* has an a-structure that requires a propositional argument for *y* in order to meet its lcs requirements.

(75) *announcement*(Ev (x (y)))

Suppose the noun appears with a CP complement. If the noun cannot support a predicate-argument relation with the CP, two things will go wrong. First, the argument position in the nominal corresponding to the CP will not be satisfied, since it will not be in a theta-marking relationship to a syntactic expression. Second, the CP argument will not be related to an a-structure position, so it will be an unlicensed argument. As a result, the CP will inevitably violate the theta criterion.

This contrasts with the case of PP arguments of a noun, discussed at the beginning of this section. In the case of Prepositional Phrases the P allows the NP to satisfy an argument position of the head and licenses the NP by relating it to the a-structure position.

To obtain this result, I have to diverge from the view laid out in Emonds (1985). Emonds assumes that nouns *do* have sentential arguments, and proposes that they are theta-marked via the complementizer. Clearly, this would give the wrong result, since it would predict that nouns do take sentential arguments. If nouns don't theta-mark directly, and if only prepositions and *not* complementizers can transmit theta-marking, the desired result will follow. (Note that unlike prepositions, the choice of complementizer does not vary with thematic role, which suggests that the two are fundamentally dissimilar.)

One important clarification is necessary here. What is the predication for languages in which a preposition can take a CP complement? Should a noun with a CP complement introduced by a preposition act like an argument-taker, and the CP like an argument? This is one possibility, but not the only one. Although prepositions *can be* theta transmitters, not all of them are. In the analysis given here, for example, *to* in (76a) and *of* in (76b, c) are not transmitters, since the heads do not even take arguments.

(76) a. John's gift to Bill
     b. A box of apples
     c. The leg of the chair

Thus it is perfectly possible for a noun to take a preposition and a CP without without the CP acting as a grammatical argument. So in cases of P + CP the behavior predicted depends crucially on whether the preposition is acting as a theta transmitter.[8] The evaluation of P + CP cases depends on how they fit into the general theory of prepositions and theta-marking. If (for either verbal or nominal theta-markers) we never find instances of P + CP where P acts as a theta transmitter, this result will itself need an explanation, presumably in terms of the lexical properties of prepositions.

To sum up, nouns are defective theta markers: they have an a-structure, but they cannot theta-mark, so they need a little help. For NP complements the help is available; for sentential complements it is not. Two things follow from this. The disparity between verbs and nouns is explained, and so is the fact that nouns take only PPs as arguments. A final point first noted in Chomsky (1970) is that nouns do not allow raising processes of any kind: subject raising, exceptional case-marking, or tough movement. Many explanations for this fact have been offered in the literature (e.g., Chomsky (1970), Williams (1982), Kayne (1984)). The fact that nouns do not take sentential arguments seems likely to provide an essential step in understanding this difference between nouns and verbs.[9] If theta-marking, or L-Marking in the Barriers system (Chomsky (1986a)), is a precondition for subject raising, for exceptional case-marking or object raising, and for the analysis of *tough* constructions, their failure to occur with nouns is an immediate consequence. Similar points hold for the deletion of the complementizer *that* under government (see Stowell (1981) and Aoun et al. (1987)). The fact that complementizers can never be deleted in sentential complements to nouns will follow if nouns do not theta-mark and therefore do not have the proper relationship of government to their complements.

3.5.2 Passive nominals
The idea that nouns cannot directly theta-mark receives further support from the analysis of passive nominals. Although passive nominals have often been treated as the NP counterpart to passive clauses, I will show here that the two are totally different. In fact, passive nominals are not complex event nominals, and they never have argument structure. This follows from the defectiveness of nouns as argument-takers.

In a passive nominal a phrase that appears to correspond to the object of the noun nevertheless appears prenominally in NP. The best-known cases involve possessive NPs in examples like those of (77).

(77) a. Reagan's defeat
      b. The defeat of Reagan
      c. John's identification
      d. The identification of John

The possessives are apparently related to the argument of the noun that corresponds to the object of the base verb, not the subject. Because of their interpretation, examples like those in (77) have been taken to illustrate a kind of passive in nominals (see Chomsky (1970), Anderson (1978, 1983–1984), Kayne (1984) and Giorgi and Longobardi (1990)).

The second set of cases involves adjectives like those in (78), which appear to behave almost like Noun Phrases (Zubizarreta (1985) and Kayne (1984)):

(78) a. The American invasion of Vietnam
      b. The American fear of failure
      c. The French defeat of the English
      d. The local attempt to boycott the election

The set includes adjectives expressing nationality and other adjectives like *local, national, liberal,* and so forth. I will call the class of adjectives that behaves this way *group adjectives,* since they seem to pick out groups with a defining characteristic.[10]

The passive use of group adjectives is illustrated in (79). Like the possessives in (77), the adjectives in (79) appear to be related to the arguments corresponding to the objects of the verbs, or the *of* phrases of the nominals, so that (79a) appears to be a paraphrase of (79b) and (79c) of (79d).

(79) a. The French defeat
      b. The defeat of France
      c. A Central American invasion
      d. An invasion of Central America

Group adjectives, like possessives, are ambiguous. Sometimes they must be analyzed as subject-like and occurring with complex event nominals. The evidence is exemplified in (80). The inclusion of a group adjective with an agentive interpretation makes the object of a noun obligatory (see (80a)), just like the inclusion of a possessive (see 3.2). The use of *constant* in (80b) forces the complex event reading of *assignment* (hence the obligatoriness of the object).

(80) a. The American love/dislike/fear * (of free speech)
      b. The (constant) American assignment * (of untrained officials) to important jobs

Both of these considerations show that group adjectives can be a-structure related and not just modifiers.

Nevertheless, group adjectives *can be* modifiers. The head in (81) is unambiguously a result nominal (hence the ill-formedness of * *an attack of a foreign country*), yet the group adjective is permitted.

(81)   The French attacks on . . .

We can conclude that group adjectives, like possessives, are ambiguous in that they behave as modifiers of result nominals and simple event nominals and are licensed by a-structure in complex event nominals.

Since both possessives and group adjectives can occur with argument-taking nominals, we expect that in principle nominals with the passive form could be either complex event nominals with internal constituents related to argument structure or result/simple event nominals with modifiers. In fact, however, the passive NPs of (77) and (79) *never* act like complex event nominals.

The evidence I will present falls into six categories: the behavior of unambiguous result and simple event nominals, the behavior of unambiguous theta-marking nominals, the effects of disambiguation toward the result/simple event reading, the effects of disambiguation toward the complex-event reading, the behavior of event control in passive nominals, and the co-occurrence of *by* phrases, possessives, and group adjectives in passive nominals

First, nouns that appear to be unambiguous result nominals nevertheless allow "preposing" of possessives and group adjectives.[11] One example is the noun *solution*, used in Anderson (1978) in examples of passive nominals. The possessive in (82a) corresponds, in pretheoretic terms, to the object of the verb *solve* in (82b).

(82) a. This problem's solution
     b. They solved this problem.
     c. The solution to/* of this problem
     d. John's solution to/* of this problem

Yet *solution*, for many speakers at least, is unambiguously a result nominal (note that the well-formed version of (82c, d) has an obvious result reading). It is because *solution* is not an argument taking noun that (82c, d) are impossible with *of*. Yet *solution* does have a passive counterpart, given in (82a). If an unambiguous result nominal can have a passive form, having this form must be a property associated with result nominals.

Similar examples can be constructed using nouns like *murder*. As (83) shows, *murder* admits a passive nominal but never behaves like an event nominal. Hence the ungrammaticality of (83c).

(83) a. Jack's murder.
     b. Someone murdered Jack.
     c. *The/John's murder of Jack

Murder contrasts with *assassination*, which is ambiguous, and occurs in all contexts of (83).

The second point is that by the same reasoning, unambiguous theta-marking nouns should not allow the preposed possessive NP. In 3.2 I argued that gerunds are always complex event nominals. Hence, they take obligatory arguments, license event adjuncts, etc. The prediction, then, is that they will never occur in the passive form if the passive form is impossible for this kind of noun. As the examples in (84) show, this is correct. Gerundive nominals lack a passive form.

(84) a. *The tree's felling
   b. *The city's destroying
   c. The felling of the tree
   d. The destroying of the city

Third, disambiguation of nouns toward the result/simple event reading leaves the grammaticality of passive nominals untouched. As we saw earlier, complex event nominals cannot be pluralized, nor can they occur with demonstratives or the posthead *of NP's*. Yet we can pluralize the head noun of a passive nominal, or add a demonstrative or posthead genitive to a passive nominal formed with a group adjective, without altering either the interpretation or the well-formedness of the example.

(85) Reagan's defeats

(86) a. The French defeats
   b. The Central American invasions
   c. All of these Central American invasions of Reagan's don't amount to a hill of beans.

(It is not possible to construct all the examples for possessive passives here because possessives are in complementary distribution with determiners and prehead and posthead possessives are in complementary distribution.)

By parity of reasoning, disambiguation in the other direction, toward the complex-event-nominal reading, *should* lead to ill-formedness. The paradigm in (87) illustrates this with modifiers of complex events.

(87) a. The politician's nomination
   b. *The politician's frequent/constant nomination
   c. The politicians' nominations

Passive nominals similarly fail to occur with the aspectual adjuncts discussed in 3.2.5, just as predicted if these nominals do not denote complex events.

(88) a. The construction of the building in three weeks,
   b. *The building's construction in three weeks.
   c. John's translation of the book in only three months,
   d. *The book's translation in only three months.

Fourth, result and simple event nominals allow possessive modifiers, like *yesterday's*, while complex event nominals do not (see 3.2.5). A possessive of this type should therefore co-occur with a group adjective in a passive nominal, since both occur with nouns of the same type. This prediction is correct, as we can see in examples like (89).

(89) Yesterday's liberal/European defeat

Example (89) contrasts with examples like (90), where the noun unambiguously takes arguments, and *yesterday's* is impossible:

(90) * Yesterday's defeat of the Europeans

Fifth, Williams (1985) has pointed out that passive nominals do not
show the same control behavior as active nominals. The hypothesis that
passive nominals are really result nominals offers an explanation for this
fact. They do not allow event control of a purpose clause, because they
do not denote complex events.

(91) a. The translation of the book (in order) to make it available to a
         wider readership
     b. * The book's translation (in order) to make it available to a
         wider readership

(92) a. The arrest of John (ostensibly) to prevent riots
     b. * John's arrest (ostensibly) to prevent riots

(93) a. The examination of the patient to determine whether. . .
     b. * The patient's examination to determine whether. . .

(94) a. The nomination of Mary in order to increase the participation
         of women on the committee
     b. * Mary's nomination in order to increase the participation of
         women on the committee

(95) a. The invasion of Grenada to rescue endangered medical
         students
     b. The Grenadian invasion was a great success.
     c. * The Grenadian invasion to rescue endangered medical
         students

Passive nominals are just like all other result/simple event nominals in
this respect, as established in 3.2. So the failure of passive nominals to
admit event control is explained.

Other accounts of the absence of control with passive nominals have
been given in the literature. Williams (1985, 308–310) proposes that
control into purpose clauses has an S or N' as controller. In a passive
nominal the possessive and the head noun do not form a constituent and
therefore cannot control. (Whether the explanation extends to (95c) depends on the constituency assigned to the adjective. If the adjective is
inside N', control should be possible.) If we assume that the noun itself
cannot act as the controller, the failure of control in passive nominals is
explained.

Another explanation proceeds as follows: The controller is usually a PRO generated in Spec of NP.[12] Yet in passive nominals the position in which PRO is usually generated is filled by a possessive. Hence, PRO is not present, and the control relationship is impossible (Roeper (1987, 279–280)). A couple of question immediately arise: Why is control impossible also in passive nominals with APs (see (95c)), since the AP is not in the position that PRO is assumed to occupy? Moreover, if PRO is present to satisfy the theta criterion, how is the theta criterion satisfied when PRO is not present?

I should point out that Roeper assumes that control in nominals can be control by an *argument* of the nominal or PRO if no overt controller is available. I take the position of Williams (1985) and Lasnik (1988) that only event control is possible (see chapter 4 for the further consequences of this point). If control is by the event, the presence or absence of PRO should not be relevant, and hence the presence or absence of a possessive in a Spec of an NP should have no effect whatsoever.

The most important problem with these solutions to the absence of control in passive nominals is that they do not generalize to all cases of control failure, nor do they connect up this property of passive nominals with their other properties. In the proposal I am defending, event control is impossible for passive nominals just as for all other nominals other than those that denote complex events, regardless of what element may or may not occupy the possessive position. Absence of control is just one of the many properties that passive nominals share with other result/simple event nominals.[13]

The final source of evidence is a little more complicated. It concerns the co-occurrence of group adjectives with possessives and the co-occurrence of each of these with *by* phrases. The basic prediction is that the passive configuration in nominals should be incompatible with the presence of an a-structure-related possessive, a group adjective, or a *by* phrase. This follows from the fact that the passive configuration is found only for nouns with no argument structure, which cannot possibly license a-structure-related elements.

Consider what happens when a group adjective co-occurs with a possessive a-adjunct. The passive reading, in which the group adjective seems to be related to an object argument, disappears when a possessive a-adjunct is included in the NP. Thus (96a) and (96b) have interpretations where the liberals are defeated, but (96c) does not allow this: it cannot be interpreted as referring to an event in which Reagan defeated the liberals.

(96) a.   Reagan's defeat of the liberals
     b.   The liberal defeat
     c.   (*)Reagan's liberal defeat
     d.   (*)Reagan's European defeat

This can be explained if passive nominals are really result/simple event nominals. The agentive possessive must be an a-adjunct to receive its subject-like interpretation, as in (96a). Hence, *defeat* must take arguments to license the possessive. But it must be a result/simple event nominal to occur in the passive form with *liberal* as a modifier, as in (96b). Since the noun cannot meet both of these conditions simultaneously, (96c) is not a well-formed nominal. This result depends crucially on the status of the passive nominal in (96b). If *defeat* were a complex event nominal, adding the possessive should have no effect on its grammaticality, since the possessive subject would be licensed by the nominal, and *liberal* would be licensed in (96c) in the same way it is licensed in (96b).

Of course, there is another possible analysis for (96c) in which the possessive is construed as a modifier associated with a result nominal. On this reading, the example means something like the defeats of a liberal flavor associated with Reagan. The availability of such readings will be a function of the availability of the modifier construal of the possessive, which varies according to the possessive and the noun itself.

Example (96d) is really just like (96c), except that its result reading makes more sense. It can mean the defeat that Reagan suffered in Europe, but this is incompatible with the defeater reading for the possessive, just as (96c) is. The second reading would be possible if agentive *Reagan's* could modify *defeat*. Note that *European* in (96d) is a modifier specifying location, not an a-adjunct, so it does not force a process reading of the noun.

The explanation for (96c, d) rests on the assumption that a possessive agentive defeater cannot modify *defeat*. This assumption can be independently supported for *defeat*, much as it was supported for *assignment* in 3.2.2 above. Sentence (97) is impossible with *Reagan* interpreted strictly as the defeater, although it is possible with *Reagan* interpreted as simply associated with the defeat. This follows because *defeat* is unambiguously argument-taking when it occurs with an agentive possessive.

(97) *Reagan's defeat

To sum up, then, we find that group adjectives in their passive use cannot co-occur with possessive a-adjuncts. This follows if they are modifiers of result nominals but not if they are a-structure related and modify complex event nominals.

The prediction for *by* phrases is completely parallel to that for possessives. *By* phrases are ambiguous between modifier status and a-structure-related status, just as possessive are. Therefore passive nominals should co-occur with the modifier *by* phrase but not with a *by* phrase licensed by a-structure.

The expected contrast is illustrated by the examples in (98) and (99):

(98) a. The defeat of the liberals by Reagan
   b. An invasion of Central America by the U.S. Army

(99) a. *The liberal defeat by Reagan
   b. *A Central American invasion by the U.S. Army

Both NPs in (98) are grammatical because the noun has an a-structure, which licenses both the *of* phrase and the *by* phrase. However, the passive nominals in (99) are not complex event nominals and have no a-structure. Hence, the *by* phrase is not licensed. Again, no similar explanation is available if passive nominals are argument-taking. Whatever licenses the group adjectives in (78) and (80) above will license them here too, and the addition of a *by* phrase a-adjunct should be perfectly legitimate in (99), just as it is in (98).

The reasoning just applied for group adjectives holds with equal force for preposed possessives: if the preposed possessive is a modifier, it should be incompatible with *by* phrases licensed by a-structure. The *by* phrase will require an a-structure to license it, and no noun with an a-structure will allow a possessive modifier. For some reason, however, the data for possessive NPs are nowhere near as clear as for group adjectives. The literature contains a number of examples, generally classified as grammatical. The most famous (in (100a)) is also the most felicitous. Other examples, which strike me as essentially ungrammatical, include (100b, c) from Kayne (1984):

(100) a. The city's destruction by the enemy
   b. It's removal by Mary
   c. During the course of its digestion by worms

Substituting a full NP for *it's* in (100b, c) greatly degrades their grammaticality (as Kayne notes).[14]

(101) a. ??The tree's removal by Mary
   b. ??During the course of the food's digestion by worms

The examples in (102) are also marginally possible, perhaps because the *by* phrase here can be interpreted as a modifier rather than as an a-structure-related element. In support of this, note that the examples in (103) are also possible:

(102) a. ??The book's publication by The MIT Press
b. ??The politician's nomination by the senate

(103) a. A new publication by The MIT Press just came in the mail.
b. A nomination by the senate led to her eventual appointment.

Problematic issues remain, however.[15] Although judgements are murky, there is a fairly sharp difference in ill-formedness between (104a), with a possessive, and (104b), with a group adjective, which is not explained by the present assumptions.

(104) a. ?America's defeat by the Soviet Union
b. *The American defeat by the Soviet Union

So the co-occurence of *by* phrases with possessive passive nominals remains something of a mystery. On the one hand, it is nothing like the free and unconstrained possibility we expect if passive nominals are argument-takers. On the other hand, it does not seem to be quite as restricted as it is with adjective passive nominals.

To sum up, the evidence overwhelmingly supports the conclusion that passive nominals do not take arguments. The apparently preposed argument is no such thing. Rather, it is a modifier or a complement participating in its usual relationship to the head.

3.5.3 Nouns as defective theta markers

The evidence just given shows that there are no argument-taking nominals with passive form. Why not? Why is NP movement to the possessive position impossible? Why do we not find true passive nominals with argument-taking heads?

The answer lies in the limited theta-marking capacity of nominals, which we saw in the behavior of nominals with sentential complements (3.5.1). There we conclude that nouns cannot theta-mark directly, but must be assisted by prepositions. In the potential passive nominal in (105) the object NP moves to the possessive position, where it presumably gets case-marked.

(105) NP's defeat e

If Nouns are defective theta-markers, an NP like this will always violate the theta criterion. There is no way to license the chain formed by movement and thus the argument now in possessive position. The noun cannot theta-mark it, since nouns can never directly theta-mark anything. The comparable structure with a verb is of course possible, because the V directly theta-marks.

The inclusion of a preposition does not improve examples like (106):

(106) *NP's defeat of . . .

But the stranding of prepositions in passivization is independently ruled out for verbs as well as for nouns, presumably by principles relating to the case-marking function of a preposition.[16]

The hypothesis that nouns are defective theta markers, then, explains why NP movement is not possible in argument-taking nominals and hence why passive complex event nominals cannot exist. Moreover, it also explains why nouns with sentential complements cannot head complex event nominals. Theta-marking is possible only in configuration (107a) and not in either configuration (107b) or (107c).

(107) a. N PP   b. N CP   c. N NP

Sentential arguments to nouns and NP complements to nouns are both ruled out by the theta criterion once we accept the defectiveness of nouns as theta markers.

This conclusion is inconsistent with the explanation given in Aoun et al. (1987) for the non-ambiguity of *each picture of John's*. They propose that the head noun of the possessive NP has been deleted and that the empty N remaining cannot govern the trace of NP movement from complement to specifier position. Hence, *John's* cannot get an object-like interpretation at least by this means (it is not clear that all other possible means are ruled out by this account). In the present system the posthead genitive is unambiguously a modifier, not an argument, so it cannot be construed as an argument of the head and has no interpretation where it satisfies an lcs argument of *picture*. It is related to the head by predication and should therefore be compatible with an interpretation of *association*. Such an interpretation should not exclude the possibility that the possessive is associated with the head by being what the head represents. My own judgment is that this reading *is* possible: consider *None of these pictures of yours will get you a job as a model*, for example.

Earlier researchers working on passive nominals have generally defended one of two views: that passive nominals involve NP movement or that they involve modification. Anderson (1978) proposes that these nominals do involve NP movement, with the class of verbs that take affected arguments. Clearly, this account cannot explain any of the properties of passive nominals discussed here, since it treats them as behaving like verbs and argument-taking nominals. Both Higginbotham (1983) and Williams (1982) took the position that there is no NP movement in passive nominals. Williams proposed that the apparent passive interpretation was just a special case of the general flexibility of interpretation associated with the possessive. Higginbotham assumed that all arguments of N are optional and proposed that this follows from the view that nouns have only modifiers. In this view, satellites of nouns can be related to the head only via identification of the external argument of the head with the external R argument of a modifier. This makes a movement analysis of the passive in NPs impossible. This is the desired result in view of conclusion of this section, but it cannot be maintained in general. Higginbotham's proposal does not offer an adequate general characterization of the relationship between nouns and their satellites. First, Higinbotham's proposal assumes that nouns have only optional arguments. I have shown here, though, that complex event nominals do take obligatory arguments when the arguments are PPs. Hence, his proposal leads us to expect the passive in precisely these cases. Second, as we will see in 3.6, even nonarguments are not uniform in their behavior: some behave like modifiers and some do not. Both Williams's account and Higginbotham's account fail if the preposed possessives and adjectives in passive nominals are not just modifiers. In 3.6 I will argue that they are not.

As for sentential complements, Stowell (1981) proposed that tensed sentential arguments of nouns are impossible because tensed clauses do not get case and case is a prerequisite for theta-marking. Infinitival clauses on the other hand, are intrinsically case-marked, according to Stowell, and hence can be theta-marked. As I pointed out above, however, this account assumes that all infinitival clauses inside nominals are arguments and that all tensed clauses are modifiers. As we have seen, this picture of the situation is not accurate, since neither is in fact ever an argument. In 3.6 we will see that both can be either a complement or a modifier. Hence, Stowell's particular attempt to reduce the theta-theoretic properties of nouns to case theory cannot ultimately succeed.

More generally, as I noted in the introduction to 3.5, it is not possible to reduce the defective theta-marking capacity of nouns to their case-theoretic properties. Such a proposal incorrectly predicts that nouns take CP arguments, since CPs do not require case. Similarly, it is not possible to reduce the case-theoretic intransitivity of nouns to their theta-theoretic intransitivity, as Emonds (1985) proposes. Emonds suggests that a case-theoretic difference between nouns and verbs is redundant, since even if nouns can assign case to NP arguments, the arguments will still violate the theta criterion. However, more general considerations argue against this interpretation of the situation: *all* nouns are intransitive, regardless of whether they are argument-taking or not. Intransitivity is shared by complex-event nominals (which are theta-markers) and by result nominals and simple event nominals (which are not theta markers). Hence, any attempt to reduce the intransitivity of nouns to theta-marking or to any property relating to argument structure must fail.

Presumably there is a relationship between the two senses in which nouns are intransitive. One possibility with many grammatical ramifications is that nouns are not governors. Hence, they can neither assign case nor theta-mark. If nouns do not govern, their behavior with respect to exceptional government will also follow, as noted at the end of 3.5.1. Moreover, the island status of complements to nouns is explained according to the position of Cinque (1990). In sum, it seems very likely that once nouns are recognized as non-theta-markers, the key known differences between nouns and verbs can be reduced to a difference in their properties with respect to government.

3.6 Complements and Modifiers

If the clauses that appear as sentential complements to nouns, as well as the specifiers of passive nominals, are not grammatical arguments of the noun, what are they? More generally, what are the various satellite phrases associated with non-argument-taking nominals? One answer is that they are appositive modifiers of some kind. The second possibility is that they are related to the lexico-semantic representation of the head like true arguments, even though their relationship is not mediated by argument structure. It turns out that both of these possibilities are realized, and there are two quite distinct ways in which the relationship between a head noun and a non-argument can be established. One is by predication, and the other by a direct relationship with the lcs. An expression predicated of the head noun will be referred to here as a *modifier*. An expression that corresponds directly to a position in the lcs of the head will be referred to as a *complement*.[17]

The essential difference can be seen if we contrast examples like *John's murder* with examples like *John's dog*. In *John's murder* the possessive is connected to the lexical meaning of the head—this is what gives the NP its passive flavor. In *John's dog*, on the other hand, the possessive is a simple modifier. Here it is not related to the lcs; it is not in any way part of the lexical meaning of *dog* that it can have a possessor. As for the affectedness constraint on nominals, I will show that it affects complements and not modifiers. Modifiers modify through identification of the external argument of the modifier with the external argument of the head (see 3.3). So a modifier modifies whatever the noun denotes—an event when the nominal is a simple event nominal, an individual when the nominal denotes an individual.

The possessive or group adjective in a passive nominal is not a modifier, since it is not predicated of the event. Similarly, the CP complement to a noun like *attempt* is not a modifier, since it is not predicated of the event. These expressions are not interpreted by predication, then, but must be analyzed as complements corresponding directly to argument positions in the lcs, even though they are not grammatical arguments regulated by a-structure. Complements are found only with simple event nominals.[18] (As we have already seen, complex event nominals do not allow sentential complements at all, because their defective theta-marking makes it impossible for them to take sentential arguments.) A phrase acting as a complement must be licensed by direct relationship to the lcs, instead of in one of the other two ways: by predication (for modifiers) or by theta-marking (for true arguments). Below we will examine the licensing of complements more precisely.

First, however, I want to establish some of the basic generalizations that follow from the proposed three-way distinction between arguments, modifiers, and complements. The essential property of a complement is that it is related to an lcs position in the representation of the head. As a result, there is a systematic relationship between verb-complement constructions and noun-complement constructions, even though argument structure is not involved. The essential property of a modifier is that is licensed by predication. This makes it possible to explain a very fundamental difference between the behavior of modifiers and that of complements. Modifiers can be separated from the head by the copula.[19] Separation is never possible for complements (or indeed for arguments). This generalization is an extension of the observation for possessives in Anderson (1983–1984).

Since modifiers occur across a copula from the head and complements observe selection, it may seem that we should never find phrases that display both (by exhibiting selectional effects across a copula). Nevertheless, such cases do exist, with lcs representations of a particular form, exactly where the theory predicts (3.6.4).

Finally, I will show that the failure of -er nominals to take sentential complements is explained by the lcs proposed for -er nominals together with the general principles of theta-marking, modification, and complement-taking.

3.6.1 A note on affectedness

The conclusion that passive nominals are never argument-taking has an interesting implication for the problem of affectedness studied by Anderson (1978). Anderson demonstrates that only a small subset of object-like expressions can occur prenominally, and she characterizes them as "affected." Affectedness is what distinguishes the examples we have been considering from those in (108).

(108) a. *That fact's knowledge (knowledge of that fact)
       b. *The book's discussion (discussion of the book)

The nature of the affectedness restriction is mysterious in a number of ways: Why should it hold, and what does it hold of?[20]

Affectedness cannot be related to a-structure, since passive nominals have no argument structure. So the affectedness restriction in passives cannot reflect a property of argument structure or a property of syntactic arguments. Nor can it be a property of modifiers. Obviously, not all possessive modifiers are subject to affectedness: it would be hard to argue that the possessive in *John's dog* is affected, for example. The true modifier possessive is typically animate and indeed human. As Williams (1982) has pointed out, it seems that just about any relation can hold between a possessor and the head. But this freedom is limited to the interpretation of the *modifier* possessive, which is subject just to real-world knowledge. It is, then, the *complement* use of the possessive, the one found with passive nominals, that is subject to an affectedness requirement. This possessive is quite unlike the possessive modifier. It is not subject to the humanness restriction and does not occur predicatively, as we will see in 3.6.3.

This casts doubt on certain recent proposals, at least insofar as they are critically formulated in a-structure terms. Anderson's own proposal is that nouns with affected objects take bare NP complements which can move to possessive position to get case. Thise proposal is inconsistent, of course, with the conclusions drawn here about the theta-marking capacities of nouns, since it assumes that nouns do theta-mark bare NPs and that passive nominals involve argument structure in the usual way. Zubizarreta (1987) suggests that affected objects are really arguments incorporated into the verb or noun and that this is what distinguishes them from other arguments. Again, since passive nominals have no a-structure, this presumably cannot be the source of the affectedness requirement in passives. Tenny (1989a) argues that affectedness must be understood as an aspectual property. Aspectual characteristics are represented in the event structure, however, and I have shown that passive nominals have no event structure. So it is hard to see how Tenny's proposal could be correct. It appears that affectedness cannot be a matter of a-structure or of event structure. Affectedness governs the behavior of the very nominals that have neither. It must then be the lcs representation that distinguishes affected participants from unaffected in such a way that unaffected lcs arguments are not subject to the complement interpretation.

3.6.2 Complements and selection

Within the present theory, a-structure cannot be what governs selection, since a-structure does not contain the information needed to establish the selectional properties of a predicate. Thematic role labels, for example, are entirely absent, yet they determine preposition choice in the regular cases. Clearly, then, lcs must be the representation responsible for complement selection. In view of this it comes as no surprise that even heads with no argument structure exert selectional control over their complements. These heads do have an lcs, even though they do not have an a-structure.

Consider *book* and *gift*, for example. Neither has an a-structure. Therefore, it must be their lcs properties that distinguish (109a) from (109b):

(109) a. *John's book to the hospital
       b.   John's gift to the hospital

These nouns show clear effects of their lexical semantic analysis: *gift* licenses a PP headed by *to*, but *book* does not. Whatever the lexical definition of *book* is, it does not include a transfer of possession, and this distinguishes *book* from *gift*. So representations like those in (110) will capture relevant properties if *to* is analyzed as marking the argument corresponding to z in these entries.

(110) *book*:   x such that y reads x
      gift: x such that y causes x to *come into z's possession*
      giving: an event in which y causes x to *come into z's possession*

A similar conclusion holds for passive nominals. Although the possessive is not an argument of the noun, as shown in 3.5.2, its interpretation
clearly implicates the semantic structure of the head. In general, passive
nominals denote simple events, and their possessives correspond to
their Patient lcs arguments. In the relevant interpretation the possessive in *John's murder* and *the book's translation* corresponds to the y
arguments in the lcs in (111).

(111) a. *murder*:   an event such that x murdered y
      b. *translation*:   an event such that x translated y

This is, of course, precisely why it has been so tempting to analyze the
passive nominals as involving NP movement of an argument.

It is easy to demonstrate for sentential complements that the complement acts like an lcs argument of the noun. The nouns that take sentential complements are related to verbs that do the same, and the type of
complement that occurs with the noun is a function of the type of complement that occurs with the verb. Nouns that take sentential complements include many, like those in (112a), with verbal counterparts. The
complement-taking properties of the verb are consistently preserved
under nominalization. Hence, the nouns in (112b) lack sentential complements, while those in (112a) allow them.[21]

(112) a. announcement, attempt, hope, wish, desire, plan, request,
          belief, hypothesis, claim, complaint, proposal, suggestion,
          statement, assertion
      b. *assignment that . . . , *assign that . . . , *description
          that . . . , *describe that . . .

The examples in (113) illustrate an additional respect in which nouns
maintain the complement-taking properties of verbs:

(113) a. They asserted that the answer was obvious.
      b. Their assertion that the answer was obvious . . .
      c. They attempted/resolved/offered to leave early.
      d. Their attempt/resolve/offer to leave early . . .
      e. They decided that he should leave early/to leave early.
      f. Their decision that he should leave early/to leave early . . .
      g. They requested that he leave early.
      h. Their request that he leave early . . .

Where the verb takes a *that* clause, the noun does the same. Where the verb takes a non-finite complement, the noun does the same. Where the verb allows either, so does the derived nominal. Even the subjunctive requirement associated with verbs like *request* is maintained, as we see in (113g, h).

All in all, it is clear that sentential complements to nouns are subject to the same lexical selection properties as complements to verbs. Since nouns with sentential complements do not have a-structure, the source of the preservation of complement selection must be the regular relationship between the lcs of the verb and the lcs of the dervied nominal. This result supports the conclusions of earlier work on complement selection. Grimshaw (1979) and Pesesky (1982) argued that complement selection is a matter of semantics and not of syntax. The argument is fundamentally that the semantic properties of complements are maintained despite variation in syntactic form. In other words, selection for properties of a complement is a matter of lcs representation, not of a-structure.

Other considerations internal to the theory I am proposing lead to the same conclusion. Theta roles are not represented in a-structure, yet it is indisputable that the preposition an argument is marked with is a function of its theta role.

(114) a. We put the book on/*to the box.
       b. We gave the book to/*on the library.

The choice of preposition cannot be a matter of satisfying a-structure, since the relevant information is simply not available there. However, the illicit preposition choices can be ruled by lcs requirements. Suppose that each semantically selected preposition can correspond to only a particular semantic type of argument. For example, we might represent *on* and *to* as in (115) with an entry that specifies that *on* introduces locations and that *to* introduces posessors.

(115) *on* z: located relative to z
       to z: come in to z's possession

If the wrong preposition occurs, the a-structure will still be satisfied, but the semantic requirements of the predicate will not be met. The lcs of the verb *give* specifies that *give* takes a possessor argument, but the preposition *on* specifies that it introduces a location argument. Hence, (114a) is incompatible with the lexico-semantic requirements of the verb when the preposition *on* occurs, and there is no need to invoke a-structure to explain the clash.

The general consequence of this view is that selectional effects will be found even without argument structure. Thus they will extend even to passive nominals and nominals with sentential complements. For the cases of sentential complements the analysis proceeds as follows. We posit an lcs like (116a) for the verb *attempt* and (116b) for the noun. "I" stands for the semantic type of infinitives like the one with *attempt*.[22]

(116) a. *attempt* (V): x attempts y (y an I)
      b. *attempt* (N): e such that x attempts y (y an I)

The noun *attempt*, then, will occur with an infinitival complement for exactly the same reason as its verbal counterpart does. The fact that the complement is also a theta-marked argument when it occurs with the verb does not affect selection. Complements show selection because selection is determined by the lcs of the head and not by its a-structure.

3.6.3 Properties of modifiers
Unlike complements, the interpretation of modifiers does not implicate the lexical semantic properties of the predicate in any direct way. For modifiers the relationship between the head and the modifier is one of predication in which the modifier is predicated of the external argument of the head noun, its *R* argument in a theory like that of Williams, (1981a) and di Sciullo and Williams (1987). For a noun like *dog* I posit the representation in (117):

(117) *dog* <R>

Anything predicated of the head will be coindexed with *R* and thus predicated of the referent of the NP. In a phrase like *large dog*, the argument of *large* is coindexed with the *R* argument of *dog*. For *John's dog* the same applies: *John's* is predicated of the *R* argument of *dog*.

An important characteristic of the relation of modification is that it can be established equally well by predication across a copula. Thus PP modifiers and possessive modifiers are all possible in contexts like those in (118).[23]

(118) a. John's dog   The dog is John's.
      b. The book by/about/on Chomsky   The book was by/about/
                                           on Chomsky.

This distinguishes modifiers from complements in a very clear way: only modifiers can be related to the head across a copula. Consider the situation with passive nominals. They denote (simple) events, and predication can therefore relate modifiers to the event, as in (119). As it is a relation of predication, this relation can be established across the copula, as in (120).

(119) a. The (man's) gruesome murder
b. The (building's) timely construction
c. The/Reagan's quick defeat
d. The unsuccessful (Central American) invasion

(120) a. The (man's) murder was gruesome.
b. The (building's) construction was timely.
c. The/Reagan's defeat was quick.
d. The (Central American) invasion was unsuccessful.

However, the possessive and the group adjective are not modifiers but complements. This means that possessive specifiers of passive nominals never occur predicatively with the passive interpretation (although, of course, other interpretations are sometimes possible):

(121) a. *The murder was the man's
b. *The construction was the building's
c. *The defeat was Reagan's
d. *The invasion was Central American

Note that this reasoning demonstrates quite clearly that the existence of passive nominals cannot just be attributed to the flexibility of interpretation shown by possessives, as suggested by Williams (1982). The possessive modifier and the possessive complement actually behave quite differently.

The same reasoning holds for nouns like *knowledge* and *attempt*. The CPs associated with them are complements, not modifiers. Hence, they cannot be related to the head across the copula:

(122) a. *The knowledge was the Dukakis was ahead.
b. *Their attempt was to climb a mountain.

Nor can possessives corresponding to their "subjects":[24]

(123) a. *The knowledge that Dukakis was ahead was ours.
b. *The attempt to climb a mountain was theirs.

Modifiers, then, are simply related to the R argument in the lcs representation, while complements are lcs arguments. Complements obey selection, and modifiers occur predicatively.

3.6.4 Selection and CP modifiers
This reasoning leads to the following puzzle. CP complements observe selectional requirements because they are related to lcs positions, and

they do not occur across the copula because they are not predicated of the head. This appears to predict that we will never find a CP predicated of a noun across the copula and obeying selectional requirements.

However, complements to nouns like *decision*, *conclusion*, and *arrangement* show exactly this cluster of properties. They do occur separted from the head by a copula, as in (124), which indicates that the relationship between the CP and the head is one of predication.

(124) a. Their conclusion/belief/hypothesis/proposal was that there is no relevant data.

b. Their decision was to leave at six/that they should leave at six.

c. The arrangement was for them to leave at six.

Yet they show the very same selectional properties as the corresponding verbs, as shown in (112) and (113) above.

Stowell (1981) suggested that finite complements to nouns do occur across a copula, while nouns with infinitival complements cannot be separated from the head by a copula. He proposed that finite complements to nouns are appositive modifiers, while infinitival complements are not. I will argue that certain apparent complements to nouns are indeed modifiers, as he proposed. However, the examples in (112) and (124) show that the correlation he proposed does not hold up: there are counterexamples in both directions. So what distinguishes the two classes?[25]

We can derive the different behavior from the nature of their lcs representations together with the assumptions already made about the relationship between the CP and the head. The crucial feature is that while nouns of the *attempt* and *knowledge* type have an event as their external arguments, those of the *decision* and *conclusion* type do not denote an event. Instead, they refer to entities that act as the internal arguments of the base verbs. Their lcs representations will therefore be like (125), which specifies that the external argument of the noun (its referent) is identified with its propositional (P) lcs argument.

(125) *conclusion*:   R< = x> such that y holds x (x a P)

The referent of the head noun corresponds to the internal argument of *conclude*, i.e., to what was concluded. Thus for such a noun, the *R* argument (which determines the reference of the phrase) is identified with the *x* argument in the lcs. The representation captures the intuition that the sentential complement specifies the nature of the conclusion itself.

When a CP modifies *conclusion*, it is coindexed with the *R* argument of the head, just like *John's* in *John's dog*. But this argument is in turn identified (or coindexed) in the lcs with the *x* lcs argument. Indirectly, then, the modifier does correspond to the lcs argument as a result of combining predication and the lcs identification of *R* and *x*. The same holds for a case like *decision*.

(125) *decision*:   R< = x> such that y decides x (x a P/I)

Sentential complements to nouns like *conclusion* and *decision* are really nothing more than modifiers, but because of the semantics of the nouns they modify, they eventually specify the content of an lcs argument of the noun, an argument that corresponds to the internal argument of the base verb. Since the CP is a modifier, it can be related to the head and across the copula via predication, just like *John's* can. Since it is coindexed with *R*, which is in turn identifed with an lcs argument, it must observe the selectional properties of this lcs slot. In sum, because of the lcs connection between *R* and *x*, the CP shows mixed properties: it acts as a modifier, yet, like an argument or complement, it respects selectional properties.

The *attempt/knowledge* class of nouns is critically different with respect to exactly the key representational point. For the *attempt* class to work like the *decision* class, we would have to posit the representations in (127):

(127) a. *attempt*:   R< = x> such that y attempted x (x and I)
       b. *knowledge*:   R< = x> such that y knows x (x a P)

But these are clearly not correct: *Attempt* refers not to what is attempted but to the (simple) event of attempting itself. Similarly, *knowledge* (at least when it takes a sentential complement) does not refer to what is known. *Attempt* and *knowledge* are crucially different from *conclusion* and *decision* in that their referent is not identified with one of their arguments, so a modifier predicated of *attempt* or *knowledge* will never be associated with one of their lcs arguments.

A similar analysis holds for passive nominals. They are like *attempt* and *knowledge* with respect to lcs representation: each refers to a simple event and not to an element corresponding to the internal argument of its verbal base. Thus the lcs representations in (128) clearly do *not* accurately reflect the meanings of the words.

(128) *murder* ≠ x such that someone murdered x
       defeat ≠ x such that y defeats x

     construction ≠ x such that y constructed x
     translation ≠ x such that y translated x

Translation does not refer to the thing translated, nor does *murder* refer to the one murdered. Thus *R* is not identified with the *x* arguments for these nominals.[26]

One final prediction. This analysis treats nouns like *conclusion* and *decision* as result nominals with modifiers. Hence, the possessive should show properties of modifiers, just as the CP does. In particular, it should occur predicatively:

(129) a. The conclusion/belief/hypothesis/proposal that there is no relevent data was theirs.
     b. The decision to leave at six/that they should leave at six was ours.
     c. The arrangement for them to leave at six was Mary's.

These examples are perhaps less than perfect. Nonetheless, they contrast sharply with the paradigms for the *knowledge* and *attempt* class give in (123) above.

Complement selection is preserved in these cases, then, because of the effects of predication combined with the nature of the lcs representation of the noun. The fact that selectional properties are strictly maintained across the copula in examples like (124) provides an extremely strong argument that selection should not be treated as a matter of a-structure. No theory of a-structure satisfaction would allow the post-copula clause to satisfy an argument of the head noun in the subject position.

3.6.5 Sentential complements to -er nominals

Carlson and Roeper (1980) pointed out a gap in the complement system of nouns. They note that *-er* nominals derived from verbs which take sentential complements lose this capacity:

(130) a. He observed the interaction/that the interaction took place.
     b. He was the first observer of the interaction.
     c. * He was the first observer that the interaction took place.

(131) a. They discovered the responsible virus/that a virus was reponsible.
     b. They were the discoverers of the responsible virus.
     c. * They were the discoverers that a virus was responsible.

The ungrammaticality of -er nominals with sentential complements can be derived from the theory of nominalization proposed here.

There are three relationships that the CPs in (130c) and (131c) could have to the head noun: the CP could be an argument of an argument-taking noun, a modifier predicated of the external argument of the noun, or a direct lcs complement. To explain the ungrammaticality of the examples, we must explain why all three possibilities are ruled out.

Suppose Levin and Rappaport (1989) are correct in arguing that -er nominals can have argument structure (see 3.3 for some discussion). Nonetheless, the examples in (130c) and (131c) cannot be argument-taking nominals, since there is no way for the sentential complement to be theta-marked. This follows from the conclusion of 3.5 that nouns cannot directly theta-mark sentential complements. If *observer* and *discoverer* have a-structure, the theta criterion will always be violated when they occur with CPs.

Could the CPs be modifiers? Since they refer to individuals, -er nominals have an lcs like that in (132):

(132) *observer*:   R< = x> such that x observed y (y a P)

Modifiers are predicated of the R argument of the head noun. In a case like (132) a modifier will be predicated of x, since R and x are identified. It is this argument that corresponds to the referent of the NP. So if the CP is a modifier, the interpretation will be one in which the content of the observer is "that. . . ." This is not a possible interpretation, because the observer argument, the x, does not have propositional content. Thus (130c) and (131c) are excluded for the same reason as (133):

(133) a. *The observer was that . . .
      b. *The discoverer was that . . .
      c. *The man was that . . .
      d. *She was that . . .

Other modifiers are possible, of course, like those in (134):

(134) a. He was the tallest observer of the interaction.
      b. The talented discoverers of the virus.

Thus there is a critical contrast between -er nominals and nominals like *observation* precisely because of their lcs. Compare the lcs structure of *observer* and *observation*:

(135) a. *observer*:   R< = x> such that x observed y (y a P)
      b. *observation*:   R< = y> such that x observed y (y a P)

The referent of *observation* corresponds to a propositional argument, but the referent of the *-er* nominal corresponds to a nonpropositionals argument. For the *-er* nominal, *R* is identified with the active subject argument rather than with the argument corresponding to the complement. Hence, predication can indirectly relate the clause only to the subject argument.

The final possibility is that the CPs in (130c) and (131c) could be complements, i.e., lcs arguments. Why is this not possible? The generalization is that the capacity to take lcs complements is limited to simple event nominals. The crucial difference between an event nominal and a result or *-er* nominal lies in the character of lcs representation in the two cases. In result and *-er* nominals, the external argument of the noun corresponds to one of its lcs participants.[27] This is expressed by having *R* identified with that argument:

(136) a. *observer*:   R< = x> x observes y
      b. *conclusion, decision*:   R < = y> x concludes/decides y

The argument bound by *R* varies according to the affix that has been added (see 3.3 and Sproat (1985)), but the lcs representations of all of these nominals have the same structural characteristic.

For event nominals, in contrast, the external argument is simply an event, so *R* is not identified with any of the lcs participants for nouns like *attempt* or *murder*.

(137) *attempt, murder*:   R < > x attempts/murders y

Apparently an unidentified or free *R* makes the Noun transparent for lcs licensing of phrases, which makes direct lcs complementation possible. Suppose, for example, that lcs complements are licensed if they receive an index from an lcs position. Suppose, moreover, that non-thematic argument structure (see 3.3) contains both the *R* slot and the extra slot indicated in angle brackets in the lcs representations given before. For a result nominal or an *-er* nominal, the extra slot, indentified with *R* , is filled in the lcs. Hence, there no way for an lcs index to be transmitted through this slot to a CP complement to the result nominal.

(138) a. [observation CP]
         (R< = y>, x observes y)
      b. [observer CP]
         R< = x>, x observes y)

Thus the head in (138b), for example, cannot license a complement corresponding to its *y* argument, since the second slot is already filled because *R* binds the *x* argument. For simple event nominals the second slot is unfilled, since *R* is not identified with an lcs position. This slot can then transmit the index (*i*) from an lcs argument of the head to a complement, which licenses the complement.

(139) $_{N'}$[attempt CP-i]

(R <i>, x attempts y-i (y an I))

The essential idea is that a simple event nominal is transparent to lcs complementation while a result or -*er* nominal is opaque and that this follows from the fact that the external argument in a result or -*er* nominal binds a position in the lcs, which makes the lcs opaque. The consequence is that direct lcs complements are possible only with simple event nominals.

Since the CP with an -*er* nominal cannot be an argument, a modifier, or an lcs complement, we have explained why -*er* nominals don't occur with CPs. This result crucially depends on several points of the theory of nominalization given here.

• Even argument-taking nouns cannot take sentential arguments.
• Sentential complements to result nominals are predicated of the external argument of the head.
• Nominals referring to individuals do not allow direct lcs complements.

3.6.6 Summary

In this section I examined the reasons for distinguishing between complements and modifiers. Complements are directly licensed by lcs, modifiers are licensed by predication, and true arguments are licensed by theta-marking. Since complements *look* like arguments in a number of respects, it is tempting to try to combine the two cases. Recall, however, that there are a number of strong reasons why complements to simple event nominals cannot be syntactic arguments:

• Unlike prepositional arguments of complex event nominals, complements to simple event nominals are always optional.
• They occur with a class of nouns (the simple event nominals) which never take syntactic arguments.
• Sentential complements to simple event nominals can be directly related to the noun (without a supporting preposition), and this is not possible for sentential arguments of complex event nominals. To admit arguments for simple event nominals we would have to allow nouns to theta-mark directly without the assistance of a preposition. But then we would inevitably lose the explanation for the lack of the passive within

nominals and the explanation for the absence of sentential arguments with complex event nominals.

The overall conclusion, then, is that sentential complements to nouns are related to lcs arguments but are not grammatical arguments. They mimic the behavior of true arguments just to the extent that this behavior is determined by the lexico-semantic representation of predicates. On the assumption that subcategorization is dependent upon argument structure, one consequence of this proposal is that nouns have no control over the realization of their sentential complement. Hence, the complements of the nouns will have to be realized in their pure form, as determined by their Canonical Structural Realization (Grimshaw (1981)). Selection for syntactic category will not be preserved under nominalization, since it is associated with a-structure, and a-structure is not preserved. We have already seen one piece of evidence that supports this: while verbs show lexical variation in the obligatoriness of sentential complements (Grimshaw (1979)), nouns do not (see 3.5). This is as expected; only the semantic properties of sentential complements to verbs are maintained under nominalization.

3.7 Some Conclusions on Nominalization

This investigation has uncovered a cluster of properties that distinguish three kinds of nominals: nominals differ in their external arguments, they differ in whether or not they have an event structure representation and hence an argument structure representation, and they have different lcs representations. Nouns are far more variable then verbs and are clearly represented quite differently. However, once this recognized, it emerges that the general principles of grammar are the same for nouns and verbs. Theta-marking, for example, is obligatory for both; that is, the theta criterion holds equally of nouns and verbs. Similarly, selection works the same in nouns and verbs, since both have lcs representations that specify properties of lcs arguments. There are two differences between nouns and verbs. The first is that only *some* nouns participate in the system of a-structure representation that lies behind theta-marking. The second is that nouns do not theta-mark directly, while verbs do, a difference that I have suggested may be due to the failure of nouns to act as governors. The next chapter examines the issue of subjects. I will argue that the apparent optionality of theta-marking for subjects in NPs indicates a major difference in the a-structure of nouns and verbs. Again the representations are different, but the principles of grammar are the same.

The diversity among nominals revealed here is only part of the picture. There are many other kinds of NPs with very different interpretations: concealed questions, exclamations and propositions, for example (Grimshaw (1979)), as well as partitives like *a box of rice/a box of the rice* (Selkirk (1977)). It is striking that despite this diversity, all Noun Phrases conform rigidly to the same basic syntactic template. This is an interesting general argument for the autonomy of syntax. Expressions that are satellites to nouns have many different relationships to them: that of argument, modifier, complement, etc. The syntax of the NP is unvarying across all of these semantically disparate cases. The noun is always intransitive, in the sense of not acting as a case assigner, and the satellite expressions appear predictably in the specifier or the complement of the phrase.

This has important implications for the formulation of general principles of phrase structure and word order, such as those involved in X-bar theory. Consider, for example, the recent proposals that word order should be expressed in terms of parameters governing the direction of theta-marking or the direction of case-marking rather than in terms of head position parameters (Koopman (1983) and Travis (1983)). How do such proposals fare with respect to nominals? No nouns assign case, so case-marking cannot be responsible for the order of elements. Result nominals and simple event nominals do not theta-mark, so directionality of theta-marking cannot determine order. The fact that these nominals have the same syntax as theta-marking nominals is strong evidence that head position is the fundamental parameter of ordering and not just the default. Otherwise, there is no way to explain why the head position is constant despite great variability in its grammatical role.

In conclusion, then, underlying the great variation in nouns is a set of invariant properties—intransitivity in particular—which maintain constant syntax for NPs regardless of their meaning.

Chapter 4
The Argument Structure of
Nominals and Passives

4.1 Introduction

Arguments in general are either completely obligatory (like the subject in English) or lexically variable. The subject of a nominal shares with the passive *by* phrase the interesting characteristic of being systematically optional. I will argue that this property reflects the a-structure representation of passive and nominal predicates, which have *suppressed* a-structure positions corresponding to the optional phrases. Suppressed positions cannot be satisfied by arguments, nor can they theta-mark arguments. However, they can license *argument adjuncts* (a-adjuncts), including the *by* phrase and the possessive. A-adjuncts, like arguments and unlike adjuncts, are regulated by relationship to an a-structure, yet like adjuncts and unlike arguments, they do not satisfy a-structure positions.

I will present evidence for a-structure representations of passive verbs in which the external argument of the verb is listed in the a-structure but is suppressed. The external argument of the verbal base is suppressed also in argument-taking nominals. Unlike passives, however, argument-taking nominals do have an unsuppressed external argument, *Ev* of chapter 3, which is a relative of the *R* argument of Williams (1981a) and di Sciullo and Williams (1987). This analysis is a development of proposals about suppression in Zubizarreta (1985, 1987), Grimshaw (1986b) and Grimshaw and Mester (1988).

The goal is to exploit these assumptions in giving an account of some central properties of passives and argument-taking nominals. These a-structure representations, together with the a-adjunct hypothesis, explain the distribution of possessives and *by* phrases as a function of the a-structure of nouns and the a-structure of active and passive verbs.

4.2 Suppressed Positions and Argument Adjuncts

A generally acknowledged and fairly clear distinction has been made between arguments and adjuncts. Arguments can be selected and subcategorized, in the sense that their presence and the form they take are under the control of individual predicates. Arguments must be licensed: they can occur only if they are theta-marked by a predicate as a function of the predicate's argument structure. Adjuncts are not theta-marked and do not need to be licensed by relationship to an a-structure; their licensing conditions pertain to other domains (McConnell-Ginet (1982)). They are not subcategorized. Hence, their form is free, and they are never required by a-structure.[1]

Possessive NPs in nominals like (1b) and *by* phrases of passives like (1c) both subjectlike interpretations in that they seem to correspond to the subject of matching active verbal predicates. If the a-structure position corresponding to the subject of (1a) is suppressed for passives and nominals, then neither the possessive nor the *by* phrase can be an argument, despite their semantic similarity to arguments. A possessive can never be given the theta-role of the subject of the corresponding verb, because this theta-role cannot be assigned by the Noun. The same reasoning holds for passive argument structures. The subject argument of the active verb is suppressed for the passive, just as for nominals. As a result, no argument need, or indeed can, fill this role. The argument structure of the active *kick* and the passive *kicked* differ, according to this proposal, in the number of open argument positions they contain.

Sample argument structures are given in (1). Annotation of an argument with $\emptyset$ indicates that the argument has been suppressed and therefore cannot be syntactically satisfied.

(1) a. The enemy destroyed the city.
        destroy (x   (y))
                   Agent Theme
     b. The enemy's destruction of the city
        destruction (R (x-$\emptyset$ (y)))
                          Agent Theme
     c. The city was destroyed by the enemy.
        destroyed (x-$\emptyset$ (y))
                     Agent Theme

Since the possessive subject of the noun in (1b) and the *by* phrase in (1c) cannot be arguments, what are they? Zubizarreta (1985, 252–259) and Grimshaw (1986b) have argued that they should be treated as a variety of adjuncts. Zubizarreta argues that *by* phrases behave like adjuncts under extraction, violating the Empty Category Principle when they are extracted from a *wh-* island. (See also Baker (1985, 576–583), Roberts (1987), and Jackendoff (1990).)

Although these elements resemble adjuncts, they also resemble arguments in one obvious way: they contribute information about positions in the a-structures of predicates. Zubizarreta (1987) views them as restricting the interpretation of the argument position they are associated with. Thus the possessive in (1b) and the *by* phrase in (1c) are both interpreted as providing information about the destroyer argument of the predicate. Developing these ideas and my proposals in Grimshaw (1986b), I will argue that these are a-adjuncts, which are licensed by a-structure and hence have an intermediate status. They resemble arguments in their mode of licensing. Yet unlike arguments they are not theta-marked, and they do not satisfy a-structure positions.

The positions that can license a-adjuncts are those that are lexically satisfied or suppressed. (We will see in 4.6 that this need not be stipulated but follows from general principles governing the licensing of arguments and adjuncts.) They include the argument of a passive verb or a nominal that corresponds to the *external* argument of the active verbal base.[2] Suppressed positions are represented in the argument structure but are not available for purposes of theta-marking. They are, in effect, "implicit arguments" (Roeper (1987)). Since a-adjuncts must be licensed by suppressed positions, they occur with nominals and passive verbs but not with actives. Since they are a type of adjunct and are not required in order to satisfy argument structure, they occur optionally.

Immediate support for the suppression proposal comes from the well-known but rarely addressed fact that both *by* phrases and possessives are optional, as (2) illustrates.[3]

(2) a. The (enemy's) destruction of the city was unexpected.

b. The city was destroyed (by the enemy).

If the possessive NP and the subject of an active verb have the same status with respect to argument structure (both syntactically satisfying an argument position), the Theta Criterion will force both to be obligatory. Similarly, if active and passive verbs have the same argument structures, the Theta Criterion will make the *by* phrase obligatory, since it will be required to satisfy an argument position. If the critical argument positions are suppressed, however, the systematic optionality of

by phrases and possessives is explained. A-adjuncts are, of course, always optional, since their presence is not required by a-structure.[4]
In this way we can explain the asymmetry between subjects of nouns and objects of nouns. In chapter 3 we saw that contrary to common belief, complex event nominals do take obligatory objects. Nevertheless, the possessive subject is never obligatory. Of course, the presence of an object invokes the complex event reading of a noun because the object must get theta-marked, but the argument structure of a noun never requires the presence of a subject for satisfaction. As a result, even an argument-taking noun will never require a subject. Examples like (3) with an object but no subject are therefore perfectly grammatical, even though their counterparts with a subject but no object are ungrammatical (see 2.2).

(3) a. The examination of the papers was long.
    b. The destruction of the city was awful to watch.
    c. The development of inexpensive housing was applauded.

Treating possessives and *by* phrases as a-adjuncts allows us to maintain the same principle of theta-marking for all argument-taking items, whether nouns, active verbs, or passive verbs, namely that argument structure must always be satisfied. The *apparent* optionality of subjects of nouns results from the a-structure representation of nouns and not from a special clause in the principle of theta-marking or the definition of a-structure satisfaction. Nouns are just like verbs with respect to the obligatoriness of their arguments: elements required to satisfy argument structure are obligatory. Possessives are optional precisely because they do not satisfy argument structure. *Arguments* of nouns, however, behave just like arguments of verbs. In sum, if we posit an a-structure difference, we do not have to posit a difference in the principles of theta-marking.

As a second piece of evidence that possessives and *by* phrases are not true arguments, consider the fact that passives of agentive verbs (like *kick*) appear to violate a general condition on argument realization to the effect that an Agent is always realized as a subject. This follows from the proposals of chapter 2, since Agents are always external arguments. However, passives of agentive predicates are counterexamples to this solution *unless* the passive of an agentive verb does not have a realizable external argument in the first place. If the argument has been suppressed, then of course the principle of realization is inapplicable, and the general formulation of the principles can be maintained. Agents (and external arguments in general) are always subjects when they are realized arguments.

The evidence suggests, moreover, that passives of agentive verbs can behave like non-agentives. Maling (1987a) shows that agentive predicates are barred from existentials in Swedish. The only apparently agentive verbs allowed are passives, which is not surprising if passive verbs do not actually assign the agent role.

A third consideration concerns the distribution of expletives. There are severe limitations on the possible occurrences of expletives, and by conjoining these restrictions with the hypothesis that the possessive position is a kind of adjunct position, it is possible to explain why expletives are barred from the subject position within NPs. In Government-Binding theory, for example, expletives never occur in adjunct positions. We expect, then, that expletives will be unable to occur in possessives, and this is a well known observation:

(4) a. *It's claim that John left.
    b. It is claimed that John left.

(5) a. *There's arrival of a man at the door.
    b. The arrival of a man at the door.
    c. There arrived a man at the door.

Similarly, we would expect raising to be impossible with nouns, since raising is generally not possible into non-argument positions. The exact source of the restrictions varies from theory to theory, but the general result is that raising to adjunct positions is impossible. This is sufficient, then, to explain the ungrammaticality of examples like (6).

(6) *John's appearance to have left.

In fact, raising in nominals is probably ruled out for other reasons: if nouns do not govern, as suggested in chapter 3, raising like that in (6) will violate the ECP. Alternative accounts as well as more detailed discussion of the failure of both expletives and raising in nominals can be found in Chomsky (1970), Kayne (1984), Williams (1982), and Rappaport (1983).

A telling fact is that not just an NP but also an AP—one of the "group adjectives" discussed in 3.5.2—can act as the subject of an NP:

(7) The American invention of the hamburger

(Evidence was cited in 3.5.2 to show that examples like these are indeed complex event nominals.) What role does *American* have here? Under the usual assumptions the adjectival modifier must somehow count as an argument of *invention* to explain why it is interpreted like its nominal counterpart *the Americans'*. If, on the other hand, there is no a-position to be satisfied, the adjective can be analyzed as an a-adjunct, and it becomes clear why nouns accept APs as subjects when verbs, for example, do not accept them as either subjects or objects. The difference is that the group adjective in (7) is not satisfying an argument position.

If possessives are adjuncts and never arguments, at least some light is thrown upon the range of uses found for possessives. Possessives can be either modifiers, as we saw in chapter 3, or a-adjuncts. These two uses can be at least partially unified. Both kinds of possessive NPs receive their semantic role from -'s (rather than from the noun), and both are optional possessive adjuncts, albeit of two different kinds.

One additional argument has been made in the literature. In the Japanese light verb construction, already mentioned in chapter 2, there is a further restriction on the positions arguments can occupy. Grimshaw and Mester (1988) show that the subject of the theta-marking noun must appear outside the direct object NP and that one additional argument must appear there also. This follows from the requirement that the a-structure of the N must contain at least one open position for it to participate in complex predicate formation. Why, then, doesn't the subject argument itself count for this purpose? The answer is that the theta-marking head is a noun and therefore has a suppressed subject position, which does not qualify as being open. Hence, one additional position must always be unsatisfied. This solution makes crucial use of the hypothesis that the a-structure of the noun has a suppressed position where an active verb would have an unsuppressed one.

4.3 External Arguments and Suppression

If nominalization and passivization suppress the external argument of a base verb, it follows that only verbs with external arguments will undergo these processes. This simple prediction explains a number of limitations on passives and nominals. First, the non-agentive psychological causatives will neither nominalize (into complex event nominals) nor passivize, and the same will be true for unaccusatives. Second, verbs with quirky-case-marked subjects will not passivize, since they lack an external. Third, the existence of a Thematic Hierarchy Condition on passives (and in fact on complex event nominals too) is a consequence.

4.3.1 The passive

Belletti and Rizzi (1988) demonstrate that Italian psych verbs of the *preoccupare* 'worry' class have no corresponding verbal passive, although they do allow the adjectival passive. The present theory predicts exactly the same for English. A form like *frightened* in (8), where the Experiencer is realized as a subject and a *by* phrase corresponds to the Theme, cannot be a verbal passive.

(8) Mary was frightened by the situation.

The non-agentive *frighten* has the a-structure of (9), and verbal passivization of this a-structure is impossible.

(9) ((x   (y))
        Exp   Theme

Passive can suppress only an external argument, but to derive (9), an *internal* argument (the Theme) would have to be suppressed instead. Thus *frightened* cannot be a verbal passive.

The prediction is, then, that all passive forms like *frightened* here must be adjectival passives, and the evidence supports this prediction.[5] First, these cases consistently pass all the tests for adjectivehood with flying colors. They allow negative *un-* prefixation, they occur as complements to the verbs that select APs (*remain*, etc.), and they are relatively unfussy about prepositions: *frightened*, for example, can occur with *about*, *by*, or *at*. Unlike Pesetsky (1987) I do not assume that a *by* phrase indicates a verbal passive, since it can co-occur with unambiguously adjectival properties:

(10) Fred remains completely unperturbed by his students' behavior.

As always, we must distinguish clearly between the agentive and non-agentive readings of the *frighten* class: agentive *frighten* verbs do have a verbal passive. Their Agent is an external argument and can be suppressed, hence nothing rules out verbal passivization on the argument structure for Agentive *frighten* shown in (11):

(11) (x   (y))
     Agent Exp

The potential ambiguity can be factored out of the situation by using verbs that are more or less unambiguously non-agentive. Examples include *worry*, *concern*, *perturb*, and *preoccupy*.

(12) a. The situation worries/concerns/perturbs/preoccupies Fred.
     b. Fred is worried/concerned/perturbed/preoccupied by the situation.

   c. Fred is/seems unworried/unconcerned/unperturbed/
      preoccupied by the situation.

A second piece of evidence concerns the behavior of the progressive
with these passive forms, illustrated in (13). The progressive, as is well
known, is incompatible with stative predicates, and English adjectives
by and large are states. In the active a psychological causative like *depress* is fine in the progressive, but in the passive it is ungrammatical.[6]

(13) a. The situation was depressing Mary.
     b. *Mary was being depressed by the situation.
     c. *Mary was being depressed about the situation.

With an agentive psychological verb the paradigm changes in the expected way, and the progressive is fully grammatical with *by*.

(14) a. The government is terrifying people.
     b. People are being terrified by the government.

The verbal passive in general does not affect the stativity of the predicate. When the input is a state, the output is a state; when the input is an
event, the output is an event:

(15) a. *Many people are believing this hypothesis.
     b. This hypothesis is (*being) believed by many people.
     c. They are discovering new ways to fight pollution.
     d. New ways to fight pollution are being discovered.

So the change in the *frighten* class cannot be attributed to effects of
verbal passivization. If the passive in (8) is verbal, it should occur in the
progressive. If, on the other hand, it is adjectival, the stativization of
the predicate is explained. The absence of a verbal passive follows from
the fact that the Theme subject of the active is not a candidate for suppression, since it is not external.[7]

    In contrast, the Experiencer of *fear* is an external argument and can
be sucessfully suppressed by passivization, which leaves the subject
position open for the Theme.

(16) a. *fear* (Exp (Theme))
     b. Mary feared the situation.
     c. The situation was feared by Mary.

Note that the ungrammaticality of the passives of the *fear* class in the
progressive (17a) does not affect the claim here, for unlike the *frighten*
class, the *fear* class is stative (see 2.3) and does not occur in the progressive even in the active (17b).

(17) a. *The situation was being feared by everyone.
    b. *Everyone was fearing the situation.

The crucial point about the *frighten* class is that they do occur in the progressive in the active, but passivization changes them from non-states to states. This is explained if the passivization that they undergo is adjectival passivization and not verbal passivization. Verbal passivization maintains the state/non-state character of the input.

The failure of verbal passivization with psychological causatives is a special case of a more general phenomenon. The general prediction concerning passivizability is this: any verb class for which the subject is not the thematically most prominent argument will fail to passivize, since it will lack an external argument. This is so because the subject will always be the thematically most prominent argument if the predicate has an external argument, since thematic prominence and aspectual prominence will coincide and map the argument onto the subject position.

In this way the effects that have been attributed to the existence of a Thematic Hierarchy Condition on verbal passives, like that proposed in Jackendoff (1972, 43) follow from the theory. Jackendoff's observation was that the *by* phrase cannot be lower in the hierarchy than the derived subject. In the prominence theory of argument structure, this follows from the organization of argument structure together with the hypothesis that the passive suppresses an external argument.[8]

Let us start by examining the case of a passive that meets the condition, such as the example in (18).

(18) a. The book was written by two linguists.
    b. (x-Ø   (y))
       Agent Theme

In the present theory the *by* phrase in a passive is an a-adjunct linked to the suppressed argument of the verb. Only the external argument can be lexically suppressed, so only the most prominent argument can have a *by* phrase linked to it. Thus the *by* phrase must be licensed by, and correspond to, the Agent argument in (18). Since the suppressed argument licensing the *by* phrase is the maximally prominent argument, the other argument, which is realized as the subject of the passive verb, will be less prominent. Thus in a well-formed passive the derived subject must be lower on the hierarchy than the *by* phrase.

The ill-formedness of the cases that Jackendoff rules out with the Thematic Hierarchy Condition follows from this reasoning if we assume Jackendoff's thematic analysis. For example, agentive *touch* passivizes, while non-agentive *touch* does not have a verbal passive. Hence the oddness of (19b).

(19) a. The lamp was touching the bookcase.
   b. ?The bookcase was being touched by the lamp.

The Theme of non-agentive *touch* is realized as the grammatical subject (*the lamp* in (19a)), and the Location is realized as the object (*the bookcase*). Thus the thematically most prominent argument (the Location) is not the grammatical subject, as it would have to be if the predicate had an external argument. Non-agentive *touch*, then, has no external argument, and (19b) can be derived only by illegitimately suppressing the Theme, an internal argument.

(20) *touch*((x   (y)))
           Location Theme

The absence of a verbal passive for non-agentive *touch*, then, follows from the fact that it has no external argument. All cases of thematic hierarchy violations follow in the same way.

Note that the thematic hierarchy effects are not tied in this account to the actual presence of the *by* phrase. It is the prominence of the suppressed argument that matters, regardless of whether an a-adjunct happens to occur. So the omission of a *by* phrase from an impossible passive should not improve its grammaticality. Hence, (21) is unambiguously agentive, even though the sentence contains no *by* phrase. This is because the (verbal) passive of the non-agentive predicate is impossible.

(21) The bookcase was being touched.

There are two important advantages of this account of thematic hierarchy effects in passives. First, the theory explains why such effects should exist to begin with. They are a necessary consequence of the organization of a-structure representation and the fact that passive suppresses an external argument. Second, the structure of this account of the passive solves a puzzle in the theory. The thematic hierarchy seems to have no relevance at all for passivization involving non-co-arguments:

(22) They are believed by everyone to have murdered the Pope.

Whatever the thematic role of the subject of *believe*, it is lower in the hierarchy than the Agent subject of *murder*. So (22) seems to violate the Thematic Hierarchy Condition, yet this does not make the passive in (22) ill-formed. The fact is that when the derived subject is not an argument of the passive verb, it makes no difference to the well-formedness of passive what the theta role of the derived subject is.

The explanation is as follows. The hierarchy constrains relative argument position in an argument structure and therefore only among co-arguments. The fact that the subject of *murder*, for example, is an Agent has no bearing on the external argument status of the subject of *believe*. Passive is fine here because the believer is external: relative positions in the hierarchy are simply not defined for the Agent of one verb and the Experiencer of another. So the irrelevance of the hierarchy for such cases is a consequence of the proposal. Passive obeys the thematic hierarchy because it requires an external argument to suppress. Semantic properties of a predicate determine whether it has an external argument. When the derived subject and the suppressed argument are not co-arguments, the prominence of each is unaffected by the other's role, and no hierarchy effects will be found.

A more general apparent paradox about the passive is that it seems to depend on, and yet be independent of, the thematic properties of the object of the active form (the surface subject argument). Passive ignores the object in one sense: it does not even matter whether the surface subject is an argument of the passive predicate (or indeed an argument of any predicate, since the phrase can be an expletive). Yet passive is sensitive to the thematic role of the object in another way. Its position in the hierarchy relative to that of the suppressed argument *does* matter, although only for co-arguments, as we just saw.

This apparent anomaly can be simply understood in the present terms. Passive is completely insensitive to properties of the underlying object or surface subject: it just suppresses the external argument. Hence, it does not matter what the status of the derived subject of the passive verb is. But passive does affect argument structure, and the organization of the argument structure itself is a reflection of thematic properties. The a-structure position of any one of a verb's arguments is a function of the other arguments of the verb: an argument cannot be external if there is another more prominent argument. So the total thematic properties of the verb determine its a-structure organization, and the a-structure organization determines which argument gets suppressed by passive. Passive itself is completely oblivious to the theta roles of all arguments. Yet its application will indirectly reflect the thematic role of the derived subject (and any other arguments) because this thematic role is reflected in the structure of argument structure and hence affects the external status of other arguments.

Finally, let us turn to the interaction between quirky case-marking and argument structure. In 2.5.2 I proposed that quirky case-marked arguments are never external, although they can be d-structure subjects. This explains the observation of Bernodusson (1982) and Yip, Maling, and Jackendoff (1987, 225) that verbs with quirky case-marked subjects in Icelandic do not passivize. They suggest that this is because they do not have agentive subjects, but this is unlikely to be the correct explanation, since non-agentive subjects do not in general block passivization. Rather, the failure of passivization is a simple consequence of the fact that these verbs lack external arguments. (By the reasoning of 3.2 they should not form complex event nominals either.)

An interesting property of the current theory is that it explains why the Icelandic passive is blocked by a quirky case-marked subject but not by a quirky case-marked object (an observation due to Joan Maling). Quirky case on a subject means that the subject is not an external argument. However, the object of the active verb is not suppressed in passivization, and its lexical case status has no effect on the promotion of object to subject, which, as suggested in Zaenen, Maling, and Thrainson (1985), from which (23) is taken, still allows the argument to be realized with its pre-associated case, albeit now in subject position.

(23) a. Eg mun sakna hans.
   I will miss him (Genitive)
   b. Hennar   var saknað
   her (Genitive) was missed
   'She was missed.'

Thus the failure of quirky case-marked subjects to suppress follows from their status as non-external arguments.

4.3.2 Nominalization

In the theory of nominals developed here, nominalization resembles passivization in that the external argument of the base verb is suppressed in both cases. The failure of passive for the *frighten* class follows from the fact that verbs in this class have no external. By the same reasoning, the *frighten* class should not undergo nominalization.

What we expect to find on the basis of syntactic parallelism between NP and S is illustrated in (24). Here the argument corresponding to *situation* or *drugs*, the Theme of the verb, is suppressed.

(24) a. The entertainment of the children
   b. The embarrassment/humiliation of the audience
   c. The depression of the patients

(25) a. The situation entertained the children.
      b. The sitiuation embarrassed the audience.
      c. The drugs depressed the patients.

Since verbs of the non-agentive *frighten* class have no external argument, the Theme arguments in (25) are *internal*, and the theory rules out this case of nominalization. At first blush this seems transparently incorrect, but it is important to bear two points in mind in evaluating the evidence. First, we know that members of the *frighten* class often have agentive counterparts. These will undergo nominalization in the usual way, just as they undergo passivization, since they do have external arguments. Second, it is only argument-taking complex event nominals that are derived from verbs by the suppression of external arguments. There is not reason at all to expect that the *frighten* class will lack result nominals. So the real prediction is that nominalizations of the *frighten* verbs will have either a result interpretation or the agentive interpretation. What is ruled out is a non-agentive argument-taking interpretation. Of course, members of the *fear* class should have argument-taking nominals corresponding to them, since they have an external argument available for suppression.

An illustrative set of data is assembled in (26). The NP in (26a) is an agentive process nominal. The NP in (26b) is a result nominal. The question concerns (26c). Is it three ways ambiguous or only two?

(26) a. John's (public) embarrassment/humiliation of Mary
      b. Mary's embarrassment/humiliation
      c. The embarrassment/humiliation of the bystanders

The present theory predicts that it has only two readings. It can be a result nominal (meaning the state of embarrassment or humiliation that the bystanders were in) or it can be a process nominal with an agentive interpretation. It should have no non-agentive process reading.

We can test the prediction by disambiguation. The NP in (26c) can be disambiguated with the addition of a possessive adjunct which cannot be an agent, which rules out the agentive process reading. As expected, the unambiguous nominal is ill-formed.

(27) *The event's embarrassment/humiliation of Mary.

The data in (28) supports the same point. The NP in (28a) is ambiguous between a result reading and an agentive process reading. (In its result reading, the noun has the sense of a state that the children are in rather than that of a process they are undergoing.) Like (26c), (28a) should be two ways, not three ways, ambiguous. The NP in (28b) is unambiguously a process nominal, as the obligatoriness of the complement shows. The contrast between (28c) and (28d) is the most informative. When the possessive adjunct is consistent with an agentive reading, the nominal is fine, as in (28d), but when the possessive is not compatible with an agentive reading, the nominal is ungrammatical, as in (28c).

(28) a. The amusement/entertainment of the children
   b. The constant entertainment *(of children)
   c. *The movie's (constant) amusement/entertainment of the children
   d. The clown's (constant) entertainment/amusement of the children

There is a further prediction here. We have seen that some *frighten* psych verbs have no agentive counterpart. Hence, they do not have argument structures with external arguments, and they should never undergo process nominalization at all. For example, *depress* (as a psychological predicate) does not have an agentive reading. Even with a human subject, as in (29), an agentive interpretation is not possible:

(29) His doctors/enemies depressed John.

As for the related nominal, *depression*, it must unambiguously be a result nominal. The interpretation of (30a) supports this clearly. Note that even the addition of *constant* here does not yield an event reading. Instead, it just modifies the state. When an argument-taking reading is forced, as by the addition of a possessive a-adjunct, the result is ill-formed, as predicted. This is illustrated in (30b).

(30) a. The (constant) depression of the patients
   b. *The drug's depression of the patients

(A point to bear in mind is that (30b) cannot be construed as a result nominal. The possessive has no sensible interpretation as a modifier and must therefore be an argument-adjunct, which cannot be licensed by a result nominal.)

By the same token, the *fear* psych verbs should nominalize, just as they passivize. Indeed, they do have argument-taking nominals, as is expected. Although their nominals are typically ambiguous, some can be put into contexts where they take an obligatory complement:

(31) Many people's dislike *(of flying)

As we know from chapter 3, the property of having obligatory arguments is unique to complex event nominals. Hence, verbs of the *fear* class do indeed form nominals of this kind.

The ungrammaticality of examples like (27) has been noted previously, in Amritavalli (1980) and Rappaport (1983), for example, and there
is also an account of the ungrammaticality of examples like (27), (28c),
and (30b) in the literature. The account is based on Anderson (1978)
and has recently been modified by Rozwadowska (1988). Basically, the
idea is that the examples violate an affectedness requirement on possessives, since the Theme argument of a psych verb is certainly not
affected. The major empirical difference between this account and the
one developed here is that the affectedness hypothesis makes no prediction about the interpretation of examples without a possessive, (26c)
and (30a) for example. The most important conceptual difference is that
in the present theory the impossibility of the examples follows from the
representation of the nouns and not from a stipulation that singles out
certain thematic roles or other semantic properties. In the present
theory the failure of nominalization is related to the failure of passivization and ultimately to the behavior of the psychological verbs with respect to anaphora (see chapter 5).

Just as with passives, the failure of complex event nominalization for
the *frighten* psych verbs should be just one instance of a general class of
impossible nominalizations—the prediction being that only verbs with
external arguments will undergo this kind of nominalization.[9] Thus
verbs whose passives violate the Thematic Hierarchy Condition should
not nominalize. This prediction is difficult to test because of the absence
of even agentive nominals for verbs like *touch* and because the affixes
that form complex event nominals do not seem to add onto these (primarily stative) predicates.

Other predictions concern -*ing* nominals. Recall that -*ing* nominals
are generally complex event nominals and do not show the ambiguities
that characterize other kinds of nouns (chapter 3). Since -*ing* nominals
are productively formed only by suppression of an external argument,
they are not derivable for the *frighten* psych verbs. The data in (32)
illustrate this point. (Note that (32d) is ungrammatical on the relevant
interpretation.)

(32) a. The situation depresses the patients.
     b. *The depressing of the patients
     c. The situation worries the public.
     d. *The worrying of the public

As expected, agentive psych verbs form much better -*ing* nominals:

(33) The entertaining/amusing of the children is my job.

We have seen throughout that agentive counterparts to the *frighten* class are predicted to behave like members of the *fear* class and not like their non-agentive counterparts. The reason is that the prominence relations in their syntax directly reflect the prominence relations in their argument structures. The Agent is both the syntactic subject and the thematically most prominent argument of the verb. The Experiencer is less prominent and is realized as the object. The argument structure for agentive *frighten* is given in (34):

(34) *frighten*(x   (y))
        Agent Exp

Members of this class of verbs should have verbal passives and should form process nominals. Hence, the passive in (35a) can be verbal, and the nominal in (35b) can take arguments.

(35) a. The children were being entertained by a clown.
        b. The entertainment of the children . . .

A final set of predictions concerns the nominalization of unaccusative predicates. Since they lack external arguments, they are expected not to form complex event nominals. Hence, they are predicted to lack *-ing* forms in general, and to have only result or simple event interpretations in other cases.

The behavior of *-ing* nominals is not as this simple reasoning would predict, since we find examples like the following:

(36) a. The (rapid) melting of the ice . . .
        b. The (rapid) freezing of the lake . . .

These certainly have the unaccusative and not the agentive interpretation. It seems that *-ing* nominalization of unaccusatives is limited to inchoatives; compare the examples in (36) with those in (37):

(37) a. ?The dropping of the stone   (Cf. *The stone dropped.*)
        b. ?The arriving of the train

Apparently *-ing* nominalization is possible for certain verb classes with no suppression at all.[10] In this view the PPs in (37) are arguments. This correctly predicts the ill-formedness of the possessive variants in (38) and the *by* phrase variants in (39), although the *by* phrase version is independently excluded because the a-adjunct is not properly licensed (see 4.5.2).

(38) a. *The ice's (rapid) melting
        b. *The lake's (unexpected) freezing

(39) a. *The melting by the ice
      b. *The freezing by the lake

Since nominalization does not suppress an argument, no a-adjunct is licensed.

It is not entirely clear what conclusion we should draw from the data in (36) and (37). If (36) does indicate that unaccusatives can undergo complex event nominalization, a revision in the theory presented so far is called for. The principle governing nominalization will now be that if there is an external argument, it must suppress. If the base has no external argument, suppression is not necessary. Thus we could view the suppression of an external under nominalization as following from the addition of a new external, which forces a former external to suppress, rather than from the operation of nominalization itself.

This conclusion would force us to reexamine the argument just given about the psychological predicates. Since they have no external arguments, it is predicted that they will not form nominals via suppression. But we might expect them to form nominals without suppression, like those in (35). This gives a number of different outputs, all of which seem to be ungrammatical:

(40) a. *The movie's depressing of the audience
      b. *The audience's depressing by the movie
      c. *The depressing of the audience by the movie

In fact, the ungrammaticality of (40a, b, c) would still be explained, even under our revised assumptions. The NPs in (40a,b) are ungrammatical because the possessive is not an argument and hence cannot satisfy an argument position in the predicate, a position that is unsuppressed by hypothesis. The NP in (40c) is ungrammatical because *by the movie* would have to be a Theme (or whatever the right label is) and *of the audience* would have to be an Experiencer, and neither of these argument realizations is possible, quite independently of the present issue. Thus, even if unaccusatives can nominalize, the behavior of the psychological predicates under nominalization still follows from the analysis in which they have no external arguments.

In sum, both passivization and nominalization involve suppression of an external argument. Since the *frighten* verbs do not have one, complex event nominals and verbal passives are impossible. Since the *fear* verbs do have external arguments, they undergo both verbal passivization and process nominalization.

4.3.3 Adjectival passives

Levin and Rappaport (1986) propose a modified version of an analysis of adjectival passives given in Bresnan (1982b). Levin and Rappaport hypothesize that adjectival passives are formed from verbal passives, by a process of adjective formation that involves simple rebracketing, in effect, by relabeling the verb as an adjective. This proposal has some attractive features, which they review. Nevertheless, there is a fair amount of evidence that it cannot be entirely correct. First, if adjectival passives are formed from verbal passives, the suppression of the external argument should be carried over to adjectival passives. Yet many adjectival passives have obligatory, not optional, *by* phrases:[11]

(41) a. This event was followed/preceded *(by another).
     b. The mountain was capped *(by snow).
     c. The volcano was rimmed *(by craters).
     d. The house was surrounded *(by mature trees).

These *by* phrases cannot be replaced by adverbials of time, place, manner, and so forth. Rather, they alternate only with other prepositional phrases, those introduced by *with* in particular. All in all, they behave simply like arguments. (They are quite different then from the obligatory adjuncts of Grimshaw and Vikner (1990), illustrated in (67) and (68).) The verbs in (40) are among those that fail to undergo verbal passivization because they lack an external argument. Obligatory *by* phrases in adjectival passives seem to be limited to adjectival passives with no corresponding verbal passive, and this is a generalization that the account I offer will explain.

Second, there are numerous adjectival passives that have no sources under the conversion hypothesis. These include not just examples like those in (40) but also unaccusatives (which Levin and Rappaport suggest may be perfect participles rather than adjectival passives) and the *frighten* verb class discussed in 4.3.1.

(42) a. a frightened man, the depressed patient
     b. a fallen leaf, a melted ice-cream, a frozen lake

Since there is no verbal passive for a verb like *frightened*, how can there be an adjectival passive? To put these points another way, adjectival passives do not show thematic hierarchy effects. Verbs whose verbal passives are excluded as violations of the Thematic Hierarchy Condition nevertheless have well-formed adjectival passives. This is shown by the *frighten* psychological verbs, the examples in (41), and cases like *touched* discussed in 4.3.1, which also form adjectival passives.

In the prominence theory the existence of the thematic hierarchy effects follows from the structure of a-structure plus the suppression of an external argument (see 4.3.1). Both the fact that the *by* phrase in (41) acts like an argument and the fact that the thematic hierarchy effects are absent in these examples suggest that adjectival passivization does not involve suppression. I conclude that these adjectival passives cannot be derived from verbal passives by relabeling.

How are they derived, then? Suppose that adjectival passives can be derived from verbs, presumably perfect participles (as Bresnan (1982b) suggests), by conversion into adjectives. Levin and Rappaport (1986) take the view that relabeling externalizes an internal argument, which is not possible in the prominence theory. Instead, conversion must add an external argument, which I call R (see 3.3).[12] R is identified with an internal argument of the base.[13] Adjectival passives of verbs like *rim* and *precede* are possible because conversion, unlike verbal passivization, does not require that the verb have an external argument. So R in (43) binds the internal Location argument, which corresponds to *the volcano* in (41c). The internal Theme argument is satisfied by the PP *by craters*.

(43) $rim((x\ (y))\ \longrightarrow\ rimmed(R\ <\ =\ x>\ (x\ (y)))$

The derived a-structure of *rimmed* in (43) explains the obligatoriness of the argument not bound by R. The *by* phrases in (41) are obligatory because they satisfy an (internal) argument of the head.

Similarly, the ungrammaticality of these adjectival passives in prenominal position follows (see (44a)), since there is no way to satisfy their a-structure in this configuration unless appropriate compounds happen to exist (44b).

(44) a. *a rimmed crater, *a preceded event, *a capped mountain, *a surrounded house
     b. a crater-rimmed volcano, a snow-capped mountain

Unaccusatives like *melt* can convert also, so this analysis follows Bresnan's proposal, and not that of Levin and Rappaport, in treating unaccusatives as forming adjectival passives in the standard way:[14]

(45) $melt((x))\ \longrightarrow\ melted(R\ <\ =\ x>\ (x))$

Finally, the *frighten* class can convert, as shown in (45):

(46) $frighten((x\ (y)))\ \longrightarrow\ frightened(R\ <\ =\ x>\ (x\ (y)))$

All of these verbs can undergo adjectival passivization because nothing prevents the addition of an external argument R to their a-structure. Now if conversion is possible *only* for a verb that has no external argument to begin with, we can derive the fact that unergatives cannot convert, although unaccusatives can:[15]

(47) $(x (y)) \longrightarrow\mkern-14mu\not\;\; (R (x (y)))$

Why is conversion limited to verbs with no external argument? The addition of an external argument is attested in two cases: nominalization and causativization. In nominalization, I have argued, the former external argument is suppressed. In causativization, I will suggest in 5.3.2, the addition of a new external argument is possible only if the former external argument suppresses or two different domains of prominence are maintained. If so, it is never possible to simply add a new external argument to a predicate that already has one. If we assume that adjectives, unlike nouns and the passive affix, are not suppressors, we can derive the conclusion that verbs with external arguments cannot convert to adjectives.

This is only part of the story, however. Unergative verbs never become adjectival passives, but transitive verbs with external arguments do convert. How is this possible? Their adjectival passives are formed by conversion from the verbal passive, essentially as Levin and Rappaport (1986) suggest. In effect, they convert because they have passive forms that meet the requirements for conversion, since they have suppressed external arguments, and as B. Levin notes in a personal communication, unergatives fail to convert because they do not undergo verbal passivization. It is also possible that conversion eliminates the external argument completely (see below). Just as a new external argument can be added when the former external argument is suppressed in nominals, so a new external argument can be added when the former external argument has been suppressed by passivization.

There is one big difference between adjectival passives formed from verbal passives and those formed from active verbs. Unlike the adjectival passives formed from verbs like *rim*, *precede*, and *cap* with no verbal passive sources, adjectival passives converted from verbal passives have only one open argument position, and this is bound by *R*.

(48) $(R < = y> (x-\emptyset (y)))$

Hence, they can *never* have an obligatory *by* phrase or *with* phrase argument. They allow *by* phrases only as a-adjuncts, so they are grammatical without *by* phrases.[16]

(49) a. The house is well built.   The book is finished.

    b. the arrested man, a well-built house, the completed manuscript

The prediction, then, is that adjectival passives derived from verbal passives will never have obligatory *by* phrases, while adjectival passives derived from active verbs with no external arguments will have obligatory *by* phrases.

If adjectival passives are derived from verbal passives, we expect that *by* phrase a-adjuncts can occur in adjectival passives, just as in verbal passives. (In light of the analysis of 4.4, they are predicted to occur only with suppressed agent arguments, since the external argument of an adjectival passive is not a suppressed position.) In fact, though, *by* phrases are extremely limited in adjectival passives. One further step makes it possible to explain this. Suppose that the adjectival passive loses the suppressed external argument of the verbal passive completely. This could plausibly follow the principles governing the addition of a new external argument, or it could follow from the semantic effects of adjectivalization, as Bresnan (1982b) and Zubizarreta (1987) suggest. It will now follow that the adjectival passive of a verb with an external argument will always have lost that argument completely. Hence, the *by*-phrase a-adjunct will never occur in adjectival passives. This explains the ungrammaticality of the *by* phrases in examples like (50) and (51). Both *murdered* and *untamed* are adjectival passives, as the first example in each pair shows, but neither allows a *by* phrase.

(50) a. This murdered man
     b. *This man is murdered by a thief.

(51) a. The lion is/seems/remains untamed.
     b. *The lion is/seems/remains untamed by the trainer.

Some *by* phrases do occur in adjectival passives. I would argue, however, that these are precisely *not* the ones that are a-adjuncts licensed by suppressed arguments, but those that are internal arguments. This is why they are typically obligatory, why they occur only with verbs that do not form verbal passives, and why they are never agentive. This is the analysis of the examples in (52):

(52) a. I am not convinced by these arguments.
     b. She is unperturbed by the situation.
     c. This book will not be followed by a second.

In addition, if the *by* phrases that do appear are the arguments of predicates lacking external arguments, as I am arguing, the fact that the *by* phrases tend to be generic may be at least partially explicable. Consider the pairs in (53), from Zubizarreta (1987).

(53) a. The island was uninhabited by humans/*by the women.
      b. The jacket was untouched by human hands/*by Paul.
      c. These facts remain unexplained by current theories/*by your
          theory.

To the extent that the change in content of the *by* phrase signals a
change in the verb's argument structure, such effects are expected. In
(53b), the clearest case of this, when *Paul* is the subject, the verb is
agentive. Hence, it has a verbal passive, and its adjectival passive is
derived from this by elimination of the suppressed argument. *By Paul*
can therefore only be an unlicensed a-adjunct. When *touch* is non-
agentive, it has no verbal passive, and its adjectival passive retains all
the internal arguments of the base, one of which is satisfied by the *by*
phrase.

In adjectival passives, then, *by* phrases are internal arguments. Following up on an argument made in Bresnan (1982b), we can see that this
provides a solution to the behavior of compounds headed by participles
in *-ed*. In 2.2.2 I showed that the prominence theory explains why external arguments do not compound. There are apparent counterexamples:

(54) a. Government-sponsored research
      b. A crater-rimmed volcano
      c. A snow-capped mountain

These are precisely cases where the non-head acts as an internal
argument of the head and not as its external argument, and the non-
compounded forms have exactly the properties of the adjectival passive
construction.

(55) a. This research is sponsored by the government.
      b. The volcano is rimmed by craters.
      c. The mountain is capped by snow.

Why then do the *frighten* class verbs have optional and not obligatory
prepositional phrases? The key lies in the event structures for verbs like
follow and the psychological causatives and in the effects of adjectival
passivization on event structure. For *follow* the event structure is a state
involving two arguments.

(56) [state]
      x follows y

Under adjectival passivization this event structure is maintained because it is already stative, so the argument structure is also unchanged.
It contains two arguments, and both arguments must be realized.

(57) *followed*((x   (y)))
          Loc Theme

For the causative psychological predicates such as *frighten* or *depress*, however, the event structure has to change, under adjectival passivization, from a complex causative event to a state:

(58) [activity state] $\longrightarrow$ [state]
      x acts   y in state   y in state

In the active event structure the cause argument is involved in the activity. Hence, when the activity component is removed by the stativization resulting from adjectival passivization, the cause argument disappears from the event structure. As a result, it is no longer projected into the a-structure, which now contains only one thematic argument position.

(59) *depressed*((y))
            Exp

Hence, state predicates with no external argument, like *follow*, require their second argument when they form adjectival passives, while causative predicates with no external argument, like *depress*, do not.

4.4 More Evidence for Suppression

In 4.2 I gave some preliminary evidence to support the claim that the a-structure of a nominal or a passive is different from that of an active verb in that the external argument of the active verb is suppressed in these derived forms and is not available for theta-marking. In 4.3 we saw that this allows us to explain the behavior of various verb classes under nominalization, verbal passivization, and adjectival passivization. The obvious and more standard alternative view is that the argument structure of a passive verb or a noun is identical to that of an active verb. There are a number of possible ways to work out this line of thought: The a-structure of a passive might be the same as that of the transitive base, with either the *by* phrase or the *-en* affix satisfying the argument position usually allocated to the external argument. Similarly, within nominals, PRO (or presumably a nominal affix) could satisfy the a-structure position satisfied by the subject of the base verb. Versions of this position have recently been taken for the passive in Hoekstra (1986), Jaeggli (1986), Roberts (1985, 1987), and in particular Baker, Johnson, and Roberts (1989), where it is suggested that the theta role normally assigned to the external argument of an active verb is assigned to *-en* in the passive. In this analysis the passive verb has the same a-structure as the active (although its arguments are satisfied in a slightly different way).

There are two kinds of reasoning that we can bring to bear in the evaluation of these alternatives, all of which involve the idea that the argument positions of a passive verb or a nominal are satisfied syntactically, just like those of active verbs. One route is to investigate the behavior of the *by* phrase and the possessive, which on these accounts should behave either like an argument (if they are satisfying the a-structure) or like an adjunct (if something else, like *-en*, is the argument). I will take these questions up in 4.6. The other route is to investigate the behavior of the nominals and passives themselves to see if they behave as if they have undergone a change in a-structure or as if they are indistinguishable in a terms of a-structure from active verbs. This is the topic of the present section.

First, we have seen that the *frighten* psychological verbs fail to undergo (complex event) nominalization and verbal passivization. The proposed explanation depends critically on a difference in a-structure between the active psychological verbs and their derived counterparts. It is because nominalization and passivization suppress an external argument and the *frighten* verbs lack one that passivization and nominalization are impossible. But if the a-structure of passives and nominals are just like those of active verbs, with unsuppressed positions satisfied with *by* phrases, possessives, *-en*, or PRO, we are left with no explanation for the gap in the paradigm.[17]

A further way in which nominals and passives behave differently from active verbs concerns control with purpose clauses. Recall the discussion of event control in 3.2. Roeper (1987) observed that a control relationship like that in (60a) is found also in passives and nominals.

(60) a. They opened the door in order to let air in.
     b. The door was opened in order to let air in.
     c. The opening of the door in order to let air in

If the control relationship in (60a) is one of control of PRO by an argument and if it is the same as the control relationships in (60b) and (60c), those in (60b) and (60c) must also involve control of PRO by an argument. Hence, the passive and nominal must contain an argument to act as the controller. This argument is used by Baker Johnson and Roberts (1989) to support their claim that *-en* is an argument.

However, Lasnik (1988) and Williams (1985) have established that the control relation is not between PRO and an argument of the noun or the passive verb (an "implicit argument") but between PRO and an event (or an N'). (This point was discussed in 3.5.2 in connection with passive nominals.) The evidence is that the predicate of the purpose clause must be the kind that can be predicated of an event and not the kind that can be predicated only of an individual:

(61) a. ??The door was opened in order to become cooler.

      b. ??The opening of the door in order to become cooler

Thus they conclude that there is no control into purpose clauses by implicit arguments.

This result in fact turns the original argument on its head. Active verbs do allow control into purpose clauses *by their external arguments*. Now if nominals and passives are just like active verbs, having PRO or *-en* as arguments just as active verbs have arguments, they ought also to allow control into purpose clauses by the arguments *-en* and PRO. The fact that such control is impossible thus indicates the existence of an important difference between actives on the one hand and passives and nominals on the other. Thus the evidence that Baker, Johnson, and Roberts cite as support for their proposal actually argues against it. Note that their hypothesis that *-en* has an arbitrary interpretation will not salvage the argument. Arbitrary PRO *does* participate in argument control. So, giving *-en* the same semantic analysis will not explain the difference between (62a) and (62b):

(62) a. To study linguistics in order to become rich is a mistake.

      b. *Linguistics should never be studied in order to become rich.

If control by arguments in passives and nominals is impossible because of suppression, we expect that even when an a-adjunct is present, control will still be impossible. This is borne out by examples like (63):

(63) a. *Caesar's invasion of Gaul (in order) to become more powerful

      b. *Gaul was invaded by Caesar (in order) to become more powerful.

Any impression of improvement is due, I believe, to the fact that a logically possible and pragmatically plausible controller is at least mentioned. Clearly, however, the control relation is ruled out. This is exactly as expected if the a-structure of a passive or a nominal contains a suppressed position even when a *by* phrase or a possessive is present. The relevant argument position of the verb or noun is still not syntactically satisfied, and so it is not available for a syntactic control relationship. The presence of an a-adjunct makes no difference.

Roeper (1987, 277) argues against the view that all control in nominals is event control, on the grounds of a difference between (64a) and (64b) (his (29) and (31) but my judgements):

(64) a. ?The doors were opened to enter the room.
     b. *The opening of the door entered the room.

His argument is that (64a) must involve argument control, not event control, or it would be as ungrammatical as (64b). However, it seems more likely that the comparative well-formedness of (64a) arises from its having a second interpretation involving an arbitrary PRO in the purpose clause.[18] The crucial point is that this reading does not involve an implicit argument—it is equally possible with expressions that have no implicit argument under any analysis:

(65) a. The doors are red to make them attractive to first graders.
     b. Grass is green in promote photosynthesis. (Williams 1985)

It this is correct, there is no difference between the control in (66a), with a passive, and the control in (66b), with an adjective. Sentence (66c), on the other hand, has an event control reading as well as an arbitrary PRO reading.

(66) a. The doors were opened to keep cool.
     b. The doors are open to keep cool.
     c. The doors were opened to keep us cool.

These examples do not support the claim that control by an implicit argument is possible, since they do not involve control in the first place. All in all, the evidence from control supports the conclusion that the a-structure of passives and nominals is *not* the same as that of active verbs but contains a suppressed position where actives have an external argument position requiring syntactic satisfaction.

A second kind of evidence that passives are fundamentally different from actives comes from the study of "obligatory adjuncts" in Grimshaw and Vikner (1990). With certain passives a *by* phrase appears to be obligatory:

(67) a. *This house was built/designed.
     b. This house was built/designed by a French architect.

A range of other expressions, including adjuncts of time, place, manner, and purpose, can substitute for the *by* phrase with well-formed results:

(68) a. This house was built in spite of many local protests.
     b. This house was built yesterday.
     c. This house was built in ten days.

    d. This house was built in a bad part of town.

    e. This house was built only with great difficulty.

Grimshaw and Vikner propose that verbs that take obligatory adjuncts in the passive have a *complex event structure* (see 2.3.4). In Pustejovsky's (1988) representational system, they contain two sub-events. Each must be syntactically *identified*.

(69)   event

   activity   state

In examples like (67a) only the Theme is syntactically represented, and it serves to identify the resulting state. The obligatory adjuncts identify the activity sub-event, which otherwise would receive no identification.

    What makes this argument of interest in the present context is the fact that obligatory adjuncts are limited to passives, never being found with active verb forms. In light of the hypothesis that the argument structures of actives and passives are different, this is no surprise. In the active the sub-events are identified by the very elements that satisfy the argument structure; in (70a) the subject identifies the activity component of *design*, and the object identifies the state component. Hence, the effects of the event structure are not noticeable in the active. They are nondistinct from those of the argument structure.

(70) a.   Bill Blass designed the dress.

       b.   *The dress was designed.

    In the passive, however, the external argument is suppressed, and only one syntactic argument is required to satisfy the argument structure. The event structure, however, remains two-part and still requires the identification of both the activity and the (resulting) state. Hence, an identifying adjunct must be provided.[19] Suppose, however, that *-en* is an argument of the passive verb. It is then impossible to explain why the passive requires an obligatory adjunct and the active does not. The affix *-en* should serve to identify the activity sub-event every bit as well as any other syntactically realized argument.[20] Thus, the active/passive difference in (70) is explained only under the suppression hypothesis.

4.5 Argument Adjuncts in Passives and Nominals

The distribution of possessive and prepositional a-adjuncts follows roughly from the ideas developed so far. Since a-adjuncts must be licensed by a suppressed argument and passive verbs, but not actives, have a suppressed argument, a-adjuncts will occur with passive verbs but not with actives. Moreover, only complex event nominals have a-structures. From this it follows that process nominals, but not result nominals, can be associated with a-adjuncts, since an a-adjunct can be licensed only by association with an a-structure. A more precise account of the distribution of a-adjuncts can be obtained when their licensing requirements are spelled out. There are two critical factors. First, an a-adjunct must be *locally* related to an a-structure (this is discussed more in section 4.6). Second, a-adjuncts are licensed by a-structure positions with particular properties: the behavior of possessive NPs and of *by* phrases in passives and nominals can be explained under the assumption that these two a-adjuncts differ slightly in their licensing requirements, if we make certain specific assumptions about the argument structure of nouns and verbs.

4.5.1 Possessives
Chapter 3 established that possessive NPs are in principle ambiguous: they can act as modifiers of non-argument-taking nouns or as a-adjuncts licensed by complex event nouns.[21] What a-structure positions can they be licensed by? The data in (71) illustrates the point that possessive a-adjuncts are not thematically restricted:

(71) a. The government's imprisonment of refugees
     b. Many people's fear of flying

The possessive can apparently be licensed by any suppressed argument, regardless of its thematic status.[22] The argument suppressed in nominals is always the one most prominent in the a-structure of the base: its external argument, according to the view of a-structure taken here. Hence, the possessives in (71) are licensed by the external argument positions of the corresponding verbs, the positions satisfied by the subjects of the active verbs. We thus account for the fact that possessive a-adjuncts correspond to subjects of verbs even though they are not themselves arguments at all.

This is illustrated in (72) for *imprison* and *imprisonment*. The external argument of *imprison* is suppressed in the nominal, which licenses a possessive a-adjunct corresponding to the Agent.

(72) a. *imprison*(x (y))
     b. *imprisonment*(x-∅ (y))

This analysis, in which the possessive is licensed by any suppressed argument, predicts that a possessive with a process nominal can in principle be associated with any theta role at all: Goal, Theme, Agent, Experiencer, Location, Source, etc.

An apparent problem lies in a restriction that has been observed with the nominals of the psychological verbs. Investigators have noted that the Theme cannot occur as a possessive and have concluded that there are thematic conditions on what can be a possessive (see the references cited in 3.3) This is illustrated in (73) and (74). When the subject of the verb is agentive, it can occur as a possessive. So (73) has the nominal counterpart in (74a). When it is not the agent of the experience, the nominal is ill-formed, as we see in (74b).

(73) a. John humiliated/embarrassed the audience.
     b. The joke humiliated/embarrassed the audience.

(74) a.   John's humiliation/embarrassment of the audience
     b.   *The joke's humiliation/embarrassment of the audience.

However, the ill-formedness of (74b) has already been explained within the current theory in 4.3.2. There we saw that the restriction need not be attributed to a thematic stipulation limiting the behavior of possessives. What is wrong with (74b) does not concern the possessive at all. Instead, the nominalization is impossible even when no possessive occurs.[23] So the restriction illustrated in (74) follows independently from the theories of nominalization and of psychological verbs, and this allows us to maintain the hypothesis that the possessive is licensed by any suppressed position. This account is clearly preferable, since it explains why we observe *this particular* apparent restriction on the possessive. If providing an account is instead simply a matter of stipulating that the possessive cannot correspond to the Experiencer argument, we have no understanding of why this semantic role is involved instead of, say, that of Agent or Goal. With the present assumptions, the generalization follows from the theories of argument structure and a-adjunct licensing.

We can conclude, then, that the possessive a-adjunct can be licensed by any suppressed argument position and that all restrictions on its occurrence are explicable in terms of independent limitations on argument suppression.

4.5.2 By phrases
Some of the basic properties of the *by* phrase follow immediately from its analysis as an a-adjunct. Since it must be licensed by a suppressed argument, it will never occur with active verbs, not even with middles or inchoatives.

(75) a. *These books read well by children.
     b. *The glass broke by the child.

Neither inchoatives nor middles have suppressed argument positions—
each simply lacks the agent position that the corresponding transitive
has. Researchers have concluded that the argument is simply not present in these forms (Roberts (1987), Pitz (1988), Condoravdi (1989)) or
that the argument is a constant (Hale and Keyser (1988)). Hence, bearing in mind the discussion of unaccusativity in chapter 2, I assign them
the a-structures in (76):

(76) a. *read*((x))
     b. *break*((x))

Beyond the requirement of a suppressed argument to license it, the
passive *by* phrase is remarkably unfussy about how it is licensed. All
Verbs that passivize allow a *by* phrase corresponding to their active subject, regardless of their thematic role structure. As a result, the *by*
phrase is subject to no thematic restrictions at all: if the verb passivizes,
it allows a *by* phrase.

(77) a. Refugees are imprisoned by the government.
     b. It is believed by linguists that . . .
     c. Flying is feared by many people.

What kind of suppressed argument position can license a *by* phrase?
Two hypotheses suggest themselves: The generalization for *by* phrases
could be the same as for possessives, with the *by* phrase linking to any
suppressed argument. Alternatively, we could hypothesize that a *by*
phrase can be licensed by any *external* argument. Since the passive always suppresses the external argument and the *by* phrase always links to
the suppressed argument, the argument it is licensed by will always be
external. Of course, this last statement does not follow from all theories
of the argument structure of passives. For example, if we were to follow
Williams's (1981) proposal, the passive would have no external argument at all, because the formerly external argument is made internal by
passivization. In the present terms, passive verbs do have external arguments, only suppressed ones, and these positions could license *by*
phrases. We will shortly see that characterizing the licensing suppressed
argument position as *external* allows us to explain a major difference in
the behavior of *by* phrases in passives and in nominals.

What about the behavior of *by* phrases in nominals like (78)?

(78) The repression of human rights by the CIA

First, we must establish the grammatical status of the *by* phrase here. Is it an argument or an a-adjunct? It must be an a-adjunct and not an argument, because the *by* phrase corresponds to the argument that is always suppressed in nominals, namely the external argument of the base verb. This can be seen in (79), which represents the a-structure operation responsible for the derivation of the noun *repression* (as a complex event nominal, of course).

(79) a. *repress*(x (y))
     b. *repression*(x-∅ (y))

The *x* variable in (79) stands for the Agent argument, which is the most prominent and is therefore external. It is suppressed under nominalization and cannot be syntactically realized. Since the *by* phrase in (78) corresponds to *x* in (79), it must be an a-adjunct and not an argument. A violation of the theta criterion would result otherwise.

One consequence is that *by* phrases absolutely must be optional in Noun Phrases, even in complex event nominals, just as they are in passive clauses and just as possessives are in nominals. So *by* phrase a-adjuncts should contrast with arguments in nominals and in clauses. This prediction seems to be correct, for although arguments of nouns can be shown to be obligatory (see chapter 3), *by* phrases are always optional.

So far we have seen that both *by* phrases in passives and in nominals are a-adjuncts linked to suppressed arguments. However, there is an interesting contrast between the behavior of *by* in passive sentences and its behavior in nominals. Rappaport (1983) argued that in nominals *by* introduces only Agents. In the present terms this means that *by* phrases in nominals are *licensed* only by Agent arguments.

The data in (80) and (81), based on Rappaport's, illustrate the contrast between passives and their corresponding nominals.

(80) a. The government imprisons refugees.
     b. The imprisonment of refugees by the government
     c. The government's imprisonment of refugees

(81) a. Many people fear flying.
     b. Many people's fear of flying
     c. *Fear of flying by many people

In evaluating the data here we must bear in mind that only *complex event* nominals are relevant to the issue, since only they can be associated with a-adjuncts in the first place. Many of the examples cited by

Rappaport certainly do not take arguments and hence are not relevant. It is possible, then, that the phenomenon has simply been misunderstood and that *by* phrases occur freely with argument-taking nouns, just as they do with passives. (This is essentially the tack taken in Zubizarreta (1987).) The ungrammaticality of the inadmissible examples can then be attributed to their status as result nominals, which are capable of licensing modifiers but not a-adjuncts or arguments.

One possible advantage of this line of explanation is that it might eliminate the reference to theta role labels inherent in Rappaport's generalization. (Note that the requirement that a *by* phrase be agentive is really a semantic requirement, identical in kind to the requirement that a PP introduced by *to* be a goal or a directional argument—see 3.3.2.) It should be noted, however, that this solution merely shifts the burden of explaining the data from the theory of a-adjunct licensing to the theory of nominalization, since it requires that we find some principled means to rule out process nominalization in the relevant set of cases. This is just the kind of reasoning that I used in the case of possessives with the *frighten* class of psychological verbs. The failure of possessives to occur in those cases follows from the fact that an argument-taking nominal is impossible in the first place. Here there is a principled means to exclude the relevant cases of nominalization. But the limits on *by* phrases in nominals observed in (81) do not reduce to limits on suppression, since any external argument can be suppressed for purposes of nominalization. The nominals in (81) are all well-formed without a *by* phrase, and it is only the inclusion of a *by* phrase that is impossible.

Moreover, although it is doubtful that some of the nouns cited in support of the agentivity of *by* phrases in nominals are argument-takers, there are some clear cases of the crucial type. Consider *dislike*, for example. As in (82a), it is ungrammatical with no complement. The obligatoriness of the complement indicates that *dislike* here is an argument-taking nominal. Nevertheless, it still does not allow a *by* phrase to correspond to its Experiencer argument, as we see in (78b).

(82) a.   Many people's dislike *(of flying)
     b.   *Dislike of flying by many people

Such examples show that the occurrence of a *by* phrase does *not* reduce to the occurrence of an argument-taking nominal.

A second issue concerns examples like (83), taken from Amritavalli (1980, 322).

(83) a. The agitation of the soap solution by the machine's rotary action
   b. The satisfaction of the nondistinctness requirement by the lexical entry
   c. The exhaustion of the country's resources by indiscriminate mining

Zubizarreta observes in a personal communication that the *by* phrases here are not agentive, although the nominals unquestionably take arguments. So this data apparently undermines the agentivity generalization.

However, a case can be made that the *by* phrases here are not really a-adjuncts but simply adjuncts. In other words, the *by* phrases are not licensed by association with suppressed arguments at all. As one piece of evidence, not that all of the examples have close paraphrases that substitute *by means of* or *through* for *by*. In all the data here the case can be made most strongly for (83c) and least strongly for (83b):

(84) a. The agitation of the soap solution by means of the machine's rotary action
   b. The satisfaction of the nondistinctness requirement through the lexical entry
   c. The exhaustion of the country's resources through indiscriminate mining.

Moreover, these *by* phrases can co-occur, more or less felicitously, with possessive a-adjuncts, something not possible for true *by* phrases (see 5.3).

(85) a. The machine's agitation of the soap solution by a/its rotary action
   b. ??The grammar's satisfaction of the nondistinctness requirement by a lexical entry
   c. The company's exhaustion of the country's resources by indiscriminate mining

The *by* phrase can even occur with active verbs, again something totally impossible for a-adjunct *by* phrases:

(86) a. ?The machine agitates the soap solution by a rotary action.
   b. ??The grammar satisfies the nondistinctness requirement by a lexical entry.
   c. They exhausted the country's resources by indiscriminate mining.

All of this suggests that the *by* phrases in (83) are really true adjuncts specifying means rather than a-adjuncts that require licensing by a-structure. As a final piece of evidence, I cite the co-occurrence of the two types of *by* phrases:

(87) a. The soap solution is agitated by the machine by its rotary action.
   b. The agitation of the soap solution by the machine by its rotary action

(88) a. The nondistinctness requirement is satisfied by the grammar by a lexical entry.
   b. The satisfaction of the nondistinctness requirement by the grammar by a lexical entry

(89) a. The country's resources were exhausted by the company by indiscriminate mining.
   b. The exhaustion of the country's resources by indiscriminate mining

These examples are certainly highly infelicitous, but I think their ill-formedness is due only to the multiple *by* phrases. They are far better than comparable examples with two a-adjunct *by* phrases, like (90), where the result is simply uninterpretable (see 4.6.3):

(90) *The country's resources were exhausted by the government by the big corporations.

All in all, then, although the evidence is admittedly rather slight, there is still some support for Rappaport's conclusion that *by* phrases in nominals are semantically restricted. I conclude that the lexical entry for *by* specifies that it introduces an a-adjunct licensed by an Agent.[24] To accommodate the semantically unrestricted occurrence of *by* phrases with passives, the entry must also allow *by* phrases to be licensed by external arguments. Hence, we must assign two alternative entries to *by*, as in (91):

(91) a. *by*, a-adjunct, external argument
   b. *by*, a-adjunct, Agent

The major question of interest concerns the relationship between these two cases. A *by* phrase corresponds to any external argument in passives but only to an Agent in nominals. Why does the domain in which the adjunct is being used (passive versus nominal) affect the range of its uses in this way? The entries in (91) could specify a domain as well, stipulating the different domains of nouns and verbs, as in (92).

(92) a. *by*, a-adjunct, external argument (verbs)

     b. *by*, a-adjunct, Agent (nouns)

The problem with this is that it treats the relationship between the argument domain (verbal versus nominal) and the type of specification (external versus agentive) as entirely accidental. We want to know why the association is free in passives and thematic in nominals, and not, for example, vice versa.

A solution lies in the a-structure representations of nouns and verbs as already developed. In the analysis given here, passive verbs have an external argument, although it is a suppressed position. Hence, an adjunct that must be licensed by an external argument can be legitimately licensed by the most prominent argument of a passive verb. However, in 3.3 I concluded that the external argument of a derived nominal does not correspond to the external argument of the base but is another element, *Ev*, for event nominals. Complex event nominalization thus adds a new external (or most prominent) argument, which is an open position and is always syntactically satisfied. As a result, the formerly external argument is no longer external, since it is less prominent than the new one. In other words, nominalization both suppresses the original external argument and internalizes it in the sense that it adds a more prominent argument that then counts as the external. The result is that the suppressed argument is not external, and the external argument is not suppressed, as we can see in (93):

(93) $(Ev\ (x\text{-}\emptyset\ (y)))$

For a passive verb, on the other hand, the suppressed argument is external, and the external argument is suppressed:

(94) $(x\text{-}\emptyset\ (y))$

Recall that a-adjuncts can be licensed only by suppressed arguments. From this, the lexical entries for *by* in (91), and the proposed argument structures for passives and nominals, the distribution of *by* phrases follows without any stipulations about *by* in NPs as opposed to passives. Case (91a), in which *by* links to an external argument, is irrelevant in nominals, since nominals do not have suppressed external arguments. This case *can* occur in passives, which gives the result that the occurence of *by* in passives is not thematically governed, since neither the suppression of the external argument nor the lexical specification of *by* is limited to particular theta roles. Case (91b), in which *by* links to an Agent, can also occur in passives, the *by* phrase being licensed by a suppressed Agent. Being licensed by a suppressed Agent in passives has no consequences, however, because it admits only a subset of the cases that are allowed anyway by (91a). This is because suppressed *Agents* in passives are a proper subset of suppressed *external arguments* in passives. The important point is that case (91b), in which *by* links to an Agent, *does* occur in nominals, since nominals do have suppressed Agents, even though they never have suppressed external arguments. The a-structure in (94), for example, will license a by phrase by (91b) if *x* is an Agent but not by (91a), since *x* is not external. It is unnecessary, then, to stipulate the different domains of the two licensing conditions for *by* phrases. Once ambiguity is posited for *by*, the domains follow from the theory of a-structure representation and adjunct linking.

Rappaport and Levin (1989) point out that *by* phrases are not possible in -*er* nominals.

(95) a. The writer of a newspaper column just walked in.
      b. *The writer of a newspaper column by a journalist just walked in.

They suggest that this shows that *by* phrases are licensed by an "event" position and not by a suppressed argument. In fact, however, the impossibility of *by* phrases in these cases follows directly from the licensing theory given here and in Grimshaw (1988). An a-adjunct is licensed by a *suppressed* position. In an -*er* nominal, the external argument of the base verb is *bound* by *R*, not suppressed. Moreover, *R* itself is not suppressed, of course. So -*er* nominals have no suppressed argument, and hence they license no *by* phrase. By the same token, they do not allow possessive a-adjuncts corresponding to the subject of the base. Hence, *the man's murderer* is not ambiguous. Thus the licensing theory for a-adjuncts has as an immediate consequence the absence of a-adjuncts in -*er* nominals.

The key assumptions in the discussion so far are that possessives are free a-adjuncts licensed by suppressed arguments, that *by* phrases are licensed by external arguments or Agents, that passives have suppressed external arguments, and that nominals have suppressed internal arguments. Hence, possessives occur freely in nominals, and *by* phrases occur freely in passives, but *by* phrases are thematically restricted in nominals. These results are obtained by positing a difference in a-structure between nominals and passives and a difference in licensing between *by* phrases and possessives that is sensitive to the difference in a-structure.

4.6 Argument, Adjunct, or Argument Adjunct?

The general contention here is that possessives and *by* phrases behave like neither arguments nor adjuncts. They have an intermediate status, which follows if they are licensed by argument structure in the way that is characteristic of arguments but do not satisfy a-structure positions in the way that is characteristic of arguments. Thus they resemble arguments in that a-structure licenses them, and they resemble adjuncts in that they fail to satisfy a-structure positions. This is the fundamental idea behind the notion of an a-adjunct.

4.6.1 The adjunct analysis

If *by* phrases were simply adjuncts, they would be completely outside the domain in which a-structure regulates occurrence, and they should co-occur freely with any verb that has a basically compatible semantics. This should certainly include middles and possibly also inchoatives. Yet, as was pointed out in 4.5.2, it is well known that such combinations are impossible.

(96) a. The window was broken by the wind/boys/balls.
     b. *Windows break easily by the wind/boys/balls.
     c. *The window broke by the wind/boys/balls.

If *by* phrases are a-adjuncts, the ill-formedness of (96b, c) follows, since the a-adjuncts are unlicensed. Neither the middle form nor the inchoative form of *break* has a suppressed argument to license the *by* phrase.

   In fact, if *by* phrases are adjuncts, it is not obvious why they cannot occur even with active verbs. In the standard view, no theta-criterion violation would result, by definition, since the theta criterion regulates arguments, not adjuncts (however, see 4.6.3 for a modification of this assumption).

(97) *The enemy destroyed the city by the army.

   Note that these very same problems arise if the *by* phrase is licensed by an "event" position in a-structure, as in Rappaport and Levin (1989). The distribution of *by* phrases is regulated by the argument structure of predicates in a way that is certainly not characteristic of adjuncts in general.

   Of course, it is possible to complicate the adjunct theory in a way that will rule out (96b, c) and (97). For example, if we hypothesize that the external theta role of a passive is assigned to the passive morpheme (Baker, Johnson, and Roberts (1989)), the behavior of the *by* phrase could be described as licensed by a verb whose argument has been satisfied by an affix or as licensed by an affix that functions as an argument. This would rule out *by* phrases with middles and inchoatives as well as with actives. The point is that this solution basically concedes that a *by* phrase is not just an adjunct, since other adjuncts are obviously not licensed by being related to affixes. Similarly, if the *by* phrase is taken to "double" the *-en* affix, why does it double only *-en* and not other arguments?

Solutions to these problems generally tend to undermine the idea that the affix syntactically satisfies the external argument of a passive by the usual process of theta-marking, just as a subject NP does in the active. The licensing of the *by* phrase must be sensitive to precisely the difference between satisfaction by an affix and satisfaction by a phrase.

A second respect in which a-adjuncts do not behave like adjuncts is in their behavior across the copula. As shown in 3.6.3, modifiers of result nominals can be separated from their heads by copulas. Arguments of event nominals cannot be. This can be derived from the fact that modifiers are related to heads by a predication relation, which itself can cross copulas, while arguments are related to heads by theta-marking, which is a function of a-structure. Theta-marking is strictly local: if it is possible only under government, for example, (98b) violates the theta criterion, since the head does not govern the PP.

(98) a.   The picture was of Bill. (modifier)
     b.   *The destruction was of the city. (argument)

The ungrammaticality of (99b) and (100b) shows that a-adjuncts behave like arguments, not modifiers or other adjuncts.

(99) a.   The book is by Bill. (modifier)
     b.   *The destruction of the city was by the enemy.

(100) a.   The book is Bill's.
      b.   *The destruction of the city was the enemy's.

Sentences (99b) and (100b) should perhaps be compared with examples involving temporal adjuncts, like (101). Although not perfect, (101) has a quite different status from the a-adjunct examples.

(101) ?The destruction of the city was on Tuesday.

This follows if the licensing requirements of the a-adjuncts can be met only locally, just as for arguments. These considerations again show that *by* phrases and possessives are not simply adjuncts but have to be licensed by a-structure in a way that is not relevant for adjuncts in general.

A third piece of evidence is based on an argument given in Roeper (1987). Roeper points out that *by* phrase modifiers can extrapose from NPs:

(102) a. An attack by the enemy occurred.
      b. An attack occurred by the enemy.

However, when the *by* phrase is associated with an argument-taking nominal, it cannot extrapose:

(103) *The destruction of the city occurred by the enemy

(Examples (102) and (103) are from Roeper (1987, 18).) Roeper takes this data to show that the *by* phrase concerned is not an adjunct, which seems to be correct. However, Roeper also claims that the data provides evidence against the a-adjunct analysis given in Grimshaw (1986b). This argument ignores the difference between an a-adjunct and an adjunct.[25] In the present terms, (102) is excluded because the PP is not governed by the head noun and therefore cannot be licensed by it. Thus the facts about extraposition support the idea that *by* phrases in argument-taking nominals are a-adjuncts and not just adjuncts.

4.6.2 By phrases and possessives as arguments

Williams (1981a) analyzes *by* phrases as arguments of passive verbs. (In Williams's account, passivization is taken to internalize, rather than to suppress, the external argument of the active form.) Roeper (1987) and Safir (1987) also treat *by* phrases in passives, or possessives in nominals, as arguments of passive verbs or of nouns. As I mentioned above, Jaeggli (1986) and di Sciullo and Williams (1987) treat *by* phrases as arguments of *-en*. Jaeggli suggests that *by* phrases are optionally subcategorized and theta-marked by the passive affix *-en*, which itself is the external argument of a passive verb, so *-en* both receives and assigns a theta role.

But regardless of whether *by* phrases are arguments of verbs or of *-en*, a major problem for this view is that the *by* phrase or its counterpart is optional in every language. Unlike Jaeggli (1986), I do not take the cases of apparently obligatory *by* phrases cited in Siewierska (1984) as counterexamples to this claim. The reason is that the constructions involved differ from recognized passives in a number of telling ways, as Ellen Woolford has pointed out to me. Woolford notes that the *by* phrases in question trigger agreement on the verbs, that the verbs undergo no morphological change, and that the verbs appear to remain transitive. Based on these observations, Woolford suggests that these are not really passive constructions in the first place (and in fact, Siewierska herself reached much the same conclusion).

Obligatory *by* phrases are found with adjectival passives (4.3.3) and also occur as the obligatory adjuncts analyzed in Grimshaw and Vikner (1990) and mentioned in 4.4. These are part of a larger system of aspectual requirements that as a whole makes adjuncts obligatory. The obligatoriness of *by* phrases is not a matter of a-structure.

The fact that passive *by* phrases are optional as far as a-structure is concerned cannot be explained under any account in which *by* phrases are arguments, since it is lexical (and hence potentially variable) properties of the argument taker (whether affix or passive verb) that determine whether a *by* phrase appears and whether it appears obligatorily. Principled optionality thus cannot be explained. This provides a major piece of evidence against the view that the *by* phrase is an argument. Other evidence has been given by Zubizarreta (1985, 1987) to the effect that *by* phrases behave like adjuncts with respect to anaphora and extraction from *wh-* islands.

The final argument that *by* phrases do not behave like arguments comes from the distribution of a-adjuncts like *widely*. When passivized, certain stative verb classes receive an interpretation in which their suppressed argument is universally, rather than existentially, quantified (Zubizarreta (1987, 56)). Compare the natural meanings of (104a) and (104b), for example:

(104) a. Carl Yastrzemski was awarded a new contract (by the general manager).
       b. Carl Yastrzemski was admired (by all the fans).

Without the *by* phrases the only possible interpretations for the missing elements are clearly existential in (104a) and universal in (104b). Those predicates that admit the universal interpretation in the passive allow a-adjuncts of a particular kind including adverbials like *widely* and *universally*.

(105) Carl Yastrzemski was widely admired.

Sentence (105) can be paraphrased as *Carl Yastrzemski was admired by all/many people*, so it appears that *widely* here is an a-adjunct with much the same function as a *by* phrase.

These adverbial a-adjuncts can co-occur with a *by* phrase:

(106) a. Carl Yastrzemski was widely admired by baseball fans.
       b. It is widely believed by linguists that PRO is ungoverned.

In these examples the content of the two a-adjuncts is merged together, so that *widely* functions like a quantifier phrase (QP) modifying *baseball fans* and *linguists* in (106). Combinations of a-adjuncts will, of course, be ungrammatical when they yield an inconsistent representation. The same is true of pure modifiers, which are not linked to arguments at all: *John's book of Fred's* is ungrammatical even though both *John's book* and *a book of Fred's* are possible. And the same is true of adjuncts (see 4.6.3). This is the basis for the ill-formedness of (107), where the information provided by the *by* phrase and *widely* is inconsistent.[26]

(107) a. *Carl Yastrzemski was widely admired by some baseball fans.
       b. *It is widely believed by (a) few linguists that . . .

So a-adjuncts can co-occur with other a-adjuncts licensed by the same suppressed argument slot if no general conditions of well-formedness are violated. This never possible for arguments, however, since it would violate the theta criterion. The well-formedness of examples like (106) shows that a-adjuncts are not subject to the theta criterion, as they would be if they were arguments. Moreover, a-adjuncts can never co-occur with a realized *argument*, even when general principles of consistency are not violated: syntactically satisfied arguments never co-occur with a-adjuncts, because a-adjuncts are not licensed by syntactically satisfied positions.[27]

(108) a. *Linguists widely believe that PRO is ungoverned.
       b. Baseball fans *widely/?universally admire Carl Yastrzemski.

The sentences in (108) contrast minimally with the passive sentences in (106), in which the *widely* a-adjunct is grammatical. The difference is that the active verbs have their subject arguments satisfied syntactically and therefore do not permit an a-adjunct, even when no obvious inconsistency of representation would result. This provides additional support for the view that the argument structure of a passive verb is satisfied differently from the a-structure of an active verb.

4.6.3 Adjuncts, argument adjuncts, and the theta criterion
Safir (1987), treating both the *by* phrase and the possessive as external arguments, raises a couple of objections to the proposal made in Grimshaw (1986b, 1988) and further developed here, that passive *by* phrases and possessives are a-adjuncts. He claims that a-adjuncts never co-occur

with each other, citing (109b) and contrasting it with (109a), which is grammatical.

(109) a. Pete's destruction of the city with Joe
b. *Pete's destruction of the city by Joe

Safir reasons that if an adjunct is possible in (109a), a *by* phrase a-adjunct should be possible in (109b). He concludes that possessives and *by* phrases must not be adjuncts (or a-adjuncts).

The observation that a *by* phrase is impossible in (109b) is, of course, correct, but its implications are not as Safir assumes. There is a crucial difference between the two cases. In (109b) a single argument position would need to license *two* a-adjuncts. In (109a), on the other hand, only the possessive is licensed by the suppressed argument, and the *with* phrase is an adjunct of the standard kind.

What such examples show, then, is that multiple a-adjuncts cannot be licensed by a single argument position when both express similiar content (see the immediately preceding discussion of multiple a-adjuncts). The question is whether this behavior is typical only of arguments. If it is, this might constitute evidence against treating possessives and *by* phrases as a-adjuncts. Safir implicitly assumes that only arguments are subject to a condition regulating multiple occurrences. In fact, this is an unwarranted assumption:

(110) *Pete destroyed the city on Tuesday on Wednesday.

The very case used by Safir to illustrate the behavior of adjuncts, a *with* phrase indicating accompaniment, fails to occur multiply, as the ungrammaticality of (111) shows.

(111) *Pete destroyed the city with Joe with Sue.

Adjuncts *can* co-occur, but only when they are in fact introducing different information:

(112) Pete destroyed the city on Tuesday at two o'clock.

Multiple adjuncts like those in (110) and (111) are ruled out, apparently because they occupy the same interpretive niche. But the same is surely true of (109b): the possessive and *by* phrase both occupy the same interpretive slot, unlike the co-occurring a-adjuncts of 4.6.2. The *with* adjunct of (109a), on the other hand, has a totally different contribution, so there is no reason why it should not co-occur with an a-adjunct licensed by the suppressed argument. Thus there is every reason to believe that the ill-formedness of (109b) receives a straightforward explanation in terms of principles regulating adjuncts, which Safir's own account must somehow express.

This line of reasoning suggests that arguments and adjuncts may be more similar in their licensing than is usually taken to be the case. The theta criterion (Chomsky (1981)), which governs the distribution of arguments only, guarantees that multiple occurrences of arguments are impossible. The fundamental idea is that each slot in the argument structure of a predicate must be associated with only one phrase. In my discussion of adjuncts I have suggested that they are subject to a similar condition requiring that only one adjunct be associated with a particular slot in the representation. How the notion of slot is to be characterized is now the critical question.

We can consider the roles taken by adjuncts to form a kind of secondary argument structure not associated with the lexical representation of individual predicates but constituting a template to which the adjunct structure of the clause must be accommodated (see Davidson (1967) and McConnell-Ginet (1982) for relevant proposals). This template licenses adjuncts just as the a-structure of predicates licenses arguments. Of course, the other clause of the theta criterion does not seem to apply to adjuncts, since adjuncts are generally optional.

Finally, we can shed light on a critical aspect of the behavior of a-adjuncts. They are licensed only by suppressed argument positions, not by syntactically satisfied a-structure positions. At this point it is clear what kind of explanation can be given for this. An unsuppressed position will always be satisfied by an argument. If we assume that arguments always completely specify all specifiable information, they will always be incompatible with any a-adjunct, just as two arguments are always incompatible with each other. Two a-adjuncts can in principle co-occur, as can two adjuncts, since neither fully specifies the potentially specifiable information. Associating both an a-adjunct and an argument with a single position would then always violate the generalized theta criterion in the form discussed above. On this assumption there is no need to stipulate that only suppressed positions license a-adjuncts, and the distribution of a-adjuncts reduces to independent principles governing adjuncts and arguments.

4.7 Conclusion

In Williams (1981a), where the theory of external and internal arguments was introduced, nominalization and passivization were both analyzed as cases of internalization of an argument. In Williams's account, the *by* phrase of the passive is an internal argument, and so is the possessive in a nominal: both are internal to the maximal projection of the element that theta-marks them, so passivization and nominalization must involve internalization of arguments in his system. In the prominence theory of a-structure, the internalization analysis is not possible. An argument is internal or external simply in virtue of its prominence relative to other arguments of the predicate, and this is not something that can be altered by a lexical operation. If the passive *by* phrase were really an internalized external argument, the prominence theory would be challenged.

I have argued here that both passivization and nominalization are really a matter of lexical suppression of an argument position. What Williams took to be an internal argument of the derived verb or noun is, on this account, an a-adjunct. Passives, then, support the prominence theory, which entails that passives cannot involve simple internalization. The theory will be supported even further if it can be shown to entail suppression for both passives and nominals. Why does the formerly external argument suppress in this theory? I have already suggested a partial answer in connection with adjectival passives: that adding a new external argument, as in nominalization, requires the suppression of an existing external argument.

The overal conclusion is that nouns and passive verbs differ from active verbs in their argument structure. Positing these different representations allows us to maintain that the principles of theta-marking, a-adjunct licensing, control, and so forth are identical for nouns and for active and passive verbs. The fact that we observe different behavior with different heads is a result of the interaction of these general principles with the lexical representation of the argument-taking heads.

Chapter 5
Argument Structure and Anaphora

One of the best known properties of the psychological predicates is their behavior with respect to anaphora, investigated recently by Giorgi (1983–1984), Pesetsky (1987), Belletti and Rizzi (1988), Hoekstra (1988), and Zubizarreta (to appear). In the analysis of psychological predicates given here, their special behavior cannot be attributed to their configurational representation, since this is no different from the configurational representation of any other group of transitive verbs. The psychological predicates differ from other transitives in the character of their argument structures and not configurationally. The challenge, therefore, is to show that this proposal supports an illuminating characterization of the facts concerning anaphora with psychological predicates. That is the goal of this final chapter.

With respect to anaphora, psychological predicates of the *frighten* class differ from other transitives in three respects. First, they do not allow reflexive cliticization. This follows, I will argue, from an analysis of Romance reflexivization under which it suppresses an external argument, together with the a-structure analysis of the experiencer verb classes given in chapter 2. Second, a weak ill-formedness results when an anaphor occurs as the object of a *frighten* psychological verb. This effect I attribute to a type mismatch between the anaphor and its antecedent. Third, the *frighten* psychological predicates are notorious for allowing antecedents in object positions to bind anaphors within their subjects despite the absence of a c-command relation between the two. This effect can be assimilated to the proposal concerning thematic prominence and anaphora developed in Giorgi (1983–1984): that the anaphors take as their antecedents arguments of maximal thematic prominence. This account extends to the behavior of anaphors in causative constructions if we posit complex argument structures for certain causative predicates.

In this way the anaphoric differences between the psychological predicates and other verb classes can be explicated and related to the other special grammatical properties of the *frighten* class.

5.1 Reflexive Cliticization

Belletti and Rizzi (1988) demonstrate that the Italian anaphoric reflexive clitic *si* cannot be bound by the subject of the *preoccupare* class.

(1) a. Gianni si teme.
        'Gianni fears himself.'
    b. *Gianni si preoccupa.
        'Gianni worries himself.'   (Belletti and Rizzi (1988, 296))

The generalization is that the *si* Experiencer of *preoccupare* cannot be bound by the Theme, while the *si* Theme of *temere* can be bound by its Experiencer, although both are apparently instances of binding of an object by a subject. Belletti and Rizzi propose that the anaphoric clitic *si* cannot be bound by a derived subject, which includes the subject of the *preoccupare* class. This result follows, they suggest, from the failure of chain formation in this configuration. In the prominence theory of the psychological predicates, all of them have non-derived subjects (see chapter 2). So the chain-formation solution cannot be adopted in this theory.[1]

As a first approximation to the solution I propose, note that one could give a descriptively adequate characterization of reflexive cliticization by proposing that it is possible only with verbs that have external arguments. This formulation excludes from participation not only the *frighten* class of psych verbs but also unaccusative predicates, subject-raising predicates, and passive predicates, since none of these have external arguments. Recall that in the prominence theory the *frighten* psychological verbs also lack external arguments, although they do have underlying subjects. In these cases, then, the external argument requirement is descriptively equivalent to the Chain Formation Algorithm proposed in Rizzi (1986).

This is only a first step. We must explain why such a restriction holds and why it holds only of reflexive clitics and not of all reflexive arguments. The proposal I will give here is a development of the idea in Grimshaw (1982) (see also Wehrli (1986), Kayne (1986), Cinque (1988)), and that is that the Romance clitics are not arguments but rather are valency reducing morphemes added to verb complexes as by-products of a lexical binding process. The evidence for this view is that verbs which have undergone clitic reflexivization of objects behave as if they are *intransitive* in many respects. In contrast, pronominal cliticization of an object does not change the transitivity of the verb, which remains transitive. This evidence is presented in some detail in Grimshaw (1982), and I will discuss only one case here.

Kayne (1975) showed that the French causative construction treats transitive and intransitive verbs differently. When the lower verb is transitive, its subject is realized as an indirect object introduced by the preposition *à*, as in (2). When the lower verb is intransitive, its subject is realized as a direct object NP, as in (3). (All data for this argument are based on examples cited in Kayne (1975).)

(2) a.   Il fera boire un peu de vin à son enfant.
    b.   *Il fera boire un peu de vin son enfant.
         'He will make his child drink a little wine.'

(3) a.   Il fera partir les enfants.
    b.   *Il fera partir aux enfants.
         'He will make the children leave.'

When the object of the verb is a clitic, its behavior depends on whether the clitic is pronominal or anaphoric. With a pronoun object the verb behaves just like the transitive verb in (2), but when the clitic is a reflexive, the subject is realized as a bare NP complement, as with the intransitive verb in (3).

(4) a.   La crainte du scandale a fait se tuer le frère du juge.
    b.   *La crainte du scandale a fait se tuer au frère du juge.
         'Fear of scandal made the brother of the judge kill himself.'

(5) a.   La crainte du scandale l'a fait tuer au juge.
    b.   *La crainte du scandle l'a fait tuer le juge.
         'Fear of scandal made the judge kill him.'

The basic idea of the analysis given in Grimshaw (1982) is that the reflexive clitic is not an object, while the pronominal clitic is. The object argument of *tuer* 'kill' is bound to its subject argument, and hence the verb has only one open argument position, just like any other intransitive. The reflexive clitic, in this view, is not theta-marked by the verb nor in any sense an argument of the verb but is a marker of the binding relationship that has been established. The key notion is that clitic reflexivization involves lexical binding of one argument of a predicate to another.

Here I develop this basic idea in a slightly different way. In Grimshaw (1982) I assumed that the internal argument of a verb like *tuer* was bound to the external argument, essentially as in (7):

(6) Le frère du juge se tue.
'The brother of the judge kills himself.'

(7) $tuer(x\ (y)) \longrightarrow se\ tuer(x\ (y = x))$

In (7) the internal argument of *tuer* is satisfied by binding and is not syntactically realized. Suppose, however, that the binding is in the other direction.

(8) $tuer(x\ (y)) \longrightarrow se\ tuer(x = y\ (y))$

In (8) the *external argument* of *tuer* is satisfied and not syntactically expressed, because it is bound to the internal argument. On this analysis, reflexive cliticization turns a verb with an external argument into a verb with no external argument: the syntactically expressed argument is the *internal* argument of the verb. Of course, NP movement will apply in the usual way, and the internal argument will eventually be realized as the derived subject.[2]

Marantz (1984, 152–165) presents a similar analysis of Romance clitics in which reflexive verbs are "[-log subj]." Kayne (1986, undated) proposes that the reflexive clitic *is* the external argument, rather than the internal. This is similar to the present proposal in that the reflexive clitic is not the internal argument. However, it treats reflexive verbs as transitives (verbs with both external and internal arguments), while the analysis in (8) treats them as unaccusative.

The essential properties of reflexive cliticization follow from the proposal that it involves lexical binding of an external argument:

1 Since reflexivization satisfies an external argument (by binding), it should not co-occur with other external-argument-affecting operations such as passive, and indeed, reflexive cliticization cannot apply to passives or subject-raising predicates, as Kayne (1975) showed. This now follows, since these verbs either have *no* external argument or, in the case of passives, have a suppressed external argument not available for binding or for syntactic satisfaction (chapter 4). By the same reasoning, reflexive cliticization cannot occur with the *frighten* verbs, since they have no external argument. The interaction of reflexive cliticization with the classification of verbs into classes is just a special case of the usual interaction between operations on argument structure and external arguments.

To look at it another way, reflexivization of a verb with no external argument violates the One Advancement Exclusiveness Law (1AEX) of Relational Grammar (Perlmutter and Postal (1984)). Marantz (1984) points out that the effects of 1AEX, which prohibits more than one promotion to subject in a given clause, follow from the theory of a-structure operations. Consider, for example, the failure of passive to co-occur with unaccusative advancement. This follows in a-structure theory from the fact that passivization requires an external, and unaccusatives have none.

In sum, the fact that reflexive cliticization is possible only with certain verb classes is explained. In particular, the fact that *frighten* verbs do not undergo reflexive cliticization follows from their lacking external arguments, which also determines their behavior under passivization and nominalization (chapter 4).

The unaccusative analysis of clitic reflexivization provides an alternative to current solutions for the problem of limiting this kind of reflexivization. Rizzi (1986) attributes these limits to the chain formation algorithm, and Burzio (1986) attributes them to anaphora being established at d-structure, where the derived subject is still in object position. Note that both of these accounts have to make some extra provision to distinguish reflexive clitics from non-clitic anaphors, as the contrast between (9a) and (9b) illustrates:

(9) a.   They appear to each other to be intelligent.

    b.   *Jean se semble intelligent.
         'Jean seems intelligent to himself.''

The fact that English reflexives and Romance non-clitic anaphors are not similarly limited to verbs with external arguments follows from the fact that they do not involve lexical binding.

2   Unlike passive verbs, reflexive verbs do not occur with *by* phrases or other a-adjuncts, because the unrealized position is satisfied by lexical binding and is not just suppressed.

3   It is predicted that reflexivized verbs like the one in (5a) will behave like intransitives. Since their external arguments are bound to their objects, which move to subject positions, they *are* intransitive, just like all other unaccusative predicates.

4   One of the most easily observable differences between unergative and unaccusative verbs concerns the selection of perfect auxiliaries. In Italian, unergatives select *avere* 'have' as the auxiliary, and unaccusatives select *essere* 'be' (Rosen (1984), Burzio (1986)).

(10) a. Gianni ha veduto un gatto.
     'Gianni has seen a cat.'
   b. Gianni è arrivato.
     'Gianni has arrived.'

In general, verbs with external arguments take *have*, and those without external arguments take *be* (Hoekstra (1984)). The fact that reflexivized verbs also select *essere*, as shown in (11), is a long-standing challenge to this generalization about auxiliary selection.

(11) a. Gianni lo ha veduto.
     'Gianni has seen it.'
   b. Gianni si è veduto.
     'Gianni has seen himself.'
   c. Gianni si è comprato un auto.
     'Gianni has bought himself a car.'

In the analysis given in Grimshaw (1982), for example, reflexive verbs like French *se tuer* 'to kill oneself' and Italian *vedersi* 'to see oneself' have external arguments, so they are incorrectly predicted to behave like the unergatives. In contrast, the present analysis, in which the external argument is satisfied by binding, assigns the reflexive verb no external argument. Hence, it should behave like an unaccusative with respect to auxiliary selection because it *is* an unaccusative.[3]

In sum, the unaccusative analysis predicts that reflexive cliticization will be impossible for unaccusatives, passives, subject-raising predicates and *frighten* psychological predicates because they all lack external arguments. It predicts that reflexive verbs will select *essere*, that they will act as intransitives when the right arguments are the binders, and that they will not license a-adjuncts. Presumably, the unaccusative status of reflexivized verbs lies behind the formal identity of reflexive verbs and the middles and inchoatives (see Cinque (1988) for a recent analysis). Middles and inchoatives also lack external arguments.

When the external argument is satisfied by binding, the verb becomes intransitive, presumably losing its case assigning properties, which forces the object NP to move into subject position. When a verb has *two* internal arguments, the external argument can be bound to either one. In (12b) the external argument of *presenter* 'introduce' is bound to the Theme, which yields an intransitive verb, while in (12d) the external argument of *acheter* 'buy' is bound to the Goal:

(12) a. Jean a présenté Pierre à Marie.
     'Jean introduced Pierre to Marie.'
  b. Jean s'est présenté à Marie.
     'Jean introduced himself to Marie.'
  c. Jean a acheté un auto pour Marie.
     'Jean bought a car for Marie.'
  d. Jean s'est acheté un auto.
     'Jean bought himself a car.'

However, the nature of the binding relation determines which NP must be in the subject position at s-structure. Descriptively, the generalization is that the *subject* is always "coreferential" with the clitic anaphor. As Zubizarreta (1987, 161) points out, anaphoric cliticization is subject-oriented: only subjects are antecedents. In other words, the binding of the external argument to the Goal argument in (12b) requires the Goal argument to be the surface subject, and the binding of the external argument to the Theme argument in (12d) requires the Theme argument to be the surface subject. Even though the external argument can be bound by the Theme z as in (13a) or by the Goal y as in (13b), the only well-formed outcome is where the NP to which the external argument is bound moves to subject position.

(13) a. *presenter*$(x = z \quad (y \quad (z)))$
        Agent Goal Theme
  b. *acheter*$(x = y \quad (y \quad (z)))$
        Agent Goal Theme

In terms of the unaccusative analysis, the generalization is that the NP that the external argument is bound to must be in the subject position at s-structure.

This cannot be the direct result of the lexical binding relationship, which will be well-formed regardless of the configurational position of the arguments. Nothing said so far connects the lexical binding relationship with the surface positions of arguments. One possible connection is case-theoretic. If case is removed from the argument that the external argument is bound to, this argument will be forced to move to the subject position, and the right result will be obtained. Whether there is any principled means of achieving this is unclear to me.

The second possibility is that the reflexive clitics are anaphors even though they are not arguments. In this case they are like the switch reference morphemes of Finer (1985), and they must bear anaphoric indices without being referential. Suppose, then, that the clitic is assigned the index of the external-argument position, which is identified with that of an interal argument by lexical binding. As an anaphor, the clitic must meet the (generalized) binding theory and have a c-commanding antecedent. Principle A of the Binding Theory (Chomsky 1981) will be met, then, only if the anaphor is c-commanded by a coindexed NP at s-structure, and this will be the case only if the NP coindexed with the clitic (the one that the external argument is bound to) moves into subject position. This hybrid analysis of the reflexive clitics, in which they are anaphors but not arguments, makes it possible to complete the account of their behavior.

5.2 Local Anaphora and Thematic Hierarchy Effects

The mild ill-formedness of examples like those in (14) has been noted by, e.g., Postal (1970, 71) and Jackendoff (1972, 146).

(14) a. ?They concern/perturb each other/themselves.

b. ?Politicians depress/worry each other.

This fairly weak ungrammaticality arises when the object of a *frighten* verb (used non-agentively) is an anaphor. A similar effect holds with Italian non-clitic anaphors, according to Belletti and Rizzi (1988), and in Dutch (M. Everaert, p.c.).[4]

The configurational properties of these examples do not supply an obvious explanation for their ill-formedness. The subject is the antecedent, and it c-commands the anaphor in object position. The sentences in (14) contrast with those in (15), where *fear* and agentive *frighten* are perfectly well behaved with respect to binding theory.

(15) a. They fear/hate each other/themselves.

b. The children frightened each other (by jumping out. . . .)

There is no configurational explanation for the examples in (14) even in a theory like that of Belletti and Rizzi (1988), in which the surface subject is a d-structure object. In their account of anaphora with psychological predicates in Italian, Belletti and Rizzi propose that principle A can be satisfied either at deep structure or at surface structure. This predicts that the examples in (14) and their Italian counterparts should be fully grammatical, since they satisfy principle A at s-structure.

In Grimshaw (1987) I proposed that the contrast between (14) and (15) reflects the relative prominence relations of argument structure. The odd anaphoric property illustrated in (14) is associated only with the nonagentive *frighten* class, the very class in which the a-structure prominence relations do not match the configurational prominence relations. Modifying the proposal in Hale (1983), I proposed that a prominence relation of argument-command (a-command) is defined over argument structure in the obvious way: a more prominent argument asymmetrically a-commands a less prominent argument. Zubizarreta (to appear) makes a similar proposal. A maximally prominent argument thus a-commands all other arguments of the same predicate.

The a-command relations relevant to (14) and (15) are sketched in (16):

(16) a. *depress, concern*: Experiencer a-commands Theme
b. *fear*: Experiencer a-commands Theme
c. *frighten*: Agent a-commands Theme

Sentences (15a, b) are perfectly well-formed, since the Experiencer of *fear* both a-commands and c-commands the Theme and the Agent of (agentive) *frighten* both a-commands and c-commands the Theme. In the examples in (14), however, the binding relation violates a-command because the anaphor corresponds to the Experiencer, which a-commands the Theme antecedent, instead of the other way round. Similar ideas about the role of a-structure (or more accurately of thematic roles) in anaphora can be found in Hellan (1988, chapter 4) and Zubizarreta (to appear).

One major problem with this view is simply that any such interaction between a-structure and anaphora is unexpected on the assumptions of current theory, since there is no reason to expect properties of a-structure to intrude upon what appear to be essentially configurational generalizations, concerning anaphors and antecedents.

A second problem is that the simple view of a-command has to be extended (as it was in Grimshaw (1987)) to cases where the anaphor is contained within an argument rather than being the argument itself. In *They like each other's friends*, for example, a-command must hold between *they* and *each other's friends* and between *they* and *each other's* even though they are not arguments of the same predicate. There are also potential problems in cases like those in (17), where the notion of a-command is simply inapplicable: cases of anaphors under exceptional case-marking or raising to object predicates, of anaphors as subjects of infinitives, and of anaphors in adjuncts.

(17) a. They expected each other to win.
b. They arranged for each other to win.
c. They send presents on each other's birthdays.

(Sentence (17c) is due to Edwin Williams.) No a-command relation holds here between the anaphors and their antecedents, yet the anaphora is perfectly grammatical.

Such considerations lead me to consider an alternative. The proposal is that the slight oddness of anaphora in cases like (14) results from a type-theoretic difference between the argument acting as subject of the verb and as antecedent for the anaphor and the argument satisfied by the anaphor in object position. My contention is that with non-agentive psychological predicates the subject is actually not an *individual* but belongs rather to the type of *properties of individuals*.[5] (See Rooth and Partee (1983) for recent discussion of semantic types.)

As evidence for this view, consider the fact that it is always possible to substitute an NP which is overtly of this type for the subject of a non-agentive *frighten* psych verb:

(18) a. John/John's behavior concerns me.
     b. He/What he does bothers them.
     c. We/Our personal characteristics irritate him.

This is, of course, not true for subjects in general:

(19) a. John murdered him.
     b. *John's behavior murdered him.
     c. He fears us.
     d. *What he does fears us.

Suppose, then, that the subject of a *frighten* verb is not of the type of individuals and that an NP which normally denotes an individual can satisfy the position by the kind of type shifting found elsewhere, as in examples like those in (20), where (20a) can be construed as a statement about solving the problem and (20b) as a statement about some property of John.

(20) a. This problem is difficult. (= Solving it is difficult.)
     b. John is incredible. (= Some property of John is remarkable.)

Suppose in addition that the anaphor *each other* and the reflexives are always of the type of individuals. This immediately explains why the anaphoric relations in (14) are not perfectly well-formed, even though the antecedent-anaphor pair fully obeys the Binding Theory. The antecedents of (14) denote properties of individuals. Hence, there is a mismatch between the type of the antecedents and the type of the anaphors. This mismatch is the source of the ill-formedness.

When the subject NP is overtly of the higher type, as in (21), the ungrammaticality becomes complete.

(21) *John's behavior concerns himself.

In such a case the entire subject NP is not even a candidate antecedent for the anaphor, since it not formally of the right type. Nor can the NP within the subject be the antecedent without a violation of c-command and hence of principle A.

The lack of ambiguity in (22a), as opposed to (22b), follows.

(22) a. The children entertained each other.
     b. The children entertained us.

Sentence (22a) is subtly ill-formed on its non-agentive reading, where it means that properties of the children or their behavior did the entertaining, but it is fine when it means that the children as individuals agentively entertained the children as individuals.

If this is the right explanation, the behavior of the *frighten* verbs with respect to anaphoric objects is attributable to the semantic types of their arguments and not to relations of a-structure prominence. Is it an accident, then, that these anaphoric properties coincide with other grammatical properties of the *frighten* class that *are* attributable to a-structure prominence? Why do the very same verbs have both funny anaphora and funny argument structure? The answer is that the subjects (Themes) of the *frighten* verbs are not individuals, despite appearances. Agentive predicates never have this kind of subject—Agents are *always* of the individual type. The type mismatch thus does not arise with agentive predicates, nor should it arise with any other predicate whose subject is an individual.

The more general issue is whether this line of explanation for the anaphoric properties of psych verbs will explain the observation, originally due to Jackendoff (1972, 148), that reflexivization seems to obey a thematic hierarchy condition: The reflexive must not be higher on the thematic hierarchy than the antecedent. (Jackendoff (1972, 150) even suggests that the failure of psychological predicates like *please* to have reflexive objects should be explained by the hierarchy.)

More recently the interaction of the hierarchy with anaphora has been explored by Hellan (1988), Sells (1988), and Wilkins (1988a). As evidence for the Thematic Hierarchy Condition on anaphora, Jackendoff cites the interpretation of sentences like (23), which can only be agentive.

(23) The children were touching each other.

In 4.3 I argued that positing suppression of an external argument as part of passivization and nominalization predicts thematic hierarchy effects on these processes, given the porminence theory of a-structure. On the a-command proposal mentioned above (see also Grimshaw (1987)), the same effects are predicted for anaphoric relations, since a-command must hold for anaphoric binding. If the anaphor is higher on the hierarchy than the antecedent, it will be more prominent in a-structure, and a-command will be violated. All well-formed anaphora will therefore be consistent with the Thematic Hierarchy Condition. The effect of the condition is to guarantee that verbs whose thematic prominence relations are not configurationally maintained will not allow anaphoric objects bound to their subjects. The *frighten* verbs are a case in point. (For those verbs where thematic prominence relations match the configurational prominence relations, the effect of the hierarchy is no different from the effect of principle A.)

So the issue that remains to be explored is where the predictions of the a-command account and the type-mismatch account differ. In cases where there is no type mismatch, no thematic hierarchy effects are expected for anaphora, although such effects should still be found for passivization and nominalization for the reasons discussed in chapter 4.

5.3 Long-Distance Anaphora and Prominence

The third respect in which psychological predicates show strange anaphoric properties involves examples like (24).

(24) a. Pictures of each other depress the politicians.

  b. Each other's pictures depress the politicians.

These examples violate the c-command requirement of principle A, at least superficially, so they appear to violate the binding theory. Yet they are relatively well-formed.

The solution I want to suggest for this and a range of related phenomena uses the idea suggested in Giorgi (1983–1984) that the anaphoric peculiarities of psychological verbs reflect the operation of long-distance anaphora in English, associated primarily with "picture Nouns":

(25) a. They think that pictures of each other should be generally available.

  b. They think it is obvious that pictures of each other should be generally available.

Giorgi argues that the antecedent for Italian *proprio* 'self's' must be the argument of maximal thematic prominence within a given thematic domain. In the prominence theory of a-structure, this corresponds to the thematically most prominent argument. Identifying the antecedent with the maximally prominent argument suggests a solution to the problem of why some types of causative constructions contain two alternative antecedents for apparently subject-oriented anaphors. This is the subject of 5.3.2.

5.3.1 Long-distance anaphora with psychological predicates

The configurational relationship between *each other* and its antecedents makes it impossible to explain the examples in (24) with the Binding Theory under the obvious assumptions. The fact that examples like those in (24) are relatively well-formed leads to one of two conclusions. One possibility is that the configurational representation of these sentences is not what it seems to be (as Belletti and Rizzi (1988) and Pesetsky (1987) conclude). However, the analysis of the psychological predicates developed in chapters 2 through 4 makes no configurational distinction between the *frighten* class of verbs and other transitives. Hence, we must look elsewhere for an explanation. The alternative is that binding can be sensitive to something other than pure syntactic configurationality. The latter conclusion is the position taken in Jackendoff (1972), Giorgi (1983–1984), and Hellan (1988).

Long-distance anaphors characteristically display a certain range of behavior (Thrainnson (1976), Maling (1984), Giorgi (1983–1984), Vikner (1985), Manzini and Wexler (1987), Sells (1987)). Many appear to take only subjects as antecedents. Yet Giorgi (1983–1984) has pointed out that this generalization breaks down for the *frighten* class of psychological predicates. Giorgi establishes that a long-distance antecedent for *proprio* 'self's' must in general be a subject, not an object:

(26) a. Gianni$_i$ ritiene che Osvaldo$_j$ sia convinto che quella casa appartenga ancora alla propria$_{i/j}$ famiglia.
'Gianni believes that Osvaldo is persuaded that that house still belongs to self's family.'

  b. *Ho convinto Maria$_i$ che la propria$_i$ casa era andata in fiamme.
'I persuaded Maria that self's house had gone up in flames.'

Giorgi also points out that there is a class of exceptions to this generalization, cases in which the antecedent is the object of one of the *frighten* verbs. Here the object can act as the antecedent:

(27) a. La propria$_i$ salute preoccupa molto Osvaldo$_i$.
'Self's health worries Osvaldo a lot.'
b. *La propria$_i$ moglia ha assassinato Osvaldo$_i$.
'Self's wife murdered Osvaldo.'
c. La salute di quelli che amano la propria$_i$ moglie preoccupa molto Osvaldo$_i$.
'The health of those who love self's wife worries Osvaldo a lot.'

Giorgi concludes that the long-distance anaphor *proprio* must be bound by an antecedent that is the most prominent in its thematic domain, where prominence is determined by a thematic hierarchy that ranks Experiencer above Theme.

In terms of the prominence theory of argument structure, this concept has official standing. We can say that *proprio* must have as its antecedent an argument of maximal thematic prominence. It will follow that the subject of a verb like *hit* or *assassinare* 'assassinate' is the only possible antecedent, since it is the external argument and hene is maximally prominent along both dimensions. Because an external argument is always the thematically most prominent, any external argument will meet this condition and will act as antecedent. Since external arguments are always subjects, the anaphor will be subject-oriented for agentive predicates.

For the psychological verbs of the *frighten* or *preoccupare* 'worry' type, the Experiencer will always be the thematically most prominent argument, regardless of the fact that it is realized in object position. Hence, it will be a proper antecedent for *proprio* even though it is neither a subject nor an external argument.

A rather startling prediction of this claim is that the subject of a *frighten* verb will *not* be a possible antecedent, even if it is a subject. This is because the object is thematically more prominent than the subject. The examples in (28), from Belletti and Rizzi (1988, 321), show that this prediction is correct.

(28) *Gianni$_i$ preoccupa chiunque dubit della propria$_i$ buona fede.
'Gianni worries whoever doubts self's good faith.'

In sum, the object of a psychological verb can be the antecedent for *proprio*, but the subject cannot. This is because the object is the thematically most prominent argument and thus the only possible antecedent. The generalization cannot be stated in configurational or relational terms and must apparently be a matter of prominence.

The facts for English anaphors are much the same.[6] Sentences (25a, b) above meet the subject requirement and are grammatical. In (29a, b), however, the antecedent is an object, and they are ill-formed.

(29) a. ??I informed them/told them that pictures of each other were available.

　　 b. ??I informed them/told them/persuaded them that it was obvious that pictures of each other should be generally available.

A pair illustrating the minimal contrast is given in (30):

(30) a. 　They informed me that pictures of each other should be generally available.

　　 b. ??I informed them that pictures of each other should be generally available.

So far, then, it appears that these are long-distance anaphors that take subjects as antecedents. In fact, however, the English pattern is the same as the Italian one discovered by Giorgi. Objects of the *frighten* psychological verbs are possible antecedents—either local antecedents, as in (31), or long-distance antecedents, as in (32).

(31) a. ?Pictures of each other annoy the politicians.

　　 b. ?Stories about herself generally please Mary.

　　 c. ?Each other's health worried the students.

　　 d. ?Each other's books amazed the men.
　　　　(Based on examples from Pesetsky (1987))

(32) a. ?It worried them that it seemed necessary for pictures of each other to be on sale.

　　 b. ?That is was necessary for each other's pictures to be on sale everywhere annoyed the politicians greatly.

Although examples like those in (31) are not usually considered fully well-formed, they contrast sharply with examples like those in (33), which do not involve experiencer verbs ((33c, d) are again based on Pesetsky's examples):

(33) a. *Students of each other hit the politicians (during the riot).

　　 b. *Stories about herself generally describe Mary accurately.

　　 c. *Each other's parents invited the students.

　　 d. *Each other's friends murdered the men.

Verbs of the *fear* class behave like the non-experiencer verbs, as the two examples in (34) show:

(34) a. *Each others' students fear the professors.
     b. Each others' students frighten the professors.

As with *proprio*, if the antecedent is the *subject* of a *frighten* psychological verb, the result should be ungrammatical, because the antecedent is not maximally prominent:

(35) a. *The students amazed each other's parents.
     b. *The children depressed each other's friends.
     c. ??They worry each other's friends.

The examples in (35) are clearly much worse than those with the *fear* class:

(36) a. The students liked each other's parents.
     b. The children hated each other's friends.

The maximal prominence proposal predicts that an external argument will be the antecedent if there is one and that the thematically most prominent argument will be the antecedent if there is no external argument or if the external argument is suppressed and hence not syntactically realized. This predicts that the subject of a passive verb can act as the antecedent.

Giorgi cites passive sentences like (37) as grammatical:

(37) Osvaldo$_j$ è stato convinto da Gianni$_i$ del fatto che la propria$_{j/*i}$ casa
     e la più bella del paese.
     'Osvaldo has been convinced by Gianni of the fact that self's house
     is the nicest in the village.'

Here the anaphor is bound by the derived subject of the passive verb, a non-theta position. This shows that *proprio* need not be bound from a theta position. The same holds for English (see (38)) and also for Japanese *zibun* 'self' (Kuno (1973, 299)), discussed more below.

(38) a. They were told that it would be reasonable for pictures of each
        other to be available.
     b. They were informed that it was unlikely that pictures of each
        other would be available.

Belletti and Rizzi (1988) argue that the long-distance anaphor *proprio* must be bound from a theta position and that this is why it cannot have the subject of a *preoccupare* psychological predicate as its antecedent. Examples like (28) are ungrammatical because they have derived subjects. Hence, the anaphor is not bound from a theta position. However, the well-formedness of long-distance anaphors bound by the derived subjects of passives, as in (37), (38), and similar examples in Japanese, shows that this cannot be right. In these circumstances the anaphor is certainly not bound from a theta position. This raises the problem of how it is possible on Belletti and Rizzi's account to distinguish between binding by the derived subject of a passive, which is grammatical, and binding by what (according to their proposal) is the derived subject of a psychological predicate, which is not grammatical.

This split between passives and psychological predicates is predicted by the prominence theory. The generalization is simply that the anaphor must be bound by the most prominent (non-suppressed) argument. In the case of a psychological predicate, both arguments are syntacticaly overt, and the object is thematically more prominent than the subject, so the subject does not qualify. But in the case of a passive predicate, the external argument has been suppressed and is not a candidate as an antecedent. This leaves the derived subject as the most prominent and so makes it a possible antecedent. There is a principled difference in this account between a passive and a psychological predicate. This is the source of the different behavior of passives and psychological predicates in long-distance anaphora.

In conclusion, in these cases of long-distance anaphora the anaphors take arguments of maximal thematic prominence as their antecedents. The requirement is not that the antecedent be a subject nor that it be in a theta position. This hypothesis explains why the antecedents vary according to the semantic class of the verb whose argument is the antecedent. If the most prominent argument of a verb were always its external argument and hence always its subject, the hypothesis that the antecedent must be a subject and the hypothesis that the antecedent must be maximally prominent would be indistinguishable. It is because the thematically most prominent argument is not always a subject that interesting examples arise. The solution thus relies crucially on identifying the Experiencer as the more prominent argument even when it does not occupy subject position. In this way the anaphoric properties of the *frighten* psych verbs are related to their theta-marking, nominalization, and passivization characteristics, explored in chapters 2 and 4.

5.3.2 Anaphora and the argument structure of causatives
The analysis of long-distance anaphora developed in the preceding section suggests a solution to a long-standing puzzle in syntactic theory concerning causativization (and complex predicate formation in general). Certain cases of causativization yield rather transparently well-behaved lexical items: the causative *break* in English and the *lexical*

causatives of Japanese (Shibatani (1976)), for example. These forms show properties typical of other verbs and pose no particular problem for the most obvious analysis. I will refer to causatives of this type as *simplex* causatives. The problematic cases are the ones that appear to show mixed properties, the most famous example being the Japanese *-sase* construction. I will refer to causatives of this type as *complex* causatives.

The problem that complex causatives pose is that they appear to be morphologically derived through affixation of a causative bound affix which is not a free morpheme. Moreover, clauses headed by causativized verbs show patterns of argument realization that are typical of single clauses—functional/stratal uniqueness is observed, for example. Nevertheless, there is one critical respect in which complex causatives differ from simplex causatives: they allow the "subject" of the internal predicate (i.e., the argument that would be the subject if the causative morpheme had not been added) to act as antecedent for anaphors which otherwise allow only subjects as antecedents. The data in (39) and (40), from Shibatani (1976, 20–21), illustrate the problem for Japanese complex causatives and *zibun* 'self'.

(39) a. Taroo wa Hanako o zibun no kuruma kara oros-i-ta.
      'Taro brought Hanako out of his/*her own car.'
   b. Taroo wa Hanako ni zibun no huku o kise-ta.
      'Taro put his/*her own clothes on Hanako.'

(40) a. Taroo wa Hanako o zibun no kuruma kara ori   -sase -ta.
                              car   from come down -cause-past
      'Taro made Hanako come out of his/her own car.'
   b. Taroo wa Hanako ni zibun no huku o ki   -sase -ta.
                          clothes wear-cause-past
      'Taro made Hanako put on his/her own clothes.'

The argument for syntactic derivation of these causatives goes like this: *Zibun* requires a subject as its antecedent and never allows an object. Hence the data in (41).

(41) Taroo$_i$ ga Hanako$_j$ o zibun$_{i/*j}$ no heya de mi -ta.
                          self   room   see past
      'Taro saw Hanako in his own room.'

The fact that *zibun* can only take the subject of the simplex causative verb as antecedent in (39) is evidence that in this sentence there is only one subject. Yet the anaphor can take *either* NP as antecedent in the complex causative, which strongly suggests that the complex causative has two subjects.

This appears to provide strong evidence in favor of a syntactic derivation. How else is it possible for a single clause to have two subjects? No respectable theory of lexical items could allow for this possibility. Hence, the complex causative cannot be a lexical item. Moreover, the contrast between simplex and complex causatives makes it difficult to appeal to semantics for a solution, since it seems that the examples are synonymous in the critical respects. Because of such problems it is widely agreed that a syntactically complex source must be posited for complex causatives (see Gibson and Raposo (1986), and Baker (1988a) for recent discussions).

It seems indisputable that the complex causative has two of something that the simplex causative has only one of. I would like to suggest an alternative hypothesis about what the complex causative has two of: not subjects but thematically maximally prominent arguments. As we have already seen in chapter 2 and in 4.3.1, this argument need not be a syntactic subject.

Why will a complex causative have two such arguments? A complex causative is formed by composing two morphemes, each of which has its own argument structure representing relations of thematic prominence. The causative affix has an a-structure that contains an Agent argument. When this combines with the a-structure of the base verb, the total number of arguments increases by one. The proposal is that in a complex causative, both the most prominent argument of the internal predicate and the most prominent argument of the causative affix remain most prominent in the sense that they are each the most prominent element in their a-structure domain. Clearly, then, the complex causative must have two prominence domains, one corresponding to the a-structure of the internal predicate and one to the a-structure of the entire complex predicate.

I represent this as in (42), where square brackets enclose prominence domains—the higher one corresponding to the entire a-structure of the complex predicate and the lower one corresponding to the internal a-structure of which y is the most prominent element. Here x is the most prominent argument of the whole domain.

(42) *-sase*(x)
      ki(y (z))
      ki-sase[x [y (z)]]

The basic idea is that complex causatives maintain two a-structure domains in a very limited sense. Hence, they can have two most prominent arguments and two possible antecedents for an anaphor like *zibun*. In this way we can derive in a reasonably principled fashion a representation that resembles the result of Farmer's (1984) subject-assignment solution, which assigned a diacritic feature to the potential antecedents for *zibun*.

The behavior of complex causatives will now follow if the antecedent for an anaphor like *zibun* is determined by *a-structure status* and not in purely configurational terms. The generalization must be that *zibun* takes a maximally prominent argument as its antecedent and not that it takes a subject as its antecedent. In this view, then, the behavior of *zibun* falls under the same principles as the behavior of *proprio* in that both anaphors select antecedents on the basis of prominence. As expected, *zibun* is like *proprio* with respect to passives, discussed briefly in 5.3.1. Following Oyakawa (1973), Ueda (1989) shows that *zibun* is like *proprio* as far as psychological predicates are concerned:

(43) a. [$_S$ [$_{NP}$ [$_S$ Kaori-ga zibun-o$_i$ kirat-te iru [koto-ga]
            self   hate   fact
     [$_{VP}$ Tatsuya-o$_i$ yuutu-ni si-ta]]
            depress
     'The fact that Kaori hates him depressed Tatsuya.'

   b. [$_S$ [$_{NP}$ [$_S$ Kenji-ga zibun-o$_i$ sit-te i-ta] koto-ga]
            self   know   fact
     [$_{VP}$ Kaori-o$_i$ odorokase-ta]]
            surprise
     'The fact that Kenji knew her surprised Kaori.'

A key assumption here is, of course, that simplex causatives differ from complex causatives in the critical respect: they do not maintain an internal a-structure, so they do not maintain the prominence of the internal subject, and their a-structures look just like those of non-derived verbs. Thus the Japanese lexical causatives exemplified above have a simple a-structure like (44).

(44) *kiseta*(x (y (z)))

Independent evidence for positing such a difference in a-structure between complex and simple causatives comes from a completely different consideration: the kinds of verbs that can undergo the two kinds of causativization. While any verb, including an agentive, can undergo complex causativization, only non-agentive predicates participate in the simple causative (see Pinker (1989) for a more detailed discussion of the semantic limits on causativization). For example, we find causatives of verbs like *break* but not of verbs like *drive*:

(45) She drove him to New York. (≠ had him drive to New York)

(Forms that look like possible counterexamples, *gallop a horse*, for example, are probably derived from non-agentive forms.)

This difference between complex and simplex causatives is explained if a simple argument structure can only include one instance of any given argument type—Agent, for example. Then a complex argument structure observes the same limitation, but for each prominence domain. As a result, complex causatives can express meanings that can never be packed into monomorphemic expressions.

This theory makes some clear predictions about the possible cases of anaphora in causatives. When the causative is complex and maintains an internal a-structure and the anaphor is one that , like *proprio* and *zibun*, has a prominence requirement (not a subject requirement), *either* of the most prominent arguments can function as an antecedent for an anaphor of the *zibun/proprio* type.

One problematic case reported in the literature is that of morphological causatives in Malayalam (Marantz (1984), based on research by Mohanan), which do not allow the internal subject to act as an antecedent. There are two possibilities within the complex a-structure proposal. One is that the anaphor is truly *subject*-oriented and not of the *proprio/zibun* type in the first place. In this case, since even complex causatives have only one subject, there will be only one possible antecedent for the anaphor, namely the subject of the entire causative. A second possibility is that the Malayalam causatives are really simplex, not complex, and do not maintain two domains of prominence. On this analysis, they simply behave like other simplex causatives with respect to anaphora. If the causative is simplex, only the argument introduced with the causative affix has maximal prominence, and it alone can be an antecedent.

Since Malayalam causatives can admit multiple agents, this would seem to contradict the claim that multiple agents are allowed only in complex causatives. It seems quite possible, however, that the construction should be analyzed as Zubizarreta (1985) treats the *faire par* construction with the internal predicate having undergone suppression of its external argument (see Rosen (1989b, 1989c)). In this case the NP cor-

responding to the subject of the internal predicate would in fact be an
a-adjunct and not an argument at all. As an a-adjunct, it would not be a
candidate for antecedent status, any more than an a-adjunct in a passive
is.[7] This analysis seems particularly plausible in view of the fact, high-
lighted in Marantz (1984), that the internal subject is realized as an instrumental in Malayalam, and not as a direct or indirect object, as in
other languages.

The complex argument structure theory also predicts that it is completely impossible for a causative to allow *only the internal* "subject" to
act as an antecedent, since the higher subject is always an external argument and hence is a possible antecedent itself. There is one case where
just this situation is reported to hold, a case discussed in Baker (1988a)
and drawn from Woodbury and Sadock (1986, 238):

(46) Isuma -mi -nik   oqalo -rqu -va   -a
     mind 3Rs INSTs speak order IND-3sS 3sO
     'He$_i$ orders him$_j$ to speak his$_{j/*i}$ own mind/thoughts.'

On the present analysis the complex verb *oqalo-rqu-va-a* either has two
maximally prominent arguments and should allow either as an antecedent, or it has just one: *he$_i$*.

Despite appearances this example does not invalidate the argument
developed here. First, Alana Johns has pointed out to me that the
meaning of the complement verb in (46) so strongly biases the interpretation as to make the alternative reading almost inconceivable, even
in English. Consider, for example, the extreme oddness of *He ordered
her to speak his own mind.* Hence, the reported judgments on (46) cannot be taken to establish much about the anaphoric properties of the
complement. Moreover, this example appears to be the *only* case of this
type: central Alaskan Yupik allows only the higher NP to be the antecedent (Woodbury and Sadock (1986, n. 6)). This behavior would follow,
of course, from analyzing the derived predicates as simplex in the sense
developed here. Alana Johns in a personal communication reports
ambiguity in extremely similar examples investigated in her fieldwork,
which suggests that in that dialect the derived predicates are complex in
the sense developed here. All in all, it appears likely that examples like
(46) represent an essentially impossible situation, in which case the fact
that they are entirely incompatible with the present approach counts
for, not against it.[8]

In a personal communication Mark Baker points out another case
reported in the literature, one from Chimwi:ni (Abasheikh (1979),

Marantz (1984), Baker (1988a)). The anaphor *ru:hu-* seems to have exactly the distribution that is predicted to be impossible here: it takes the lower subject as antecedent and not the higher subject. However, it is not clear that this anaphor is of the same type as *proprio, zinbun,* and the picture-noun anaphors: apart from everything else, it requires a local antecedent.

In conclusion, I have suggested a solution for the problems of anaphoric antecedents and complex predicates that allows us to characterize the word-like properties of complex causatives while also explaining why they are more liberal in their support of anaphors than underived forms. The two key points of the analysis are the existence of complex a-structures and the hypothesis, based on Giorgi's work, that thematic prominence can determine antecedenthood.

5.4 Conclusion

These proposals for anaphora raise a couple of important theoretical questions. The first is why the thematic prominence of an argument should affect its ability to act as an antecedent when it is not directly encoded in the configurational representation. It seems likely that the place to look for insight into this issue is the theory of discourse (see, for example, Kamp (1981), Sells (1987), and Zribi-Hertz (1989)). Perhaps this theory accords a special status to arguments of maximal thematic prominence, and prominence-dependent anaphora depends on discourse representation. The second question is why the analysis in which the Romance reflexive clitics are external argument binders should be the right one. What rules out the alternative proposed in Grimshaw (1982), where they are *internal* argument binders? It seems clear that the answer must be that lexical operations can affect external arguments in ways that they cannot affect internal arguments. While operations on external arguments are numerous and relatively well understood, there are only a few examples of lexical operations affecting internal arguments, including antipassive constructions (see Goodall 1989), and the passive-like constructions that violate the 1AEX (discussed in Baker, Johnson, and Roberts (1989)). Such phenomena have not yet been studied as intensively or extensively as the more familiar passive constructions. It seems likely, then, that the child, more fortunate than the linguist in knowledge of what lexical operations are possible, will be able to easily decide on the external-argument proposal without either negative evidence or great difficulty.

Notes

Chapter 2

1. The details of (1) are obscure and/or controversial in some places, especially with respect to the relationship between Theme and the Goal/Source/Location group and with respect to relationships within that group. For example, Carrier-Duncan (1985, 7) and Baker (1989) represent the Theme as higher than the Goal (see also Larson (1988)). Evidence to be presented in 2.2 supports the representation in (1). Note also that Barss and Lasnik (1986) discuss a number of respects in which Goal NPs in English datives behave as though they are more prominent than Themes.

2. English verbs in this class include *despise, scorn, abhor, resent, adore, admire, like, love, hate, respect, deplore, appreciate, detest, enjoy.*

3. English verbs in this class include *disgust, amaze, astonish, (dis)please, appall, terrify, annoy, anger, enrage, irritate, infuriate, shock, entertain, amuse, intrigue.*

4. There is one area where theta roles seem to be obviously implicated, and that is the realization of arguments. It is indisputable that the way arguments are realized is in part a function of their theta roles, the preposition a particular argument is marked with, for example. Clearly, preposition choice cannot be expressed as a matter of a-structure prominence, but this does mean that theta roles must be represented in the a-structure, since preposition choice can be, and I will argue should be, construed as a matter of lcs selection (3.2).

5. I am abstracting away from the issue of the suppression of the subject position in the argument structure (see Grimshaw and Mester (1988) and chapter 4 below).

6. One prediction of this reasoning is that no effects of the hierarchical organization of a-structure will be found in root compounds, since such effects are a consequence of theta-marking. Root compounds do not involve theta-marking.

7. Examples like (13a) are predicted to be ungrammatical according to the *First Order Projection Condition* of Selkirk (1982, 37), since only one (non-subject) argument is satisfied within the compound. The compound in (13a) does have a faint air of illegitimacy. Nonetheless, it contrasts very clearly with (13b).

8. *Frighten* predicates with an available agentive reading should allow compounding of the Theme with the Agent satisfied outside.

9. Note that *god-frightening man* is also ill-formed with the meaning a god that frightens man, even though with this analysis the compound does respect relative thematic prominence. The explanation for this will be given in 2.3.4.

10. Noting that indirect objects are almost never included in idioms, M. Everaert suggests in a personal communication that the structure of idioms might provide further support for the relative prominence of Theme and Goal. He also reports that where the indirect object *is* idiomatized, the direct object tends to be part of the idiom too.

11. Selkirk in fact argues that the correct generalization involves the notion *subject* rather than *external argument*, but the argument probably does not go through in the present context (see chapter 4).

12. The case of noun-headed compounds is a little more complicated because it interacts with two other points of analysis. The first is the analysis of the external argument of a noun (3.3). The second is the proposal that the argument of a noun that corresponds to the external argument of the base verb is suppressed (chapter 4). If we assume the results of these later discussions, the argument structure of the noun *hunting* will be (Ev(x-∅ (y))) and that of a compound like *bear-hunting* (with a nominal head) will be (Ev(x-∅)). Because of the effects of suppression, a synthetic compound like *student-shouting* is not possible. The a-structure of *shouting* is (Ev(x-∅)), and this a-structure cannot theta-mark an argument inside the compound, because the *x* position is suppressed. Hence *student-shouting* always violates the theta criterion on the relevant interpretation. The remaining question concerns unaccusative nominals (see 4.3.2).

13. Sara Rosen points out in a personal communication that in languages that have incorporation of the kind that she analyzes as "classifier incorporation" (Rosen 1989a), it is in fact possible to incorporate a classifier corresponding to the single argument of an unaccusative. This is the expected result, since classifier incorporation does not involve theta-marking, according to her proposal. However, external arguments apparently do not undergo this kind of incorporation, contrary to what we expect under the proposal made here. Classifier incorporation should behave like root compounding (see 3.4) if neither involves a-structure satisfaction.

14. Baker (1988c) sketches an interesting alternative thematic analysis for these predicates.

15. Note that this principle applies only to simple predicates and not to complex predicates (see 5.3.2).

16. Pesetsky points out in a personal communication that examples like (i) are also impossible, even though under a plausible analysis the subject here is an Agent, the object an Experiencer, and the oblique argument a Theme, and hence thematic uniqueness is not obviously violated.

(i) *John frightened Mary of/at the ghost.

It is tempting to suggest, as M. Everaert does in a personal communication, that (i) is ruled out because it contains two causes, in which case a similar analysis might be given for (33b).

17. Certain technical problems still arise with this view, and these are hard to evaluate or solve without more evidence about the character of event structure. For example, an activity like *x works on y* does not break down into two sub-events in Pustejovsky's (1988) proposal—both arguments are associated with the same subevent. But then which is more prominent? One possibility is that either can be, and the thematically more prominent argument is the one that is chosen. Another possibility is that a finer-grained aspectual analysis does assign them relative prominence, perhaps one that represents "affectedness," as B. Levin suggests (personal communication). Yet a third possibility is that some arguments have no status at all in the aspectual representation and hence do not interfere with the computation of prominence.

18. It is possible that "affectedness" (Anderson (1978)) should be represented in the aspectual dimension, which would perhaps explain the strong tendency for an affected argument to occur in object position (see Tenny (1989c)).

19. More exactly, the proposed solution explains why the Theme of *frighten* is its subject but not why its Experiencer is an NP object rather than, say, a PP, which would yield examples like *The weather frightens to John*.

20. A. Belletti points out in a personal communication that without the lexical case feature on the Experiencer arguments in Belletti and Rizzi's account, generating the Theme in the VP would make it impossible to predict which of the two arguments moves to subject position to receive case.

21. One of the most influential arguments Marantz presents is based on predicates like *throw a party, throw a fit*, the argument being that the theta role of the subject is determined compositionally by the VP in a way that is special to external arguments. However, idioms like *hit the roof* and *kick the bucket* show that the same holds for internal arguments, since these predicates have unaccusative meanings and hence presumably have internal arguments, not external arguments, as their surface subjects.

22. I should point out that including the external argument in an a-structure does not entail that it is theta-marked in the same way as all other arguments (although it makes this a possibility). The external argument can be theta-marked by VP, or by V' if the subject is generated in Specifier of VP.

23. In an earlier version of this work (Grimshaw (1987)) I proposed that the thematically most prominent argument counts as external, analyzing the *frighten* psychological class as having an Experiencer external argument. This external argument was distinguished from other externals in being lexically associated with Belletti and Rizzi's [acc] case. The fundamentally stipulative character of this account makes it less interesting than the present one, since it can never explain the differences between the *fear* and *frighten* classes.

24. There is one problem with this explanation: it predicts that the agentive counterparts to *frighten* verbs should participate in the alternation, since they have an external argument. Perhaps there is a deeper solution hinging on the

interpretation of these predicates, which seem to lack an inchoative meaning altogether.

25. It may be more accurate to say that these dative subjects have maximal thematic prominence than to say that they are true externals. Arguments of maximal thematic prominence can act as antecedents for anaphors even if they are not external (chapter 5). Whether the dative subjects of Georgian are external or not depends on how Georgian fits into the cross-linguistic variation found with Experiencer state predicates (see 2.3.4).

26. Van Valin (1989b) argues that the existence of this semantic difference between unaccusatives and unergatives renders any syntactic account of unaccusativity superfluous. This is not the position I take here. To defend a position like Van Valin's, one must show that the semantic distinction *explains* the differences between the two verb classes. This has not been done and probably cannot be done. A more promising view is that the semantic distinction entails an a-structure difference which entails a d-structure difference. Thus unaccusatives and unergatives differ in representation in several respects, allowing the wide-ranging asymmetries between them to be explained.

27. Because of the complications discussed in 2.3.4 I will not include verbs like *fear* and *please* in this analysis.

Chapter 3

1. Sentence (i) seems grammatical even without the object:

(i) Only frequent examination by the doctors kept John healthy.

The correct analysis of this example is not clear to me.

2. On the assumption that these determiners also project their properties to the entire NP, this point should carry over to determiners that are not possible in event nominals.

3. Note that using *in order to* rather than just *to* gives the clearest results because *in order to* is not ambiguous between the purpose clause interpretation of interest and an irrelevant infinitival relative interpretation.

4. It might be possible to view R as occurring just in the lcs of result and simple event nominals and blocking the projection of lcs positions as arguments rather than as occurring in the a-structure strictly conceived.

5. These argument structures do not represent the suppression of the external argument of the verb, a point that I will discuss in chapter 4.

6. One outstanding question is how *-er* nominals should fit into the system as a whole. The determiners they occur with are those of the result nominals, they pluralize, and they can be predicative. In the present system, then, they will have R as their externals. It has recently been argued (see Levin and Rappaport (1988)) that *-er* nominals nonetheless have an event interpretation and a syntactic a-structure. The interpretation of this is tricky, however—these nominals do not refer to events and do not take aspectual modifiers like *in* PPs or *for* PPs (see 3.2.5), although they do seem to occur with *constant/frequent*. Apart from *constant* and *frequent*, the evidence for an event interpretation cited by Levin and

Rappaport amounts to the claim that the proposed event must have happened. This is, however, irrelevant to the event interpretation, as can easily be seen from examples like:

(i) The proposed destruction of Rome

(ii) The potential purchaser of this house

7. There is one exception to this: nouns can theta-mark within synthetic compounds without a preposition, as in examples like *gift giving*, discussed in chapter 2. That these have nominal heads is shown first by the fact that they exist at all, since there are no verb-headed compounds in English, and second by the fact that they take NP and not verbal modification: *His unexpected gift giving*, **His unexpectedly gift giving*. The fact that theta-marking inside the lexical category is possible even for nouns is probably related to the fact that compound internal arguments do not have to receive case.

8. This issue arises in English with interrogative and exclamative complements which can appear as complements to prepositions, unlike *that* clauses and infinitives.

9. Abney (1987) points out that *belief* is a result nominal and argues that the absence of raising with *belief* does not show anything about raising with Nouns. This reasoning is correct but misses an important issue, which is *why* there is no complex-event nominal corresponding to *believe* or to any other raising verb. This is explained if nouns are defective theta-markers, as argued here.

10. These group adjectives are a-adjuncts, and not arguments, when they occur with complex event nominals (see chapter 4).

11. Speakers vary to some extent in which nouns they treat as ambiguous, so not all judgements given here will be shared by all speakers. The prediction is that nouns that are unambiguous for an individual speaker will behave in the way characterized here.

12. Of course, this analysis is not possible within the theory of a-structure proposed here. PRO in NP is ruled out if nouns cannot theta-mark.

13. Another example is discussed by Hegg (in prep.), who argues that the "tough" predicates select events. This proposal explains the contrast in (i) once passive nominals are understood to be non-event nominals:

(i) a.   The translation of the book was an arduous task.

   b.   *The book's translation was an arduous task.

14. This difference has never been explained. It suggests that English may have some kind of second-order system in which pronominal possessives are treated as adjectival, like the Romance prehead pronominal possessives.

15. One simple prediction of the present account is not straightforwardly borne out. In *the city's destruction by the enemy* the possessive NP should be freely omissible, and *the destruction by the enemy* should have the same grammaticality status as the passive nominal. Two factors may be relevant to evaluating this point. The first is that other nouns do seem to behave exactly as expected. The second is that the inclusion of *the city's* as a possessive does have the effect of

disambiguating the nominal into a reading in which no argument is required. Thus the apparent difference in well-formedness between the two cases may really just reflect the effects of this disambiguation.

16. C. Cinque points out in a personal communication that verbs and nouns differ in that while verbs become reanalyzed with a preposition, nouns never do. Perhaps this is another reflex of the intransitivity of nouns—if government is required for reanalysis and nouns do not govern, the absence of reanalysis with nouns will be explained.

17. The notion of *complements* employed here is similar to the "thematic roles system" discussed in Dowty (1989) in that it is a non-grammatical mode of associating a predicate and its semantic arguments/participants.

18. Nominals that refer to individuals do allow sentential *modifiers*, as we will see below, but they do not allow direct lcs complements. This becomes crucial in explaining the absence of CP complements to *-er* nominals in 3.6.5.

19. Some non-deverbal nominals occur only in this configuration. They include *upshot, outcome,* and *situation.*

20. Group adjectives seem to be subject to affectedness also: *French knowledge* cannot mean 'knowledge of France/French things'.

21. There are a few unexplained gaps. For example, the noun *thought* seems to take CP complements in contexts like *the mere thought that . . .* but not with a subject **John's thought that. . . .* Similarly, *knowledge* allows a CP complement but resists a possessive: *The/??John's knowledge that. . . .*

22. It is, of course, a simplification to treat all infinitives as of one semantic type. See Pesetsky (in prep. b)

23. Not all modifiers occur in this configuration. Possessive modifiers of the form *of NP's* do not, and neither do possessives expressing part-whole relations:

(i) a. This book of John's   *This book was of John's.
    b. The car's roof   *The roof was the car's.

24. When an adjective like *first* appears in the subject, the postcopula possessive is much improved.

(i) The first attempt to . . . was John's.

It seems that the possessive in this case is under the control of *first* (compare (ii)).

(ii) John's was the *(first) attempt to . . .

25. One piece of evidence suggests that the verbs themselves may differ in their representations: the generalization known as "Visser's generalization" (Bresnan (1982a)) is respected by *attempt* but not by *decide.*

(i) a. *It was attempted to leave at six.
    b. It was decided to leave at six.

26. The posited representations makes sense of a point raised in 3.5.1: with Nouns of the *decision* class a plural head seems to require multiple complements.

(i) a. *Their decisions to leave early were not popular.
   b. Their decisions to leave early and to go straight to the next meeting were not popular.

A Noun like *attempt*, on the other hand, shows no such limitation.

27. B. Levin points out in a personal communication that zero-derived nouns like *break* and *hit* do not have this property.

Chapter 4

1. It is often assumed that adjuncts must be optional, but this is factually incorrect (Grimshaw and Vikner (1990)). The important point is that they are not regulated by a-structure, so when they are obligatory, it is for other reasons.

2. It does not seem that external arguments are the only arguments that can be suppressed in this way. Antipassive constructions exemplify the same phenomenon with respect to an object argument. In Greenlandic, for example, transitive verbs alternate with intransitive antipassive constructions in which the phrase corresponding to the direct object of the transitive verb appears optionally and in the instrumental case (Woodbury (1977, 322–323)). In the present system, this involves lexical satisfaction of the object argument, and the instrumental phrase simply acts as an a-adjunct licensed by the suppressed argument in the normal way.

3. Some languages *appear* to obligatorily require an expression like the *by* phrase (Siewierska (1984, 35)). See 4.6.2.

4. Like other adjuncts, *by* phrases are obligatorily required by event structure under certain conditions (Grimshaw and Vikner (1990)).

5. Martin Everaert has informed me that in Dutch there is evidence that verbs like *irriteren* 'irritate' form both adjectival and verbal passives (den Besten (1981, 1982), Everaert (1982)). Everaert points out a number of possible factors here: first, den Besten (1982) suggests that the verbal passive might be related to the agentive predicate; second, the *by* phrase seems to be obligatory in such examples (Everaert (1982)), which makes them similar to the adjectival passives discussed in 4.3.3.

6. The fact that there is a slight improvement with *by* I attribute not to any true difference in grammaticality but to the fact that the *by*-phrase cases (unlike those with other Ps) are in principle ambiguous between agentive and non-agentive readings. In the agentive version a progressive is perfectly acceptable, of course.

7. Of course, the Experiencer is not external either, so it cannot be suppressed by passivization. If the Experiencer in (i) were suppressed, the Theme would be realized as the subject of the passive, and the Experiencer should optionally appear as a *by*-phrase a-adjunct. Hence, the passive version of (i a) would be (i b), which is obviously impossible.

(i) a. The situation frightened Mary.
   b. The situation was frightened (by Mary).

8. The claim that passive is governed by the thematic hierarchy has been challenged, for example, by Gee (1974). Gee discusses a variety of problematic examples, some of which are analyzed here as adjectival passives (see 4.3.3). Others involve Goal-Theme pairs and are not analyzed here. See also Hust and Brame (1976), and Pinker (1989).

9. A rather similar prediction follows from Zubizarreta's proposal that nouns lack a level of lexico-syntactic representation, which verbs use to realize their arguments in non-canonical ways (Zubizarreta (1987)).

10. For other kinds of nominalization it is considerably more difficult to determine whether unaccusative verbs participate. The paucity of nominals corresponding to unaccusatives other than -ing cases makes the question hard to investigate.

11. Such examples have been pointed out in many places in the literature. See, for example, Emonds (1976), Bolinger (1977), Gross (1979), Bowerman (1987), and Pinker (1989). Although they are apparent counterexamples to the Thematic Hierarchy Condition on passives, in fact they are adjectival passives and hence not counterexamples. Note that the obligatoriness of the by phrase itself sets them apart from verbal passives.

12. It is not clear how this proposal should be reconciled with the existence of unaccusative adjectives (Cinque (1990)) or how unaccusative adjectives should be represented in this system.

13. Levin and Rappaport argue that it is always the "direct" argument that is externalized and that this follows from the way theta-marking works. I simply adopt this conclusion reformulated in my terms: R always binds the direct argument. The other possibilities are allowed by conversion itself but are ruled out by the theta criterion.

14. Kevin Hegg has pointed out to me that adjectives like fallen in a fallen leaf do not occur predicatively, as in *The leaf is fallen. This could support the view that they are really perfects, not adjectival passives. However, other adjectival passives based on unaccusatives do occur predicatively: The ice cream is melted, The lake is frozen, etc. The generalization seems to be that change-of-state predicates like melt and freeze can be predicative and those like fall and drop cannot be. A similar generalization seems to be operating in adjectival passives based on transitive verbs: the arrested man is possible, but the state interpretation of The man is arrested is at best dubious.

15. One problem with Levin and Rappaport's position that unaccusative participles are perfects and not adjectival passives is that it seems to leave completely unexplained the fact that unergative participles do not occur adjectivally. After all, unergatives have perfect participles.

16. As Grimshaw and Vikner (1990) show, some adjectival passives take obligatory adjuncts for reasons of event structure, but this is not relevant to the present point.

17. Within Baker, Johnson, and Roberts's proposal it might be possible to analyze -en as only an external argument. It would then follow that it cannot

satisfy any argument of a *frighten* class psych verb. This does seem to involve some retreat from the claim that *-en* is a syntactic argument just like any other, however.

18. This leaves open, as does Roeper's account, the question of why examples with purpose clauses like *in order to become a hero* do not allow the same possibility.

19. Nominals never seem to have obligatory adjuncts, even though they too have a suppressed argument. This appears to be due to the event structure representation of nominals, which has an extra layer of structure. See Grimshaw and Vikner (1990).

20. I. Roberts suggests in a personal communication that the failure of *-en* to act as a normal argument here might be due to its impersonal semantics (see Cinque (1988) for a recent analysis of impersonal and arbitrary constructions).

21. The possessive system of Romance nominals does not have the same analysis as that of English (see Cinque (1980), Zubizarreta (1987), and Giorgi and Longobardi (1990)).

22. Posessives are by and large not very good in *-ing* nominals, as examples like *?The/*Their solving of the problem* indicate. One possible explanation is that *-ing* nominalization removes, rather than suppresses, the external argument of the verb. However, this predicts that *by*-phrase a-adjuncts should be impossible in *-ing* nominals also.

23. Another class of cases, discussed in Zubizarreta (1987), may not fall under this generalization, since they seem to involve non-argument-taking nominals:

(i) a.   Mary's horror of the ghost
    b.   *The ghost's horror of Mary

24. Strictly, the a-adjunct will be licensed by any suppressed argument but will have a use semantically restricted by the preposition. As a result, the use of *by* with a non-agent will violate selectional restrictions (see 3.6.2).

25. Roeper asserts that *by* phrases—indeed all prepositional phrases in NPs— are analyzed as adjuncts in Grimshaw (1986b). This is not true. *By* phrases are there analyzed as *argument* adjuncts, not as adjuncts. Moreover, other PPs, such as *of* phrases that serve as object-like elements, are explicitly analyzed as *arguments*.

26. Sentence (i) is also ill-formed and presumably for a similar reason.

(i) *The army's American invasion of Europe.

This example could mean that the American army invaded if the information from the possessive and the adjective were simply combined. The solution must lie in the special character of those adjectives that occur as subject adjuncts. They are primarily adjectives of national origin and have a quasi-referential character, which seems to forbid merger with another referential element.

27. The judgment in (108) is shared by many speakers, including all speakers of British English that I have consulted, but it is not unanimous. Why should some speakers accept (108)? I believe that the answer lies in the character of their

analysis of *widely*. Many other adverbs like *frequently* and *generally* also appear to have the property of contributing information about lexically bound arguments, yet they do co-occur with a realized argument, as in (i):

(i) a. It is frequently believed by linguists that . . .
    b. The frequent belief of linguists that . . .
    c. Linguists frequently believe that . . .

I suggest that *frequently* is not really an argument adjunct at least in (i c), although it could be ambiguous in (i a, b). Rather, it is a normal adverbial with the expected interpretation. The interpretation it receives in (i c) must be indirectly obtained, presumably because the sentence is most likely to be true if many linguists hold the belief. For some speakers, *widely* may be analyzed just like *frequent(ly)*, which would make (104) acceptable. Speakers who do not allow (104) treat *widely* and its related adjective unambiguously as an argument adjunct.

Chapter 5

1. The ungrammaticality of the clitic examples cannot be reduced to the type mismatch discussed in 5.2, because the judgments are quite different. Cases like (1b) are sharply ungrammatical, not just weakly so, like the non-clitic examples.

2. There is a complication here, however. As examples (11c) and (12d) show, reflexive cliticization differs from passivization in that an indirect object can be moved to subject position when the external argument is bound to a Goal, for example. In the analysis of Grimshaw (1982) these examples just represent the binding of the Goal by the external argument, but in the unaccusative analysis given here, the binding relation is reversed and the Goal is moved to subject position. Two possibilities come to mind. One is that the movement is somehow legitimized by the binding relation, which does not exist in the case of passives. The second is that movement is not involved at all, and the Goal, which is in a sense simultaneously satisfying both an external and an internal role, is generated in subject position. I leave the problem unsolved here.

3. There is one remaining problem. G. Cinque observes in a personal communication that reflexive verbs do not allow *ne* cliticization from their inverted subjects, unlike unaccusatives and middles.

4. The examples in (i) illustrate the situation in Dutch:

(i) a. *Marie intrigeerde zichzelf.
      'Marie intrigued herself.'
    b. *Zij choqueerde zichzelf.
      'She shocked herself.'

This data was brought to my attention by Martin Everaert, who notes that (i b) becomes relatively well-formed if it is construed agentively.

5. Zubizarreta (to appear) argues that there is a relationship of metonymy between the subject of a *frighten* psychological predicate and an implied causal adjunct, as in "John frightened Bill (*by his behavior*)." Although the specific

conclusion drawn is not accepted here, Zubizarreta's insight about the interpretation of the subject is the same as the one that lies behind the present proposal.

6. Norbert Hornstein observes in a personal communication that examples like *Pictures of each other held the men's attention* seem to be well-formed even though the antecedent is embedded within the object and is not the object itself. This cannot be explained by the prominence account.

7. Ueda (1989) argues against an earlier version of the analysis of causatives I am giving here, on the grounds that while a passive *by* phrase cannot be the antecedent for *zibun*, a possessive NP can. Neither is a maximally prominent argument. The difference may lie in the fact that a possessive is in Specifier position and may qualify as an antecedent for at least local binding of *zibun* for this reason.

8. In fact, if Baker's and Woodbury and Sadock's theories do accommodate such examples, it seems likely that this is counterevidence rather than support.

References

Abasheikh, M. (1979) *The Grammar of Chimwi:ni Causatives*, doctoral dissertation, University of Illinois, Urbana.

Abney, S. P. (1987) *The English Noun Phrase in Its Sentential Aspect*, doctoral dissertation, MIT.

Allen, C. (1986) "Reconsidering the History of *like*," *Journal of Linguistics* 22, 375–409.

Amritavalli, R. (1980) "Expressing Cross-Categorial Selectional Correspondences: An Alternative to the X-Bar Syntax Approach," *Linguistic Analysis* 6, 305–343.

Anderson, M. (1978) "NP Preposing in Noun Phrases," in M. J. Stein, ed., *Proceedings of the Eighth Annual Meeting of the North Eastern Linguistics Society*, Graduate Linguistics Student Association, University of Massachusetts at Amherst, 12–21.

Anderson, M. (1983–1984) "Prenominal Genitive NPs," *Linguistic Review* 3, 1–24.

Andrews, A. (1982) "The Representation of Case in Modern Icelandic," in Bresnan (1982c).

Aoun, J., N. Hornstein, D. Lightfoot, and A. Weinberg (1987) "Two Types of Locality," *Linguistic Inquiry* 18, 537–577.

Bach, E. (1986) "The Algebra of Events," *Linguistics and Philosophy*, 9, 5–16.

Baker, M. (1988a) *Incorporation: A Theory of Grammatical Function Changing*, University of Chicago Press, Chicago.

Baker, M. (1988b) "Theta Theory and the Syntax of Appplicatives in Chichewa," *Natural Language and Linguistic Theory* 6, 353–389.

Baker, M. (1988c) "On the Theta Roles of Psych Verbs," ms., McGill University.

Baker, M. (1989) "Object Sharing and Projection in Serial Verb Constructions," *Linguistic Inquiry* 20, 513–533.

Baker, M., K. Johnson, and I. Roberts (1989) "Passive Arguments Raised," *Linguistic Inquiry* 20, 219–252.

Barss, A., and H. Lasnik (1986) "A Note on Anaphora and Double Objects," *Linguistic Inquiry* 17, 347–354.

Belletti, A., and L. Rizzi (1988) "Psych-Verbs and Θ-theory," *Natural Language and Linguistic Theory* 6, 291–352.

Bernodusson, H. (1982) "Opersonnlegar Setningan," M.A. thesis, University of Iceland.

Bolinger, D. (1977) "Transitivity and Spatiality: The Passive of Prepositional Verbs," in A. Makkai, V. B. Makkai, and L. Heilmann, eds., *Linguistics at the Crossroads*, Jupiter Press, Lake Bluff Illinois, and Liviana Editrice, Padua, Italy.

Borer, H., ed. (1986) *The Syntax of Pronominal Clitics*, Syntax and Semantics 19, Academic Press, New York.

Bottari, P. (1989) "On Derived Nominals Displaying a Predicate-Argument-Structure Level of Representation," ms., University of Venice.

Bowerman, M. (1987) "Commentary: Mechanisms of Language Acquisition," in B. MacWhinney, ed., *Mechanisms of Language Acquisition*, Erlbaum, Hillsdale, New Jersey.

Bresnan, J. (1982a) "Control and Complementation," *Linguistic Inquiry* 13, 343–434. Reprinted in Bresnan (1982c).

Bresnan, J. (1982b) "The Passive in Lexical Theory," in Bresnan (1982c).

Bresnan, J., ed. (1982c) *The Mental Representation of Grammatical Relations*, MIT Pess, Cambridge.

Bresnan, J., and J. Kanerva (1989) "Locative Inversion in Chichewa: A Case Study of Factorization in Grammar," *Linguistic Inquiry* 20, 1–50.

Burzio, L. (1986) *Italian Syntax*, D. Reidel, Dordrecht.

Carlson, G., and T. Roeper (1980) "Morphology and Subcategorization: Case and the Unmarked Complex Verb," in T. Hoekstra, H. van der Hulst, and M. Moortgat, eds., *Lexical Grammar*, Foris, Dordrecht.

Carrier-Duncan, J. (1985) "Linking of Thematic Roles in Derivational Word Formation," *Linguistic Inquiry* 16, 1–34.

Carter, R. (1988) "On Linking: Papers by Richard Carter," edited by B. Levin, and C. Tenny, Lexicon Project Working Papers 25, Center for Cognitive Science, MIT.

Chomsky, N. (1970) "Remarks on Nominalization," in R. A. Jacobs and P. S. Rosenbaum, eds., *Readings in English Transformational Grammar*, Ginn and Co., Waltham, Mass.

Chomsky, N. (1981) *Lectures in the Theory of Government and Binding*, Foris, Dordrecht.

Chomsky, N. (1986a) *Barriers*, MIT Press, Cambridge.

Chomsky, N. (1986b) *Knowledge of Language*, Praeger, New York.

Cinque, G. (1980) "On Extraction from NP in Italian," *Journal of Italian Linguistics* 1, 47–99.

Cinque, G. (1988) "On *Si* Constructions and the Theory of Arb," *Linguistic Inquiry* 19, 521–581.

Cinque, G. (1990) *Types of A' Dependencies*, Linguistic Inquiry Monograph, MIT Press, Cambridge.

Cinque, G. (1990) "Ergative Adjectives and the Lexicalist Hypothesis," *Natural Language and Linguistic Theory* 8, 1–39.

Condoravdi, C. (1989) "The Middle: Where Semantics and Morphology Meet." MIT Working Papers in Linguistics 11, 16–30.

Davidson, D. (1967) "The Logical Form of Action Sentences," in Nicholas Rescher, ed., *The Logic of Decision and Action*, University of Pittsburgh Press, Pittsburgh, 81–95.

Den Besten, H. (1981) "A Case Filter for Passives," in A. Belletti, L. Brandi, and L. Rizzi, eds., *Theory of Markedness in Generative Grammar*, Scuola Normale Superiore, Pisa.

Den Besten, H. (1982) "Some Remarks on the Ergative Hypothesis," *Groninger Arbeiten zur germanistischen Linguistik (GAGL)* (University of Groningen) 21, 61–81.

Di Sciullo, A. M., and E. Williams (1987) *On the Definition of Word*, Linguistic Inquiry Monograph 14, MIT Press, Cambridge.

Dowty, D. R. (1979) *Word Meaning and Montague Grammar*, D. Reidel, Dordrecht.

Dowty, D. R. (1987) "Thematic Proto-Roles, Subject Selection, and Lexical Semantic Defaults," ms., Ohio State University, Columbus, Ohio.

Dowty, D. R. (1989) "On the Semantic Content of the Notion 'Thematic Role'," in G. Chierchia, B. H. Partee, and R. Turner, eds. *Properties, Types, and Meaning*, Kluwer, Dordrecht.

Emonds J. (1976) *A Transformational Approach to English Syntax*, Academic Press, New York.

Emonds, J. (1985) *A Unified Theory of Syntactic Categories*, Foris, Dordrecht.

Emonds, J. (1986) "Θ-Role Assignment in Derived Nominals," *Revue québecoise de linguistique* 15, no. 2, 91–107.

Everaert, M. (1982) "A Syntactic Passive in Dutch," Utrecht Working Papers in Linguistics 11.

Everaert, M. (1986) *The Syntax of Reflexivization*, Foris, Dordrecht.

Farkas, D. (1987) "On Obligatory Control," *Linguistics and Philosophy*.

Farmer, A. (1984) *Modularity in Syntax: A Study in Japanese and English*, MIT Press, Cambridge.

Fassi Fehri (1987) "Generalized IP Structure, Case, and VS Word Order," MIT Working Papers in Linguistics, 10.

Fillmore, C. (1968) "The Case for Case," in E. Bach and R. Harms, eds., *Universals in Linguistic Theory*. Holt, Rinehart and Winston, New York.

Finer, D. (1985) "The Syntax of Switch Reference, " *Linguistic Inquiry* 16, 35–55.

Freidin, R. (1975) "The Analysis of Passives," *Language* 51, 384–405.

Gee, J. P. (1974) "Jackendoff's Thematic Hierarchy Condition and the Passive Construction," *Linguistic Inquiry* 5, 304–308.

Georgopoulos, C. (1987) "Psych Nouns," in *Proceedings of NELS 17*, Graduate Linguistics Student Association, Department of Linguistics, University of Massachusetts at Amherst, 211–321.

Gibson, J., and E. Raposo (1986) "Clause Union, the Stratal Uniqueness Law, and the Chômeur Relation," *National Language and Linguistic Theory* 4, 295–331.

Giorgi, A. (1983–1984) "Toward a Theory of Long Distance Anaphors: A GB approach," *Linguistic Review* 3, 307–361.

Giorgi, A., and G. Longobardi (1990) *The Syntax of Noun Phrases*, Cambridge University Press, Cambridge.

Goodall, G. (1989) "Evidence for an Asymmetry in Argument Structure," *Linguistic Inquiry* 20, 669–674.

Grimshaw, J. (1979) "Complement Selection and the Lexicon," *Linguistic Inquiry* 10, 279–326.

Grimshaw, J. (1981) "Form, Function, and the Language Acquisition Device," in C. L. Baker and J. J. McCarthy, eds., *The Logical Problem of Language Acquisition*, MIT Press, Cambridge.

Grimshaw, J. (1982) "On the Lexical Representation of Romance Reflexive Clitics," in Bresnan, (1982).

Grimshaw, J. (1986a) "A Morpho-syntactic Explanation for the Mirror Principle," *Linguistic Inquiry* 17, 745–749.

Grimshaw, J. (1986b) "Nouns, Arguments, and Adjuncts," ms., Brandeis University.

Grimshaw, J. (1987) "Psych Verbs and the Structure of Argument Structure," ms., Brandeis University.

Grimshaw, J. (1988) "Adjuncts and Argument Structure," Lexicon Project Working Papers, no. 21, and Center for Cognitive Science Working Papers, no. 36, Massachusetts Institute of Technology.

Grimshaw, J., and A. Mester (1988) "Light Verbs and Θ-Marking," *Linguistic Inquiry* 19, 205–232.

Grimshaw, J., and S. Vikner (1990) "Obligatory Adjuncts and the Structure of Events," ms., Brandeis University and University of Geneva.

Gross, M. (1979) "On the Failure of Generative Grammar," *Language* 55, 859–885.

Hale, K. (1983) "Warlpiri and Grammar of Non-configurational Languages," *Natural Language and Linguistic Theory* 1, 5–47.

Hale, K., and S. J. Keyser (1986a) "Some Transitivity Alternations in English," Lexicon Project Working Papers 7, Center for Cognitive Science, MIT.

Hale, K., and S. J. Keyser (1986b) "A View from the Middle," Lexicon Project Working Papers 10, Center for Cognitive Science, MIT.

Hale, K., and S. J. Keyser (1988) "Explaining and Constraining the English Middle," in Tenny (1988), 41–57.

Hale, K., and M. Laughren (1983) "The Structure of Verbal Entries: Preface to Dictionary Entries of Verbs," Warlpiri Lexicon Project, MIT.

Hegg, K. (1990) "Adjectival Predicates: A Case Study in Tough Adjectives," ms., Brandeis University.

Hellan, L. (1986) "Reference to Thematic Roles in Rules of Anaphora in Norwegian," *University of Trondheim Working Papers in Linguistics* 3, 55–68.

Hellan, L. (1988) *Anaphora in Norwegian and the Theory of Grammar*, Foris, Dordrecht.

Hermon, G. (1985) *Syntactic Modularity*, Foris, Dordrecht.

Higginbotham, J. (1983) "Logical Form, Binding, and Nominals," *Linguistic Inquiry* 14, 395–420.

Higginbotham, J. (1985) "On Semantics," *Linguistic Inquiry* 16, 547–593.

Hoekstra, E. (1988) "Psych-Verbs, Unaccusativity, and the Binding Theory," Groningen Papers in Theoretical and Applied Linguistics, Instituut voor Algemene Taalwetenschap, Groningen.

Hoekstra, T. (1984) *Transitivity: Grammatical Relations in Government-Binding Theory*, Foris, Dordrecht.

Hoekstra, T. (1986) "Verbal Affixation," ms., University of Leiden.

Hornstein, N. (1977) "S and X′ Convention," *Linguistic Analysis* 3, 137–176.

Hust, J., and M. K. Brame (1976) "Jackendoff on Interpretive Semantics," *Linguistic Analysis* 2, 243–277.

Jackendoff, R. (1969) "Les constructions possessive en anglais," *Langages* 14, 7–27.

Jackendoff, R. (1972) *Semantic Interpretation in Generative Grammar*, MIT Press, Cambridge.

Jackendoff, R. (1983) *Semantics and Cognition*, MIT Press, Cambridge.

Jackendoff, R. (1985) "Believing and Intending: Two Sides of the Same Coin," *Linguistic Inquiry* 16, 445–460.

Jackendoff, R. (1987) "The Status of Thematic Relations in Linguistic Theory," *Linguistic Inquiry* 18, 369–411.

Jackendoff, R. (1990) *Semantic Structures*, Linguistic Inquiry Monograph 18, MIT Press, Cambridge.

Jaeggli, O. (1986) "Passive," *Linguistic Inquiry* 17, 587–622.

Kamp, J. A. W. (1981) "A Theory of Truth and Semantic Representation," in J. Groenendijk, T. Janssen, and M. Stokhof eds., *Formal Methods in the Study* of Language, part 1, Mathematical Centre Tracts, Amsterdam, 277–321. Also in J. Groenendijk, T. Janssen, and M. Stokhof, eds. (1984) Truth, Interpretation, and Information, Foris, Dordrecht, 1–41.

Kayne, R. (1975) French Syntax, MIT Press, Cambridge.

Kayne, R. (1984) "Unambiguous Paths," in Connectedness and Binary Branching, Studies in Generative Grammar 16, Foris, Dordrecht. Reprinted from J. Koster and R. May, eds., Levels of Syntactic Representation, Foris, Dordrecht, 1981.

Kayne, R. (1986) "Participles, Agreement, Auxiliaries, Si/Se, and PRO," paper presented at the March Workshop on Comparative Grammar, Princeton University.

Kayne, R. (undated) "Thematic and Case-Assigning Properties of Past Participles," ms., MIT.

Koopman, H. (1983) The Syntax of Verbs, Foris, Dordrecht.

Koopman, H., D. Sportiche (1988), "Subjects," ms., UCLA.

Kratzer, A. (1989) "Stage-Level and Individual-Level Predicates," in E. Bach, A. Kratzer, and B. Partee, eds., Papers on Quantification, NSF Report, grant BNS 8719999, University of Massachusetts at Amherst.

Kuroda, Y. (1986) "Whether We Agree or Not," ms., UCSD, La Jolla, California.

Landau, B., and L. R. Gleitman (1985) Language and Experience, Harvard University Press, Cambridge.

Larson, R. (1988) "On the Double Object Construction," Linguistic Inquiry 19, 335–391.

Lasnik, H. (1988) "Subjects and the Θ-Criterion," Natural Lanuage and Linguistic Theory 6, 1–17.

Lebeaux, D. (1984) "Nominalizations, Argument Structure, and the Organization of the Grammar," ms., University of Massachusetts at Amherst.

Lebeaux, D. (1986) "The Interpretation of Derived Nominals," in A. M. Farley, P. T. Farley, and K.-E. McCullogh, eds., CLS (Papers from the General Session at the Twenty-Second Regional Meeting of the Chicago Linguistics Society) 22, 231–247.

Legendre, G. (1989) "Inversion with Certain French Experiencer Verbs," Language 65, 752–782.

Levin, B. (1987) "Psych Verbs, Further Dilemmas," ms., Center for Cognitive Science, MIT.

Levin, B., and M. Rappaport (1986) "The Formation of Adjectival Passives," Linguistic Inquiry 17, 623–662.

Levin, B., and M. Rappaport (1988) "Non-event -er Nominals: A Probe into Argument Structure," Linguistics 26, 1067–1083.

Levin, B., and M. Rappaport (1989) "An Approach to Unaccusative Mismatches," in Proceedings of NELS 19.

Levin, L. (1985) *Operations on Lexical Forms: Unaccusative Rules in Germanic Languages*, doctoral dissertation, MIT.

Li, Yafei (1990) "On Chinese V-V Compounds," *Natural Language and Linguistic Theory* 8.

McConnell-Ginet, S. (1982) "Adverbs and Logical Form: A Linguistically Realistic Theory," *Language* 58, 144–184.

Maling, J. (1984) "Non-Clause-Bounded Reflexives in Modern Icelandic," *Linguistics and Philosophy* 7, 211–241.

Maling, J. (1987a) "Existential Sentences in Swedish," MIT Working Papers in Linguistics.

Maling, J. (1987b) "Existential Sentences in Swedish and Icelandic," Working Papers in Scandinavian Syntax 28, Department of Scandinavian Languages, Lund.

Maling, J., and S. W. Kim (to appear) "Case Alternations in Korean," in D. Gerdts and J. Yoon, eds., *Topics in Korean Syntax*, Syntax and Semantics, Academic Press, New York.

Maling, J., and A. Zaenen, eds. (1990) *Modern Icelandic Syntax*, Syntax and Semantics 24, Academic Press, New York.

Manzini, M. R., and K. Wexler (1987) "Parameters, Binding Theory, and Learnability," *Linguistic Inquiry* 18, 413–444.

Marantz, A. (1984) *On the Nature of Grammatical Relations*, Linguistic Inquiry Monograph 10, MIT Press, Cambridge.

Marantz, A. (1989) "Relations and Configurations in Georgian," ms., Linguistics Curriculum, University of North Carolina at Chapel Hill.

Miyagawa, S. (1987) "Lexical Categories in Japanese," *Lingua* 73, 29–51.

Miyagawa, S. (1989) "Light Verbs and the Ergative Hypothesis," *Linguistic Inquiry* 20, 659–668.

Nishigauchi, T. (1984) "Control and the Thematic Domain," *Language* 60, 215–260.

Ostler, N. D. M. (1979) *Case-Linking: A Theory of Case and Verb Diathesis Applied to Classical Sanskrit*, doctoral dissertation, MIT.

Oyakawa, T.(1973) "Japanese Reflexivization 1," *Papers in Japanenese Linguistics* 2, 49–135.

Perlmutter, D. (1978) "Impersonal Passives and the Unaccusative Hypothesis," in *Proceedings of the Fourth Annual Meeting of the Berkeley Linguistics Society*, Berkeley, University of California, 157–189.

Perlmutter, D., and C. G. Rosen, eds., (1984) *Studies in Relational Grammar*, vol. 2, University of Chicago Press, Chicago.

Perlmutter, D., and P. Postal (1984) "The One-Advancement Exclusiveness Law," in Perlmutter and Rosen (1984), 81–125.

Pesetsky, D. (1982) *Paths and Categories*, doctoral dissertation, MIT.

Pesetsky, D. (1985) "Morphology and Logical Form," *Linguistic Inquiry* 16, 193–246.

Pesetsky, D. (1987) "Binding Problems with Experiencer Verbs," *Linguistic Inquiry* 18, 126–140.

Pesetsky, D. (in prep. a) "Psych Predicates, Universal Alignment, and Lexical Decomposition," Department of Linguistics and Philosophy, MIT.

Pesetsky, D. (in prep. b) "Infinitival Complement Selection," Department of Linguistics and Philosophy, MIT.

Pinker, S. (1989) *Learnability and Cognition*, MIT Press, Cambridge.

Pitz, A. (1988) "Middle Constructions in German," in *Working Papers in Linguistics*, vol. 6, University of Trondheim, 1–31.

Postal, P. (1970) "On the Surface Verb *Remind*," *Linguistic Inquiry* 1, 37–120.

Postal, P. (1971) *Cross-Over Phenomena*, Holt, Rinehart and Winston, New York.

Pustejovsky (1988) "Event Semantic Structure," ms., Brandeis University.

Randall, J. (1984) "Grammatical Information in Word Structure," Roundtable on Word Formation and Meaning II, *Quaderni di Semantica* 5, 313–330.

Rappaport, M. (1983) "On the Nature of Derived Nominals," in L. Levin, M. Rappaport, and A. Zaenen, eds., *Papers in Lexical-Functional Grammar*, Indiana University Linguistics Club, 113–142.

Rappaport, M., M. Laughren, and B. Levin (1987) "Levels of Lexical Representation," Lexicon Project Working Papers 20, MIT.

Rappaport, M., and B. Levin (1986) "What to Do with Theta Roles," Lexicon Project Working Papers 11, MIT. Also in Wilkins (1988b).

Rappaport, M., and B. Levin (1989) "-*Er* Nominals: Implications for the Theory of Argument Structure," in E. Wehrli and T. Stowell, eds., *Syntax and the Lexicon*, Syntax and Semantics 24, Academic Press, New York.

Rizzi, L. (1986) "On Chain Formation," in Borer (1986).

Roberts, I. G. (1985) *Implicit and Dethematized Subjects*, doctoral dissertation, University of Southern California.

Roberts, I. G. (1987) *The Representation of Implicit and Dethematized Subjects*, Foris, Dordrecht.

Roeper, T. (1983) "Implicit Arguments," ms., University of Massachusetts at Amherst.

Roeper, T. (1987) "The Syntax of Compound Reference," ms., University of Massachusetts at Amherst.

Roeper, T., and M. E. A. Siegel (1978) "A Lexical Transformation for Verbal Compounds," *Linguistic Inquiry* 9, 199–260.

Rooth, M., and B. H. Partee (1983) "Generalized Conjunction and Type Ambiguity," in R. Bäuerle, C. Schwarze, and A. von Stechow, eds., *Meaning, Use, and Interpretation of Language*, de Gruyter, Berlin.

Rosen, C. G. (1984) "The Interface between Semantic Roles and Initial Grammatical Relations," in Perlmutter and Rosen (1984), 38–77.

Rosen, S. T. (1989a) "Two Types of Noun Incorporation: A Lexical Analysis," *Language* 65, 294–317.

Rosen, S. T. (1989b) "The Argument Structure and Phrasal Configurations of Romance Causatives," MIT Working Papers in Linguistics 11, Department of Linguistics, MIT.

Rosen, S. T. (1989c) *Argument Structure and Complex Predicates*, doctoral dissertation, Brandeis University.

Rozwadowska, B. (1988) "Thematic Restrictions on Derived Nominals," in Wilkins (1988b).

Ruwet, N. (1972) *Théorie syntaxique et syntaxe du français*, Éditions du Seuil, Paris.

Safir, K. (1987) "The Syntactic Projection of Lexical Thematic Structure," *Natural Language and Linguistic Theory* 5, 561–601.

Selkirk, E. (1977) "Some Remarks on Noun Phrase Structure," in A. Akmajian, P. Culicover, and T. Wasow, eds., *Formal Syntax*, Academic Press, New York.

Selkirk, E. (1982) *The Syntax of Words*, Linguistic Inquiry Monograph 7, MIT Press, Cambridge.

Sells (1987) "Aspects of Logophoricity," *Linguistic Inquiry* 18, 445–479.

Sells, P. (1988) "Thematic and Grammatical Hierarchies," in H. Borer, ed., *Proceedings of the West Coast Conference on Formal Linguistics*, vol. 7, CSLI, Stanford Linguistics Association, 293–303.

Shibatani, M. (1976) "The Grammar of Causative Constructions: A Conspectus," in Shibatani ed. *The Grammar of Causative Constructions*, Syntax and Semantics 6, Academic Press, New York.

Siewierska, A. (1984) *The Passive: A Comparative Linguistic Analysis*, Croom Helm, London.

Sigurðsson, H. A. (1989) "Verbal Syntax and Case in Icelandic," doctoral dissertation, University of Lund.

Sportiche, D. (1988), "A Theory of Floating Quantifiers," *Linguistic Inquiry* 19, 425–449.

Sproat, R. W. (1985) *On Deriving the Lexicon*, doctoral dissertation, MIT.

Stowell, T. (1981) *Origins of Phrase Structure*, doctoral dissertation, MIT.

Tenny, C., ed. (1988) *Studies in Generative Approaches to Aspect*, Lexicon Project Working Papers 24, Center for Cognitive Science, MIT.

Tenny, C. (1989a) "The Aspectual Interface Hypothesis," Lexicon Project Working Papers 31, Center for Cognitive Science, MIT.

Tenny, C. (1989b) "Event Nominalizations and Aspectual Structure," ms., Center for Cognitive Science, MIT.

Tenny, C. (1989c) "The Role of Internal Arguments: Measuring Out Events," ms., Center for Cognitive Science, MIT.

Thrainnson H. (1976) "Reflexives and Subjunctives in Icelandic," in *Proceedings of the Sixth Annual Meeting of NELS*, L'Association linguistique de Montréal, Université de Montréal, Montreal, Quebec, 225–239.

Torrego, E. (in prep.) "The Interaction between Wh-Phrases and Determiners in Romance," University of Massachusetts at Boston.

Travis, L. (1983) "Word Order and Parameters," MIT Working Papers in Linguistics 5.

Tsujimura, N. (1988) "Ergativity of Nouns and Case Assignment," ms., Indiana University, Bloomington.

Ueda, M. (1989) "Notes on Reflexives and Argument Structure," ms., University of Massachusetts at Amherst and Harvard University.

Van Valin, R. D. (1989a) "Another Look at Icelandic Case-Marking and Grammatical Relations," ms., University of California at Davis.

Van Valin, R. D. (1989b) "Semantic Parameters of Split Intransitivity," ms., University of California at Davis.

Vendler, Z. (1967) *Linguistics in Philosophy*, Cornell University Press, Ithaca.

Vikner, S. (1985) "Parameters of Binding and Binding Category in Danish," Working Papers in Scandinavian Syntax, University of Trondheim.

Vikner, S. (in prep.) "Three Types of Passive in Scandinavian."

Wehrli, E. (1986) "On Some Properties of French Clitic *se*," in Borer (1986).

Wilkins, W. (1988a) "Thematic Structure and Reflexivization," in Wilkins ed. (1988b).

Wilkins, W., ed. (1988b) *Thematic Relations*, Syntax and Semantics 21, Academic Press, New York.

Williams, E. (1981a) "Argument Structure and Morphology," *Linguistic Review* 1, 81–114.

Williams, E. (1981b) "On the Notions 'Lexically Related' and Head of Word," *Linguistic Inquiry* 12, 245–274.

Williams, E. (1982) "The NP Cycle," *Linguistic Inquiry* 13, 277–295.

Williams, E (1985) "PRO and Subject of NP," *Natural Language and Linguistic Theory* 3, 297–315.

Williams, E. (1987a) "Implicit Arguments, the Binding Theory, and Control," *Natural Language and Linguistic Theory* 5, 151–180.

Williams, E. (1987b) "The Theta Structure of Derived Nouns," *Proceedings of the Chicago Linguistics Society*.

Woodbury, A. (1977) "Greenlandic Eskimo, Ergativity, and Relational Grammar," in P. Cole and J. M. Sadock, eds. *Grammatical Relations*, Syntax and Semantics 8, Academic Press, 307–336.

Woodbury, A., and J. Sadock (1986) "Affixal Verbs in Syntax: A Reply to Grimshaw and Mester," *Natural Language and Linguistic Theory* 4, 229–244.

Yip, M., J. Maling, and R. Jackendoff (1987) "Case in Tiers," *Language* 63, 216–250.

Zaenen, A. (1987a) "Unaccusative Verbs in Dutch and the Syntax-Semantics Interface," ms., Xerox PARC, Palo Alto, and CSLI, Stanford.

Zaenen, A. (1987b) "Unaccusativity in Dutch: An Integrated Approach," ms., Xerox PARC, Palo Alto, and CSLI, Stanford.

Zaenen, A., J. Maling, and H. Thrainsson (1985) "Case and Grammatical Functions: The Icelandic Passive," *Natural Language and Linguistic Theory* 3, 441–483.

Zribi-Hertz, A. (1989) "Anaphor Binding and Narrative Point of View: English Reflexive Pronouns in Sentence and Discourse," *Language* 65, 695–727.

Zubizarreta, M. L. (1985) "The Relation between Morphophonology and Morphosyntax: The Case of Romance Causatives," *Linguistic Inquiry* 16, 247–289.

Zubizarreta, M. L. (1987) *Levels of Representation in the Lexicon and in the Syntax*, Foris, Dordrecht.

Zubizarreta, M. L. (to appear) "The Lexical Encoding of Scope Relations among Arguments," in E. Wehrli and T. Stowell, eds., *Syntax and the Lexicon*, Syntax and Semantics 24, Academic Press, New York.

Zucchi, A. (1988) "The Syntactic and Semantic Status of the By-Phrase," in *Proceedings of NELS*, vol. 19, Graduate Linguistics Association, University of Massachusetts at Amherst, 467–484.

Index